Accounting
and
Financial Disclosure

A Guide to Basic Concepts

By

Stanley Siegel
Professor of Law
University of California at Los Angeles

David A. Siegel
Certified Public Accountant

ST. PAUL, MINN.
WEST PUBLISHING CO.
1983

COPYRIGHT © 1983 By WEST PUBLISHING CO.
50 West Kellogg Boulevard
P.O. Box 3526
St. Paul, Minnesota 55165

Printed in the United States of America

Library of Congress Cataloging in Publication Data

Siegel, Stanley, 1941–
    Accounting and financial disclosure.

    1. Accounting.   2.   Disclosure in accounting.
I.   Title.
HF5635.S587   1983   657   83–12505

ISBN 0-314-74733-8

3rd Reprint—1991

Siegel Acct. & Fin.Disclosure

To

PHYLLIS A. SIEGEL, ESQ.

and

ROSE M. SIEGEL

She openeth her mouth with wisdom;
And the law of kindness is on her tongue.

*

FOREWORD

Accounting has been called the language of business, the medium of communication by which enterprises of all forms report on their performance and status to investors, creditors, government and the general public. Knowledge of accounting is essential in order to understand the financial reports of enterprises because, like other languages, it loses much in translation.

But accounting is more than merely a language; it is also a profession, a process and a powerful analytical tool. Therefore no single text can hope to train its readers to be accountants, and this text makes no attempt to achieve that result. Nevertheless, our object is ambitious. We seek nothing less than to make our readers fluent in accounting: familiar with its vocabulary, conversant with the structure and meaning of financial statements, comfortable with analysis of financial information and aware of the strengths and limitations of the accounting process.

We have intentionally avoided the traditional textbook emphasis on the mechanical aspects of bookkeeping. Indeed, the fifteen chapters of this book contain the terms *debit* and *credit* in only a single paragraph. However, we have provided an appendix for readers who wish to study the elements of bookkeeping, from original entry of financial transactions through closing of the books and preparation of financial statements.

This text brings together the central themes of accounting, beginning with the fundamental structure of the financial statements and progressing through the major elements of accounting theory. We have included detailed discussion of the areas critical to income determination, including inventories and depreciation. Chapters are devoted to analysis of financial statements and cash flow. The subject of reliability of financial information is introduced in a chapter on auditing and is further examined in a chapter on accountants' liabilities.

Since accounting has relevance to the activities of all businesses and professions, we have attempted to be universal in our discussion. The chapters that deal with legal matters are therefore important not only to lawyers and law students, but to all readers who wish to understand the setting in which financial statements are issued and used.

FOREWORD

Throughout the text, we have sought to answer the questions that are usually asked by readers of financial statements. For example, the effects of inflation are the subject of an entire chapter, as are the problems of income tax accounting. Wherever possible, we have avoided over-simplification. As a result, some sections will prove to be challenging reading. We have also avoided unnecessary detail. Our approach is expository; with rare exceptions we have left reference materials for the end of each chapter, rather than interrupting the discussion with citations and footnotes.

This text is designed for use by students and professionals alike. It may be used as a principal or supplementary text for courses in accounting, or as a supplement to courses on business associations, taxation, finance and business planning. It should also be helpful to attorneys and other professionals who wish to learn accounting independently. We hope that this book will provide to its readers a broad understanding of the processes of financial reporting and the uses and limitations of accounting.

The authors are indebted to many people for the ideas that are embodied in this book, but our debt is greatest to Phyllis A. Siegel and Rose M. Siegel who analyzed and edited our drafts and encouraged and supported our efforts.

STANLEY SIEGEL
DAVID A. SIEGEL

June, 1983

TABLE OF CONTENTS

Chapter One

AN INTRODUCTION TO FINANCIAL DISCLOSURE

Chapter Two

CREATION OF FINANCIAL RECORDS: THE FUNDAMENTAL EQUATION

Chapter Three

THE ACCRUAL SYSTEM OF ACCOUNTING

TABLE OF CONTENTS

Chapter Four

INVENTORIES

Chapter Five

FIXED ASSETS: DEPRECIATION AND DEPLETION

Chapter Six

OTHER ASSETS

Chapter Seven

LIABILITIES

Chapter Eight

CAPITAL ACCOUNTS: PARTNERSHIPS AND CORPORATIONS

Chapter Nine

ANALYSIS OF FINANCIAL STATEMENTS

Chapter Ten

CASH FLOW AND FUNDS FLOW: THE STATEMENT OF CHANGES IN FINANCIAL POSITION

Chapter Eleven

AUDITING

Chapter Twelve

ACCOUNTANTS' LIABILITIES: THE ACCOUNTANT AND THE SEC

Chapter Thirteen

CORPORATE ACQUISITIONS AND COMBINATIONS; CONSOLIDATED STATEMENTS

Chapter Fourteen

ACCOUNTING FOR INFLATION

Chapter Fifteen

FEDERAL INCOME TAX ACCOUNTING

Appendix A

ILLUSTRATIVE FINANCIAL STATEMENTS

Appendix B

DOUBLE-ENTRY BOOKKEEPING: THEORY AND OPERATION

Accounting
and
Financial Disclosure

A Guide to Basic Concepts

*

Chapter One

AN INTRODUCTION TO FINANCIAL DISCLOSURE

If a man look sharply and attentively, he shall see Fortune; for though she is blind, she is not invisible.

Francis Bacon, Of Fortune

Financial Disclosure: Presentation of Status and Performance in Monetary Terms

Enterprises of all forms must summarize their status and performance in meaningful terms to their members, employees, investors and others. The owners and creditors of a business wish to know what the business owns and what it owes, how much it has earned, and whether it is likely to pay its debts. Employees of a large manufacturing company seek to know its performance—its "profits"—so they may have a basis for negotiating their wages. Members of a social club want to know its assets and obligations in order to determine its dues structure and its building plans for the future. Residents of a city are concerned with its revenues and expenses to determine the need for new or increased taxes.

In these cases and many others, participants in collective activity—whether in traditional business form or otherwise—summarize the status and performance of the enterprise in monetary terms. Values are assigned to the items of value that the enterprise owns, its "assets", and to the debts that the enterprise owes, its "liabilities." Similarly, values are assigned to the revenues that the enterprise receives and to the expenses that the enterprise incurs.

Accounting is the process of accumulating information concerning assets, liabilities, revenues and expenses, and summarizing and presenting the results in various forms. It is based on the assignment of monetary values, and it produces a picture of status and performance based on those values. As you will see, it is an analytical tool of enormous power when properly used. But we must recognize at the outset a number of important limitations, the most significant of which is that it measures only monetary phenomena. One cannot derive from financial statements a measure of the wisdom of business activity, or of community responsibility. Some elements of enterprise activity are difficult or impossible to quantify; others, though quantifiable, cannot be measured in financial terms. Therefore, at the beginning of our study we must appreciate that accounting represents only one measure of a collection of human activities, a financial measure.

Financial Statements

Our study will focus on the documents that relate financial status and performance, the *financial statements*. We will focus our analysis at three levels: terminology, format and calculation. Accounting may be viewed as a separate language, categorizing certain tangible and intangible items and phenomena under a unique morphology. As examples, the accounting item called "cash" includes currency (bills and coins) as well as demand deposits (checking accounts); a debt payable within one year is generally categorized as a "current liability"; a mortgage payable is generally classed as a "long term liability." These terminology problems need not concern us immediately, but they will have to be mastered soon in order to proceed with our analysis.

Format is also important, since it provides a structure for analysis. Financial statements take any of several forms. Revenues and expenses are shown in one statement, while assets and liabilities are shown in another. On the statements themselves, assets are listed in one place and liabilities in another, revenues in one place and expenses in another. This, too, requires some early mastery.

Calculation, the bane of many beginning accounting students, is really not as difficult as it appears. Nearly every accounting problem can be solved with simple arithmetic; the most complex can be dealt with by means of elementary algebra. Accounting complexity, as we shall see, is not occasioned by difficulties of calculation, but rather by difficulties of principle. As an example, it is not complex to divide the price of a car—say $10,000— by five to allocate its value at the rate of $2000 per year over its useful life. But is its useful life five years? And is it appropriate to allocate its purchase price *evenly* over its useful life? And in a period of inflation, is it appropriate to base our calculations on the $10,000 original cost of the car?

As you may now have guessed, some aspects of accounting must be based on opinions and estimates, rather than objectively verifiable facts. After all, accounting is merely a quantification of human activities, and human activities do not lend themselves to certainty in measurement. Readers who are attorneys or law students are familiar with uncertainty in law; the same must be said of medicine, dentistry, and most other professions. Be ready to see the same uncertainty in accounting, despite the fact that the numbers look precise. The addition and subtraction on the financial statements should be accurate, but the numbers that are added and subtracted represent a collection of judgments that can only be categorized as reasonable or fair, and not materially at variance from established standards of accounting.

Our study is directed at understanding and interpreting the financial statements, not at constructing them. To be sure, we will need to know how the statements are constructed in order to understand them fully. However, it is not the intention of this text to turn its readers into accountants or bookkeepers. Appendix B explains in detail the *double entry bookkeeping system* that lies at the heart of the accumulation of accounting data. You may wish to read Appendix B and learn how to establish bookkeeping records, but you need not do so in order to understand the remainder of this book.

The Uses of Financial Statements

Financial statements are very widely used for a great variety of purposes by an equally great variety of users. The most obvious users of financial statements are investors and creditors of businesses. Recent accounting literature has emphasized heavily the "informativeness" aspect of financial statements, that is to say, their ability to communicate to investors and creditors relevant information on the enterprise. Investors and creditors use this information to determine whether, and to what extent, to extend credit or refuse it, or to invest or disinvest. They do so based on conclusions drawn from the statements. As an example, a potential creditor considering extending a $1,000 loan to a company should draw some reassurance from a balance sheet showing assets of $100,000 and liabilities of only $20,000. The creditor might have even more confidence in his potential loan if the company shows net income of $20,000 per year. A potential investor in the company would be pleased by a series of annual income statements showing net income rising steadily from year to year; he might draw different conclusions if the income fluctuated widely from year to year or declined over the last few years.

This informativeness character of the financial statements needs some amplification. Note that both the creditor and the investor have drawn conclusions about *future* expectations of the business based on financial statements reflecting *past* events (the earning of income last year or in previous years), or at best reflecting *present* status (the listing of assets owned and liabilities owed). The users of these statements must draw inferences about future events from the historical data contained in the statements. Accounting, then, is basically an historical recording and reporting process, although we shall see some attempts within the accounting profession to produce forward-looking information. One major reason for understanding accounting is not only to interpret these statements, but also to appreciate their limitations. Excessive or uninformed reliance on the statements may be almost as dangerous as complete ignorance of their contents.

Apart from investors and creditors, other outsiders make significant use of the financial statements. The most prominent examples of these are governments that impose taxes—based on value, income or other financial criteria—calculated on the basis of accounting information. Here we encounter another troublesome phenomenon, sometimes known as "maintaining two sets of books." We have already noted that accounting involves a myriad of judgments; now we are introduced to the notion that accounting principles may be differently determined or applied, depending upon the purpose to which they will be put. Since governments raise revenues based on these calculations, it can be expected that they will often, by statute or regulation, prescribe the principles of accounting that will apply. And they do just that, requiring, quite legitimately, that the enterprise create different financial statements for use by revenue authorities than those that are distributed to investors. Other outside users of financial statements include regulatory authorities, labor unions and consumer groups.

Among the most significant users of financial statements, not often specifically mentioned in the accounting literature, are the firms themselves, the generators of the statements. Some uses of the statements by these firms are obvious when mentioned. For example, the entire discipline of *cost accounting* is concerned with the internal development of cost information with respect to products and services for purposes of pricing, purchasing and manufacturing decisions. On a larger scale, however, businesses gauge their performance on the basis of the so-called "bottom line", the figure for net income as determined by the accounting process. Activities that increase net income tend to be continued and extended, while those that decrease it tend to be eliminated. A simple and obvious concept, isn't it? But is it that straightforward? Suppose an activity—such as long-range research—is unprofitable for a decade, but generates increases in net income thereafter. Is it likely that the continued pressure of reductions in reported income will cause management to abandon the activity despite its long-range potential? Some highly regarded economic theorists have suggested that this very result has prevailed in America, and has thwarted long-range planning while encouraging short-range profits. Accounting, then, becomes not only a matter of reporting results, but also a phenomenon that may affect the substantive character of business conduct.

Forms of Financial Statements

The financial statements, as we have seen, portray what an enterprise is and what it has done. There are three principal financial statements and a collection of additional statements and schedules that serve this task. The three principal statements portray what might be called the three dimensions of the enterprise:

(a) *Balance Sheet* or Statement of Condition: depicts the assets (items of value, both tangible and intangible) owned by the enterprise, the liabilities (debts and obligations) owed by the enterprise, and the interests of the owners of the enterprise (its proprietor, partners or shareholders).

(b) *Income Statement:* lists the items of revenue (such as sales, fees or services income) and shows as deductions from them the items of expense incurred by the enterprise as part of its operations. The resulting figure of "net income" summarizes for the period the performance of the enterprise.

(c) *Statement of Changes in Financial Position:* describes the inflows and outflows of cash and cash-like assets (such as accounts receivable from customers) for the period. It provides a basis for evaluating the enterprise's handling of its funds and its ability to pay debts as they come due, buy assets as needed, and extend credit as appropriate to its business affairs.

In addition to these principal statements, supplementary statements and schedules will include such information as breakdowns of income by industry segment, aging of accounts receivable, listing of long-term debt and other commitments, and analysis of sales backlog. This information is often essential to understand and interpret the Balance Sheet, Income Statement and Statement of Changes in Financial Position. The supplementary statements and schedules will often be found in notes to the financial statements or in commentary associated with the statements.

Sources of Definitive Accounting Rules

One of the more troublesome aspects of accounting with which we will have to contend during our study is that the rules are not contained in one place. Indeed, the rules often allow many different forms of accounting treatment of the same transaction, and—surprisingly—remain silent with respect to the treatment of many items.

The core of accounting rules, known as *Generally Accepted Accounting Principles,* or GAAP, consists of the accepted practices of the accounting profession. These are not codified. Rather, they can be found in a collection of definitive publications and in the practices of the profession itself.

The accounting profession in the United States, through its national professional association, the American Institute of Certified Public Accounts (the AICPA), has since 1938 published definitive pronouncements on accounting principles. The first series of these, known as the Accounting Research and Terminology Bulletins, was promulgated by the AICPA Committee on Accounting Procedure from 1938 through 1959. Thereafter, the AICPA established the Accounting Principles Board (the APB), whose definitive APB Opinions and Interpretations were promulgated from 1959 through 1973. In 1972, as part of the process of making the determination of accounting principles more independent, there was established the Financial Accounting Standards Board (the FASB), which today carries the responsibility for issuance of definitive pronouncements of accounting principles, in the form of FASB Opinions and Interpretations. Over the years, these three series of pronouncements have often been revised, revoked or amended. However, they stand today as the most definitive statements of GAAP in the areas that they address.

It is particularly interesting—and not without controversy— that the accounting profession has on the whole set its own rules, rather than having rules set for it by the legislature or by an administrative agency. This state of affairs is not accidental. Indeed, since 1933 the Securities and Exchange Commission (the SEC) has had statutory authority to prescribe accounting principles, but has followed the general practice of leaving the development of GAAP to the accounting profession. However, acting under the authority granted to it under the Securities Act of 1933 and the Securities Exchange Act of 1934, the SEC has issued definitive accounting pronouncements, particularly where it has determined that the pronouncements of the profession left gaps. The SEC's Accounting Series Releases have spoken to such important issues as accounting for inflation and auditing procedures, both of which we will discuss in detail in later chapters. Often the SEC has acted as a gadfly, proposing or disseminating regulations that were later withdrawn after the accounting profession developed its own. A recent and controversial example concerns proposed regulations with respect to auditing and internal control, disseminated by the SEC pursuant to its statutory authority under the Foreign Corrupt Practices Act.

Other state and federal laws and regulations affect accounting principles and auditing procedures in particular areas. For example, the Interstate Commerce Commission has particular accounting rules applicable to its regulatory proceedings, as do some other federal regulatory agencies and many state rate-making bodies. And, of course, the Internal Revenue Service by virtue of the provisions of the Internal Revenue Code and the Treasury Regulations implements an accounting system for tax purposes that is often quite different from GAAP.

The result of this diverse set of rules and regulations is that there is no one recognizable set of accounting principles. The principles vary with the application, as perhaps one might expect in a complex society. Unfortunately, the variability of the principles doesn't make the study of accounting, or the evaluation of financial statements, any easier. In this text, we will attempt to simplify the process by focussing on Generally Accepted Accounting Principles, and by identifying where appropriate the major variations from those principles.

The Role of the Accountant and the Auditor in Preparing and Attesting to the Financial Statements

The process of accounting can be divided into roughly four steps:

1. Generation of original financial records from the transactions carried on by the enterprise.

2. Accumulation and summarization of the financial records preparatory to reporting the results of operation.

3. Preparation and dissemination of the financial statements, including notes and comments thereto.

4. Independent examination of the financial statements and expression of an opinion on the fairness of their presentation.

Although these steps are roughly chronological—except perhaps the last two—in practice they may all be going on, in various stages, at the same time.

Generation of the original financial records is usually the province of the bookkeeping department of an enterprise. Using methods varying from a pencil and paper through automatic recording by "intelligent" computer terminals, the financial data concerning every transaction are entered into books of original entry, or their equivalent on magnetic tape or disc. Every sale, purchase, bill, payment, receipt and other transaction is compiled in these books for later summarization and reporting. For all but the smallest enterprises, this process is elaborate and results in massive collection of data. For rather obvious reasons, several industries have developed around accounting systems and data collection.

Just as important as the generation of the original financial data is reasonable assurance that the data are correct and complete. Error and fraud begin at the cash register; the processes of accounting and audit must begin there as well.

The process of accumulation and summarization may, in some smaller enterprises, merge with either generation of original entries or preparation of the financial statements. However, in most instances the summarization step justifies examination on its own. For example, a chain of department stores will have thousands, if not millions, of cash and credit sales each day. Summarizing the sales by product or department, by cash or credit, by store or region, is essential before any further step can be taken. Later, we will see that the process of accumulation and summary involves many judgment calls. For now, it is sufficient to note that the reliability of the financial statements will be heavily dependent on verification of this process. This process, too, would generally be carried on by the bookkeeping department of the enterprise.

It is an article of faith of the accounting profession that the third step, preparation of the financial statements themselves, is also the responsibility of the enterprise. Accountants within the enterprise perform the final step of summarization and produce the annual (and, often, quarterly or monthly) statements that portray the status and performance of the company. However, the financial statements as the end product of the accounting system are based on a large mass of data and a large number of professional judgments. Their generation is only in small part a mechanical process. Accordingly, while the financial statements are, indeed, representations by the management of the enterprise, their preparation and dissemination invariably merges with the fourth step.

Although we will examine auditing in detail later, an introduction will assist us in understanding the entire accounting cycle. Auditing is uniquely the role of the accountant, usually the independent certified public accountant. The process actually begins with the financial statements and works backward. Each item on the financial statements—cash, accounts receivable, sales, expenses, etc.—is audited by examination backward from the financial statement number to the original transactions. For example, in auditing sales an examination is made of the summary sales records, the original sales records, and original sales invoices justifying those records. Of course, the examination must be made on the basis of samples, but the sampling technique, together with the auditor's evaluation of the enterprise's accounting system and system of internal controls, provides reasonable assurance with respect to the fairness of the financial statements.

Auditing is governed by *Generally Accepted Auditing Standards* (GAAS), a few of which we should mention here. The central standard is independence, which demands that the auditor, an outside independent professional, have essentially no connection with the firm other than as auditor. Another crucial standard is professional competence and supervision. As an illustration of specific standards, we might mention that in auditing inventories, the auditor is required to make a physical examination of the inventories, at least on a test basis. Another example concerns accounts receivable, amounts due to the enterprise from others; the auditing standards require that these be independently confirmed, at least on a test basis, by direct verification by the auditor with the customers of the enterprise.

The outside independent auditor can play only a limited role, since he is present to examine the financial statements for a short time, and on a test basis. To achieve the necessary assurance of reliability and fairness of records it is necessary that the enterprise have a system of *internal control* that provides for division of responsibility, cross-checking of records and functions, and often internal auditing by the company itself. The

[*9*]

outside auditor examines the system of internal control as part of the audit process.

One might expect that the audit process will unearth adjustments that must be made to the financial statements, and it does. One result is that while the statements are prepared by the management of the enterprise, they will not be disseminated with the auditor's opinion until the audit has been completed and appropriate adjustments have been made based on its findings.

The audit does more, however, than merely discover errors in entry and calculation. The auditor must express an opinion with respect to fairness of presentation in accordance with Generally Accepted Accounting Principles. Thus, the central professional role of the auditor is to evaluate the accounting judgments implicit in the financial statements and to give an opinion as to their fair presentation and consistency with GAAP. One result of this is that further changes, occasionally of great significance, may have to be made in the financial statements. These may not be entirely to the liking of management, but may be required to obtain the desired auditor's opinion. Another result is that the statements will invariably be accompanied by notes that describe the accounting principles used in their generation, and that provide supplementary information concerning the results and numbers that they contain. We will see later that these disclosures, along with the auditor's opinion, will often provide us with the most important information needed to evaluate the financial statements.

The Relevance of Accounting in the Era of "Efficient Markets" and Contemporary Economic Theory

Recent economic theory, in particular the "efficient market hypothesis", has occasionally lent itself to the suggestion that the financial statements of enterprises may no longer be relevant to investment decisions. This suggestion, though not widely voiced, merits discussion at the outset.

A central hypothesis of efficient market proponents is that the market for corporate securities is, on the whole, efficient in the sense that it rapidly absorbs and reflects in the prices of securities the information relevant to those prices. In general, by the time an investor reads and acts upon the financial statements, the information contained in them will already have been reflected in the prices of securities. Some investors, of course, will make profits on "quick strike" transactions, having spent the time and effort to obtain and act on the relevant information quickly, before others obtain it. But, the hypothesis goes, the costs of gathering the information in advance of its public dissemination, if that can be done, generally exceed the investment profits that can be made based on it. The efficient market hypothesis, like other economic theories, is of course not universally accepted. Still, it is a theory of sufficient strength to require that we address its principal conclusions.

Whatever value the efficient market hypothesis may have in understanding or rationalizing the movement of securities markets, it would be a misreading of the hypothesis to suggest that readers no longer gain value from financial statements. A central point, not addressed by the hypothesis, is that many of the users of financial statements and the information contained in them do not operate in the context of any market, much less an efficient one. The Internal Revenue Service determines taxes based on income; labor unions negotiate wage rates based on reported corporate performance; managers determine the course of future enterprise activities based on evaluation of performance as reflected in the financial statements. None of these are using the financial statements, except personally, for investment decisions. For these users, the efficient market hypothesis does not reduce the importance of financial statements.

Even those who invest and disinvest in business enterprises may find little solace in efficient markets, if the securities they purchase have a very limited market. Investors in closely-held corporations, in many limited partnerships, and in other narrowly distributed enterprises cannot look to the market for evaluation of their investments, since the market is too narrow to be efficient or informative. For them, too, the financial statements are the principal source of meaningful investment information.

Finally, where the market is in fact efficient, the source of much of the relevant enterprise information is the accounting process. To be sure, most investors will receive the information after market professionals and others have already purchased or sold on the basis of that information. Still, were the information not gathered and disseminated by the accounting process, there would be considerable doubt whether the market would be able to act on it. Put another way, it has been demonstrated that where there is an efficient market, it reflects reported corporate performance before the final financial statements are issued, probably on the basis of dissemination, or leaks, of interim or preliminary data. Perhaps, from the market's viewpoint, the final audited financial statements are unnecessary. However, would the market react as quickly and efficiently if the data on which those statements were based were never collected as part of the accounting process? We doubt it. The accounting process emerges, then, as the crucial first step in producing much of the firm-based information upon which the market acts.

REFERENCES

Official Pronouncements:

American Institute of Certified Public Accountants, Committee on Accounting Procedure, Accounting Research Bulletins No. 43–51 (1953–1959).

American Institute of Certified Public Accountants, Accounting Principles Board, Opinions No. 1–31; Statements No. 1–4 (1962–1973).

Financial Accounting Standards Board, Statements of Financial Accounting Standards No. 1–49; Interpretations No. 1–35 (1973–1982).

Secondary Sources:

Carey, The Rise of the Accounting Profession (1970).

Previts & Merino, A History of Accounting in America: An Historical Interpretation of the Cultural Significance of Accounting.

Dyckman, Downes & Magee, Efficient Capital Markets and Accounting: A Critical Analysis (1975).

Chapter Two

CREATION OF FINANCIAL RECORDS: THE FUNDAMENTAL EQUATION

Few have heard of Fra Luca Pacioli, the inventor of double-entry bookkeeping; but he has probably had much more influence on human life than has Dante or Michelangelo.

Herbert J. Muller, The Uses of the Past

Introduction: Why Do We Need to Know This?

You will remember that our objective in writing this book was to instruct the readers on how to understand financial statements, and not to turn them into accountants or bookkeepers. Why, then, is it necessary to study, in some detail, the bookkeeping system? The answer lies in concepts which were introduced in the first chapter. The financial statements represent the end product of a process of accumulation, summarization and reporting of data, and bookkeeping, in one form or another, is the beginning—or input—of that process. If we do not know how the input end of the financial reporting process works, and how to evaluate its reliability, honesty and fairness, then we cannot know what reliance to place on the financial statements that represent the end product of that process.

Moreover, the financial statements are structured in accordance with certain fundamental rules derived from the bookkeeping process, to which we now turn.

Double-Entry Bookkeeping

In the simplest of enterprises, it may be unnecessary to maintain any financial records, since the owner may be able to keep in his mind a sense of what he owns and owes from time to time. Not many enterprises are so simple, and nearly all eventually keep some records of ownership, debts, income and expenditures. At the very least, taxpayers must maintain some records for purposes of federal and state income tax reporting. These records may be as simple as a shoebox full of receipts and a checkbook register. The checkbook register is a form of bookkeeping, the maintenance of a record of events, or transactions, affecting the enterprise.

The checkbook register, however, tells us only what cash came in and what cash went out, but not what became of the things for which the cash was spent. We may learn from it, for example, that $750 was spent for a television set in January, 1980, but we cannot determine whether the set is still owned. Moreover, while we can determine at any time the cash balance of the enterprise, we cannot find out from the checkbook register what other things of value, and what obligations, the enterprise has.

Double-entry bookkeeping was first described in writing by Luca Pacioli, an Italian mathematician and Franciscan Friar, in Summa de Arithmetica, Geometria, Proporcioni e Proporcionalitá, published in 1494. It is a method of recording transactions designed to accumulate and generate comprehensive financial status reports of a kind not available by means of checkbook registers and other simple lists. The principles of double-entry bookkeeping are found in a simple formula, usually referred to as the "Fundamental Equation":

$$Assets = Liabilities + Net\ Worth$$

The terms of the Fundamental Equation have the following meanings:

Assets are the items of value owned by the enterprise, including tangible items such as cash, land and machinery, and intangible items such as copyrights and business goodwill.

Liabilities are the debts and obligations owed by the enterprise, which might include such items as trade accounts payable, mortgage debts and unpaid income taxes.

Net Worth is a residual, representing the difference between assets and liabilities. Indeed, we might rewrite the Fundamental Equation as follows:

$$Assets - Liabilities = Net\ Worth$$

In other words, net worth is defined as the difference between assets and liabilities. More importantly, however, net worth represents the owner's interest in the enterprise, the interest in the assets left over for the owner after recognizing the interests of its creditors.

The Fundamental Equation arrays on the left side the items of value of the enterprise and on the right side the interests in those items. This is illustrated in the *Balance Sheet*, which shows the financial position of the enterprise as of a given date.

A. V. Justice, Attorney
Balance Sheet
December 31, 1982

Assets		Liabilities and Net Worth	
Cash	$ 1,000	Accounts Payable	$ 3,500
Accounts Receivable	4,000	Note Payable	2,000
Office Supplies	2,500	A. V. Justice,	
Office Equipment	7,500	Net Worth	9,500
		Total Liabilities and	
Total Assets	$15,000	Net Worth	$15,000

The left side of the balance sheet shows that A. V. Justice, Attorney, has total assets (items of value used in the business) of $15,000. All but one of these items, *Accounts Receivable*, are familiar to you. Accounts receivable represent amounts of money owed to Justice by others, probably clients, on which he has not yet received payment.

The right side of the balance sheet lists first the debts owed by Justice. *Accounts Payable* are ordinary commercial debts, amounts that Justice owes, but has not yet paid, to others for goods and services. The *Note Payable* is another form of debt, evidenced by a written instrument. The last item, *A. V. Justice, Net Worth*, represents Justice's interest in the enterprise. Although the total assets are $15,000, Justice has debts totalling $5,500. Therefore, his interest in the enterprise is $9,500.

Notice how the balance sheet exactly follows the tenets of the Fundamental Equation. The balance sheet is "in balance" (that is, the left and right sides are equal) *by definition.*

If the Fundamental Equation must remain in balance, it follows that the recording of any transaction will require two entries, hence the "double-entry" system of bookkeeping. For example, if Justice pays off $500 of his accounts payable, both sides of the balance sheet (representing both sides of the Fundamental Equation) will be affected: an asset (cash) will be reduced by $500 on the left side, and a liability (accounts payable) will be reduced by $500 on the right side.

It is not always necessary that entries be made on both sides of the Fundamental Equation for the balance to be maintained. For example, if Justice spent $500 cash to buy books for his law library, he would affect only the left side of the equation. The result would be an increase in one asset (library) and a corresponding decrease in another asset (cash), leaving the Fundamental Equation in balance once again.

[*15*]

In fact, the entire accounting process may be encompassed in nine basic transactions, of which all others are merely variations:

1. Increase Assets, Increase Net Worth.
2. Increase Assets, Decrease Assets.
3. Increase Assets, Increase Liabilities.
4. Decrease Assets, Decrease Liabilities.
5. Decrease Assets, Decrease Net Worth.
6. Increase Liabilities, Decrease Liabilities.
7. Increase Liabilities, Decrease Net Worth.
8. Decrease Liabilities, Increase Net Worth.
9. Increase Net Worth, Decrease Net Worth.

In order to understand the material that follows, it is necessary that we examine briefly the nature of these transactions. You may find it helpful at this point, or later in your reading, to study Appendix B on bookkeeping, which examines in detail the operation of the double-entry system derived from the Fundamental Equation. For the purposes of the remainder of this book, however, the abbreviated descriptions in this chapter will suffice.

The Forms of Transactions

Each of the nine forms of transactions may be simply illustrated, and each should be completely understood before progressing further. Let us use the example of Joan Wisdom, who is just opening a new business. We will look at the effects on that business of each of the transactions.

1. Increase Assets, Increase Net Worth. This is the transaction in which the owners of the business contribute items of value to it. Suppose Wisdom establishes a consulting business with $4,000 of her cash. The effects on the Fundamental Equation would be:

+ $4,000 Cash   =   + $4,000 Wisdom Net Worth
   (Increase Assets)   (Increase Net Worth)

2. Increase Assets, Decrease Assets. This very common transaction might take the form of Wisdom purchasing some office supplies for $500 cash:

+ $500 Office Supplies
    (Increase Assets)   =
– $500 Cash
    (Decrease Assets)

Note that in this illustration, as we saw in our earlier discussion, the Fundamental Equation remains balanced, though both entries were made on the same side.

3. Increase Assets, Increase Liabilities. Not all purchases, of course, are made for cash. Suppose Wisdom buys $5,000 of furniture on credit:

+ $5,000 Furniture   =   + $5,000 Accounts Payable
    (Increase Assets)   (Increase Liabilities)

4. Decrease Assets, Decrease Liabilities. The payment of a liability generally looks like the reverse of transaction 3. If Wisdom now pays in cash $2,000 of the debt she incurred to buy the furniture, the effect will be:

– $2,000 Cash   =   – $2,000 Accounts Payable
    (Decrease Assets)   (Decrease Liabilities)

5. Decrease Assets, Decrease Net Worth. Suppose that Wisdom decides that she would like for her personal use one of the items of furniture that was purchased for her business. She removes a $400 chair from the office and brings it to her home. As a result, she has reduced her investment in the business, and this is reflected in the Fundamental Equation as follows:

– $400 Furniture   =   – $400 Wisdom Net Worth
    (Decrease Assets)   (Decrease Net Worth)

6. Increase Liabilities, Decrease Liabilities. This transaction takes place when one debt is substituted for another. Remember that Wisdom incurred a debt of $5,000 for furniture (transaction 3), and paid $2,000 of that debt in cash (transaction 4). Suppose now that the furniture supplier insists that Wisdom give a promissory note for the unpaid balance of $3,000. Although the amount of the debt has not changed, its form has. This would be reflected in the Fundamental Equation:

                            + $3,000 Note Payable
                                (Increase Liabilities)
                        =   – $3,000 Accounts Payable
                                (Decrease Liabilities)

7. Increase Liabilities, Decrease Net Worth. Suppose misfortune strikes Ms. Wisdom, and a client is injured in her office. Ms. Wisdom agrees to pay the client's medical expenses, which are expected to be to $500. The effects:

> \+ $500 Expenses Payable
> (Increase Liabilities)
> = − $500 Wisdom Net Worth
> (Decrease Net Worth)

Note how this transaction differs from transaction 3, where liabilities increased and assets increased. In this transaction, however, the business received nothing of value (no asset) in return for the increase of its liabilities. Therefore, since the business has incurred a liability and it receives no value in return, Wisdom's ownership interest in the business has declined.

8. Decrease Liabilities, Increase Net Worth. Every cloud has a silver lining. Suppose that the injured client (transaction 7) recovers her entire expenses from medical insurance, and forgives Wisdom's debt. The effects:

> − $500 Expenses Payable
> (Decrease Liabilities)
> = \+ $500 Wisdom Net Worth
> (Increase Net Worth)

How do we explain the increase in Wisdom's Net Worth? She has received something of value: not an asset, but the forgiveness of an indebtedness. Since she gave up nothing of value (no asset) to reduce the liability, her ownership interest in the business has increased.

9. Increase Net Worth, Decrease Net Worth. Wisdom decides to take in a partner, Sharp. She sells to Sharp a $2,000 interest in the business receiving payment personally in the amount of $2,000. Since no assets were contributed to the business by Sharp, the left side of the Fundamental Equation remains unchanged. However, the ownership interests have changed, as follows:

> \+ $2,000 Sharp Net Worth
> (Increase Net Worth)
> = − $2,000 Wisdom Net Worth
> (Decrease Net Worth)

Although each of these transactions has been explained in terms of its effects on the Fundamental Equation, in practice the transactions would be recorded in the books of the business by means of *entries,* in each case reflecting both sides of the transaction. These entries are explained and examined in detail in Appendix B on bookkeeping.

Debit and Credit

Accountants call the left side of the Fundamental Equation *Debit* and the right side *Credit*. A great deal of needless anguish has been suffered by students who have sought deeper meanings of these terms. Be assured, they have none. We use the terms "debit" and "credit" in our discussion of bookkeeping in Appendix B, since the terms are widely accepted, but your understanding of accounting will not be the least compromised if you prefer "left" and "right".

Income and Expense

As you studied the nine basic transactions, you may have been struck by the fact that none of them involved operation of the business, as opposed to setting it up. Where are the fees from clients, the expenses of secretaries, staff and utilities? Recall that we spoke earlier of variations on the nine transactions. Now it is time to explore those variations.

If a business receives one asset in exchange for another, and both are of equal value (transaction 2), the business itself has neither increased nor decreased in value. Increase in value occurs when the business receives more than it gives up, or receives something and gives up nothing. In the first instance, the business is generally selling goods at a profit; in the second, it is generally rendering services for a fee.

Returning to the Fundamental Equation, we remember that it must stay in balance. If, therefore, a business receives a cash fee of $1,000 and gives up no assets and incurs no liabilities in return, its net worth is by definition increased. Similarly, if the business sells goods for $10,000 which cost it $8,000, its net worth has increased by $2,000. In both cases, we might simply reflect the increases in net worth directly every time they occur. For a moderately active service or sales business, however, it might be necessary to reflect net worth changes many times daily. Moreover, such a recording process would forsake an opportunity to collect separately and analyze some of the most important information with respect to the activities of the business.

We are speaking, of course, of income or revenue. Indeed, at least one very important purpose, if not the principal purpose, of most businesses is generation of income. Therefore, instead of recording income items directly as increases in net worth (which, in fact, they are) the accounting process maintains them separately. Income appears on the right side of the Fundamental Equation as a subcategory (positive) of net worth. Eventually, it becomes a part of net worth, as we shall see below.

Income usually cannot be generated without expense. Expense is for all practical purposes the opposite of income: a business disburses its assets and does not receive in return something of continuing value. As an example, a business might spend $250 cash in a given month on telephone service. To be sure, the telephone service is of value to the business, or else the cash would not have been expended for it. But it is not an asset, since it is no longer an item of *continuing* value to the business. One might view the telephone expense as an expired asset, having been used up as it was paid for. If assets (cash) were reduced and no other assets were increased or liabilities reduced, it follows that there must have been a reduction in net worth. Indeed there was, as there is with any item of expense. As with income, however, the accounting process does not reflect expense directly as a reduction of net worth. Rather, expenses are separately maintained on the right side of the Fundamental Equation as a subcategory (negative) of net worth.

Enterprises generally report on their status and results of operations periodically, with the most general period being one year. Many report on the calendar year (January 1–December 31) but many report on a *fiscal year*, which may be any one-year period (such as July 1–June 30). Income and expenses are aggregated and categorized for the year, and are shown on the Statement of Income. The excess of income over expense, usually called *Net Income*, is then added to net worth, and the cycle of aggregating income and expense is started over again for the new year. Of course, if expense exceeds income, there is a *Net Loss*, which results in a reduction of net worth.

The Accounting Cycle

The accounting process begins with transactions that affect assets, liabilities and net worth, or the two subcategories of net worth, income and expense. These transactions are recorded in so-called *books of original entry*, or *journals*, that reflect in each case both sides of the transaction. As with every element of accounting, the balance of the Fundamental Equation is always preserved.

Since almost all enterprises are more complex than the illustrations we used earlier, it is necessary to summarize the transactions not only into the elements of the Fundamental Equation, but also into separate categories of each element. Accordingly, the information recorded in the journals is transferred (*posted*) to separate accounts, generally in a set of documents known as *ledgers*. For example, separate accounts are maintained for cash, inventories, equipment, buildings and land. Separate accounts are maintained for accounts payable, and—indeed—for each person or firm to whom money is owed.

Similarly, separate accounts are maintained for each category of income and expense. At the end of the year, various adjustments will usually be made to the income and expense accounts, as we will see in later chapters. Thereafter, the accounts are added up, summarized, and reported on the statement of income. The balance of net income or net loss is transferred to net worth, and the income and expense accounts for the year are *closed*. In other words, the income and expense accounts are used to collect information about enterprise activities during the year, and once that information is collected, the accounts are closed—to be reopened for collection of information in the succeeding year. Accountants occasionally refer to these accounts as *nominal accounts*, as contrasted with asset, liability and net worth accounts, which are called *real accounts*.

The balances in the accounts for assets, liabilities and net worth are not closed, but rather are maintained as running balances throughout the life of the enterprise. Periodically, usually annually, the account balances are determined and summarized, and are then reported on the balance sheet. As you might expect, the balance sheet reflects both the form and the balance of the Fundamental Equation.

It is important to remember that income and expense accounts relate to *activities* that take place *over a period of time*, whereas asset, liability and net worth accounts relate to *status at a given time*. This difference is highlighted by the dating of the Times Mirror Statement of Income ("for the year ended . . . .") and Balance Sheet ("as of . . . ."), that appear in Appendix A (pages 206–208).

Financial Statements: The Balance Sheet

We have seen how the accounting process accumulates information concerning transactions in assets, liabilities and net worth, and about transactions involving income and expense. We are now ready to examine the principal financial statements and to draw some preliminary conclusions about their construction and their purposes.

Refer in Appendix A (pages 206–207) to the Consolidated Balance Sheets of Times Mirror Company and Subsidiaries. You will note immediately that the statement is in the form of the Fundamental Equation. Taking the figures (in thousands) for December 31, 1981, total assets on the left ($1,917,212) equal total liabilities and net worth on the right ($1,917,212). No surprises. However, the statement is a bit intimidating, so we shall spend a few paragraphs examining it.

The heading "Consolidated Balance Sheets" is in the plural, since it is customary to show balance sheets as of the end of two or more years for comparative purposes. Later, we will compare balance sheets and income statements from year to year to evaluate the progress of the enterprise. "Consolidated" refers to the fact that the balance sheets show, in combined form, the status of several companies. Times Mirror Company owns several subsidiary corporations—including companies involved in newspaper publishing, broadcast and cable television, and newsprint and forest products—all of whose assets, liabilities and net worth have been combined in the consolidated balance sheets.

The balance sheets speak as of a date, December 31, 1981 and 1980. We will later learn that it takes some time to accumulate and verify the information in these statements. In the case of Times Mirror, though the latest balance sheet is dated December 31, 1981, it was not published until February 8, 1982. Recall our discussion in Chapter 1, where we noted that financial statements reflect what has already happened.

The assets side of the balance sheet is organized in the order of relative *liquidity* of the assets, that is, their closeness to being cash. *Current Assets* include cash and other assets that are expected to be converted into cash within the operating cycle of the business, usually one year. Cash is the first asset listed. Directly beneath it are Marketable Securities (stocks and bonds) and Accounts Receivable, which are amounts owed to the company, usually by its customers, expected to be received within the year. Of course, not every trade creditor actually pays, so the company has reduced the amount of accounts receivable by an estimate for doubtful accounts and returns.

The next listing is Inventories, which represent the assets— in this case mostly books, newsprint and logs—that are held for sale to the company's customers or for use in manufacturing the company's products. These, too, are current assets, since the company expects to convert them into cash by manufacture and sale within the next year.

Below inventories are prepaid expenses, expense items that have already been paid for but have not been consumed. These items will be discussed in detail in the next chapter.

Following the heading Current Assets, the balance sheet lists Timberlands, which represent a long-term asset for Times Mirror Company, but one that is being used up or *depleted* as the timber is cut and processed. The timberlands are shown on the balance sheet reduced in value by the estimated depletion.

Next are listed Property, Plant and Equipment, often known generically as *Fixed Assets*. These are assets of relatively long life, ordinarily part of the productive capacity of the business. Times Mirror shows these assets under separate categories for Buildings, Machinery and equipment, and Land. The phrase "less allowance for depreciation and amortization" reflects the fact that while the buildings, machinery and equipment have long lives, their lives are not infinite. In Chapter 5, we will discuss in detail how the purchase price of these assets is allocated as an expense over the useful life of the assets. That process of allocation is known as *depreciation*, and is reflected in both the balance sheet and the income statement. Land does have infinite life, and is therefore not subject to depreciation.

The last assets listed, "Other Assets," consist principally of the asset called Goodwill, an asset whose origins and accounting treatment will be examined in Chapter 6.

Turning to the right side of the balance sheet, we note that Liabilities are listed first, and that they—in a manner similar to the assets—are listed in the order in which they must be paid. Liabilities due to be paid within the coming year are *Current Liabilities*, and these include accounts payable, employee compensation and taxes.

The next item on the right side of the balance sheet is Long Term Debt, the details of which can be found in Note G (pages 215–216) in the notes following the financial statements. These Notes provide further details concerning the summarized data to be found in the balance sheet and the other financial statements. Later chapters will explain the contents of other notes to the financial statements.

Finally, the balance sheet lists other liabilities, including principally Unearned Income and Deferred Income Taxes, both of which will be discussed in Chapter 7.

The final section of the balance sheet, also on the right, details Net Worth, for which Times Mirror uses the alternate terminology *Shareholders' Equity*. In a corporation, like Times Mirror, Net Worth is no single figure. Instead, it is divided into three separate categories representing the three legal and financial forms of net worth in a corporation. These will be discussed later in Chapter 8, but you may note now that a separate figure is given for the *Retained Earnings* of Times Mirror, representing the accumulated income of the company that has not been distributed to its owners.

We have chosen to introduce the balance sheet at this point, with all its complexity and attendant confusion, to provide a sense of the nature of the end product of accounting and the degree of detail offered by financial statements. By the end of this book, you should have little difficulty understanding the Times Mirror Balance Sheets, but you should expect some confusion now. Refer to the appropriate sections of the Times Mirror financial statements as they are discussed in succeeding chapters, and the confusion will disappear.

Financial Statements: The Statement of Income

The Statement of Consolidated Income that appears in Appendix A (page 208) is fundamentally a far simpler document to understand. Unlike the balance sheet, it reports on operations *for a period of time*, in this case each of three years. The first item, *Revenues*, represents the inflow of income items to the company for the year. From revenues are subtracted *Costs and expenses*, listed under three categories, to arrive at a figure for *Income before income taxes*. From this figure is subtracted *Income taxes* to arrive at the figure for *Net Income*. Generally Accepted Accounting Principles have adopted the concept of the *all inclusive income statement*, containing all items of income, expense, gain and loss for the year. If a company has unusual or nonrecurring items of gain or loss (such as the destruction of a manufacturing plant by fire), they will appear separately on the income statement and will be included in the calculation of net income.

The last item on the statement of income is a figure for *Earnings per share*, which represents a calculated figure of the amount of net income allocable to each outstanding share of the company's stock. This is one of many figures used by readers of financial statements to summarize the performance of the company. Later, in Chapter 9, we will study the calculation of earnings per share and examine other analytical tools for evaluating the financial statements.

Financial Statements: The Statement of Changes in Financial Position

Of the three principal financial statements, the Statement of Changes in Financial Position is probably the most difficult to understand. The Times Mirror Statements of Consolidated Changes in Financial Position in Appendix A (pages 210–211) detail the sources and applications of *funds* and the changes in *working capital* for three years. Funds and working capital are used synonymously to refer to the excess of current assets (including cash, accounts receivable and inventories) over current liabilities. The purpose of this statement, therefore, is to describe the company's performance in terms of the inflows and outflows of assets and liabilities. Later, in Chapter 10, we will study this statement and the related concepts of cash and funds flow.

Other Statements, Schedules and Notes

The Times Mirror Statements also include Statements of Shareholders' Equity (page 209), detailing changes in the net worth accounts, a collection of notes to the financial statements (pages 212–222), and Management's Discussion and Analysis of Financial Condition and Results of Operations (pages 196–205). The statements are preceded by schedules (pages 192–195) that provide summary information for ten years and business segment information for five years. These notes and schedules contain a wealth of additional information that explains and elaborates upon the financial statements.

The Report of Independent Accountants appears on the last page of the financial statements (page 223). That report, and the auditing process that preceded it, are the subject of Chapter 11.

Chapter Three

THE ACCRUAL SYSTEM OF ACCOUNTING

As those persons who despair of ever being rich make little account of small expenses, thinking that little added to a little will never make any great sum.

Plutarch, Of Man's Progress in Virtue

The Concepts of Realization and Recognition

Possibly the most complex and important issue faced by the accounting system is when—and how—to reflect the effects of economic activity. Some events, of course, lend themselves to clear accounting treatment. If a business renders a service and is promptly paid in cash, income has been earned and the income should be reflected in the accounting records. The receipt of the cash and its recordation in the accounting records is called *recognition.* However, it was the rendering of the services that gave rise to the right to receive the income; that event is known as *realization.* In our illustration, realization and recognition occurred nearly simultaneously. That is not always so.

Let us suppose that a business renders a service in 1982, for which it is not paid until 1983. The receipt of cash cannot be shown until 1983. When is the income realized? When should it be recognized by an entry in the accounting records? Alternatively, suppose that in 1982 a business receives an advance payment of cash on services it does not render until 1983. The receipt of cash must be reflected in 1982, since it actually occurred in that year. When should income be recognized by an entry in the accounting records?

We have already introduced the concepts that every event recorded in the accounting records has two effects under the double-entry system, and that the Fundamental Equation must remain in balance. Is it possible to maintain the balance of the Fundamental Equation and at the same time to record cash in one year and income in another?

The principle of realization rests on the notion that the events giving rise to recognition of income or expense are not necessarily tied to the date when cash is paid or received. In the case of services income, the realization principle would call for recognition *when the services are rendered,* irrespective of the date of payment. If services are rendered in 1982 they give rise to income in 1982, and if rendered in 1983 they give rise to income in 1983.

How the cash is handled, and how the Fundamental Equation is kept in balance, are the subjects of the remainder of this chapter.

Accrual Accounting Principles

The principle of realization requires that recognition be given to income when it is earned, and that recognition be given to expenses when they are incurred. To achieve these results, accounting uses the mechanical processes of *accrual* and *deferral.* Accrual refers to recognition of income or expense before cash is paid or received, and deferral refers to recognition after cash changes hands. Accrual and deferral, the two basic techniques of the accrual accounting system, allow recognition to be given to transactions while preserving the balance of the Fundamental Equation.

Suppose that Arthur Patience, an architect, rendered services to a client in December, 1982. He billed the client $1,000 in December, but did not receive payment until February, 1983. He might simply recognize the income in 1983, when he was paid. As we will later see, recognition on payment, called "cash basis accounting," is occasionally acceptable for certain accounting purposes, most importantly federal income taxes. For purposes of Generally Accepted Accounting Principles, however, cash basis accounting is not acceptable, and recognition of the income in 1983 would be erroneous. Since Patience performed all the services required for payment in 1982, the $1,000 is income in 1982 *even though it was received in 1983.*

The transaction is reflected in the accounting records twice, first at the time when the services are completed and a bill is rendered, and second when payment is received. The first transaction, in 1982, shows an increase in net worth of $1,000, to reflect the income, and an increase in an asset: fee receivable. The asset might alternatively be called account receivable, or fee income receivable, or some other appropriately descriptive term.

[*27*]

The effects on the Fundamental Equation are a variation of transaction 1 in Chapter 2:

> \+ $1,000 Fee Receivable   =   + $1,000 Fee Income
> (Increase Assets)   (Increase Income, a
>   subcategory of Net
>   Worth)

The second transaction, receipt of cash in 1983, represents an increase in the asset cash, coupled with a decrease in the asset fee receivable, with effects similar to those of transaction 2 in Chapter 2:

> \+ $1,000 Cash
> (Increase Assets)   =
> − $1,000 Fee Receivable
> (Decrease Assets)

It may look as though we have gone to a good deal of trouble to reflect a simple transaction, but the effects are quite important. When Patience prepares his balance sheet as of December 31, 1982 and his income statement for the year ended December 31, 1982, one item will appear on each statement that would not have been present had he waited until 1983 to recognize the fee:

— The balance sheet will show an asset, fee receivable, of $1,000.

— The income statement will show $1,000 more in fee income.

Correspondingly, his 1983 income statement will show $1,000 *less* fee income, since the $1,000 cash received in February will be shown as received in return for an asset.

Are these differences of any importance to the readers of the financial statements? In the long run, there is no difference between cash basis accounting and accrual accounting: if we were to produce an income statement for the entire life of a business (10, 50 or 150 years), it would make no difference whether income was recognized in 1982 or 1983. However, accounting generally is not designed to report on the long run. A principal purpose of the income statement is to disclose *periodic* income. Correspondingly, the balance sheet is intended to disclose the status of the business *as of a given date*. Failure to reflect income that has been earned, though not received in cash, results in a distortion of both of these statements. Moreover, the distortion, as we shall later see, is capable of easy manipulation by the unscrupulous or overeager business.

The accrual system, therefore, is a key element in assuring meaningful and fair disclosure of status and periodic performance. We will now examine the other elements of accrual accounting.

Accrual of Income and Expense

When income is earned prior to its receipt, the income is reflected in the accounting records as of the time when it is earned. Similarly, when expense is incurred prior to its payment, the expense is reflected as of the time it is incurred. In these instances, accountants speak of *accrued income* or *accrued expense*. Accrued income was illustrated above.

To illustrate accrued expense, suppose that Patience moved into his offices on September 1, 1982, with a lease providing for rent at the monthly rate of $1,000, payable at the end of each three-month period. On November 30, 1982, he will therefore pay $3,000, representing the rent for the preceding three months. As of December 31, 1982, he will prepare his income statement. If it reflects only $3,000 of rent expense, it will understate his expenses for the year, since he will have occupied his offices for four months. Accordingly, Patience should *accrue* an additional $1,000 of rent expense (reflecting the unpaid rent of one month since his last rental payment) and show a liability of $1,000 on his balance sheet. The Fundamental Equation effects are as follows:

$$+ \ \$1,000 \text{ Rent Payable}$$
(Increase Liabilities)
$$= \quad - \ \$1,000 \text{ Rent Expense}$$
(Reduction of Income, a subcategory of Net Worth)

You will realize that the rent expense transaction is quite similar to transaction 7, in Chapter 2.

The reflection of expenses in the accounting records deserves some further explanation. We have shown rent expense above as a negative entry to net worth. Note, however, that rent expense *increased*, even though its effect on the Fundamental Equation was negative. That is because expenses of any kind constitute *reductions* in the net worth of the enterprise. Keep in mind the concept that increased income = increased net worth, and increased expense = decreased net worth. How these concepts translate into the accountant's debits and credits is explained in Appendix B on bookkeeping.

[*29*]

What happens when Patience pays his rent on February 28, 1983 for the three months then ended? Although Patience will pay $3,000, only $2,000 will be expense for the year 1983, representing rent for the months of January and February. The remaining $1,000 will be paid to discharge the liability, rent payable, that was recorded at the end of 1982.

The accrual process has succeeded, therefore, in allocating to each year the portion of rent expense that was in fact incurred in that year. The date of payment does not affect the allocation.

Deferral of Income and Expense

Often, cash is paid or received prior to the rendering of services or the incurring of an expense. The same process of allocation of income and expense is followed, but this time it is called *deferral*. Suppose that in November, 1982, Patience contracts with a client to perform services and receives an advance of $5,000. He begins the services in January, 1983, completes them in February, and charges a total fee of $12,000. Since the client has already paid $5,000 in advance, he pays Patience the remaining $7,000 in March, 1983. How are these transactions reflected in Patience's accounting records?

Although cash was received in 1982, the services for which the cash was paid were not rendered until 1983. Accordingly, the $5,000 advance was not *earned* in 1982, and income should not be recognized in 1982. All of the income, the entire $12,000, is attributable to 1983.

The $5,000 cash advance is, of course, an asset owned by Patience. However, there is a corresponding liability, which might be called "professional services owed" or "fees received in advance," a liability that Patience did not discharge until he actually rendered the services in 1983. Accountants refer to this item as *deferred income*, and it is shown as a liability on the balance sheet. It will be listed under current liabilities or long-term liabilities, depending upon when the obligation to render services is expected to be performed. A similar item appears on the Times Mirror Company Balance Sheet, in Appendix A, (page 207) under the heading "Unearned Income."

[*30*]

In terms of the Fundamental Equation, the cash advance has the following effects:

$$+ \$5,000 \text{ Cash} \qquad = \qquad + \$5,000 \text{ Deferred Income}$$
$$\text{(Increase Assets)} \qquad\qquad \text{(Increase Liabilities)}$$

When Patience completes the job and receives the remaining $7,000 in 1983, the liability (deferred income) is discharged and an additional asset (cash) is received. The effects:

(1) $-$ $5,000 Deferred Income
            (Decrease Liabilities)

            $=$

            $+$ $5,000 Fee Income
                (Increase Income, a
                subcategory of Net
                Worth)

(2) $+$ $7,000 Cash $=$ $+$ $7,000 Fee Income

In this illustration, the deferral process has succeeded in allocating to the year 1983 the entire $12,000 fee income, which is as it should be, since all of the income was earned in 1983.

A similar analysis leads to the deferral of expenses that have been paid in advance. Let us suppose that Patience purchases a fire insurance policy on June 1, 1982, with a term of one year, and that he pays in advance the entire premium of $1,200. By December 31, 1982, when Patience prepares his financial statements, a portion—but not all—of the insurance policy will have been consumed. To be precise, seven months of the policy coverage will have expired, and five months of coverage will remain for 1983. Therefore, it would be a misallocation of the expense to show the entire $1,200 premium as an expense of 1982. Instead, only $700 (seven months at $100 per month) is shown as an expense in 1982. The remaining $500 is *deferred*, to be shown as an expense in 1983. What is the $500? An item of value to the business, whether tangible or intangible, is an asset. Therefore, the $500 will appear as an asset on Patience's balance sheet, under the heading *Deferred Expense* or, more commonly, *Prepaid Expense*. Prepaid expenses appear on the Times Mirror Company Balance Sheet, Appendix A (page 206) as the last of the current assets.

The combined effect of accrual and deferral is that income and expense are *recognized* by entry in the accounting records *when they are realized*, irrespective of when payment is made or received. As a result, the periodic financial statements pro-

[*31*]

vide a more realistic view of the economic effects of the enterprise activities.

Accrual Accounting and Preparation of the Financial Statements

The general principles of accrual accounting will be applied daily, as each transaction of the enterprise is recorded in the accounting records. For example, when services are rendered and a bill is submitted, income will be recognized as described above. However, it is neither necessary nor feasible to make regular adjustments for accrued and deferred income and expense as time passes. Consider the rent expense illustration above: should Patience reflect the accrual or deferral of rent expense at the end of each month? Ordinarily, he would not, because he is not preparing financial statements each month. He reflects the accruals and deferrals at year-end, since he prepares financial statements annually. In other words, the accruals and deferrals, called *adjusting entries* by accountants, are made at the end of a financial reporting period, in order to provide more meaningful information on the results of operations for that period and for succeeding periods.

The last point deserves amplification. Every adjusting entry will have effects on at least two reporting periods. If income is deferred from 1982 to 1983, the result is a *decrease* in the reported income for 1982 and a corresponding *increase* in the reported income for 1983. Many of the adjusting entries can be made virtually with mathematical precision, as in the case of accrual or deferral of rent expense based on the portion of the lease term that has expired. Other adjustments, however, involve substantial judgment questions, as we shall see later.

The preparation of the financial statements at year-end (or at the end of any different reporting period used by the enterprise) can be summarized in four steps:

1. The year-end balances in the accounts of the enterprise are summarized in a document called a *trial balance*. The trial balance is simply a listing of all asset, liability, net worth, income and expense accounts.

2. Adjusting entries are made to reflect the accruals and deferrals as of the end of the year.

3. The income and expense items, as adjusted by the adjusting entries, are assembled to prepare the income statement; and the balance of all of the items—*Net Income or Net Loss*—is transferred to the net worth or capital ac-

count. This is the process that was earlier described as *closing the books.*

4. The asset, liability and net worth items, as adjusted by the adjusting entries and after closing the books, are assembled to prepare the balance sheet.

You will find a complete description and illustration of these steps, in the form used by accountants, in Appendix B on book-keeping.

Following these steps, the income statement and balance sheet are prepared and disseminated, and a new year is begun in the accounting books. As of the beginning of the new year, the balances in the income and expense accounts are zero. The balances of the asset, liability and net worth accounts are carried forward.

Variations on a Theme: Businesses With Inventories

So far, we have dealt with enterprises that earn their income by performing services. In those enterprises, fees or services income are clearly income items. Now we turn to enterprises that sell goods.

Let us suppose that Helen Honesty opens a book store in January, 1982, and that she purchases an initial inventory of books at a cost of $30,000. Since she will sell many different books, her costs and her selling prices will be different for each title. Suppose also that during the course of the year, Honesty purchases an additional $50,000 of books. Honesty's sales for the entire year of 1982 amount to $100,000. How should she calculate her income?

Obviously, Honesty has not given us enough data with which to calculate income, since we do not know the *cost* of the books that she sold. We might determine those costs in either of two ways:

1. *Perpetual Inventory.* If Honesty kept separate records of each book sale and identified both the selling price and the cost of each book sold, she could determine her profit on each sale. The total of the individual profits would be her profit on sales for the year, known as *Gross Profit.* The system of keeping track of the cost of each item sold is known by accountants as *perpetual inventory.* The term is something of a misnomer, but it refers to an inventory system that keeps a running balance as each purchase and each sale is made.

[*33*]

2. *Periodic Inventory.*   As an alternative, Honesty might simply keep records of her sales (without recording the associated cost of each book sold) and her purchases in the aggregate.   Indeed, she has already kept those records.   In order to calculate her profit on sales for the year, *Gross Profit*, she would determine by physical examination the dollar amount of inventory remaining at the end of the year.   If her physical examination shows, for example, that the end-of-year inventory is $15,000, she would calculate her profit on sales as follows:

Sales		$100,000
Less Cost of Goods Sold:		
Opening Inventory	$30,000	
Plus Purchases	50,000	
Total Available for Sale	$80,000	
Less Ending Inventory	15,000	
Cost of Goods Sold		65,000
Gross Profit		$35,000

In other words, Honesty began her year owning goods with a cost of $30,000, and she purchased an additional $50,000 during the year, giving her a total of $80,000 of goods *available for sale* during the year.   Since her physical examination showed $15,000 of goods remaining at year-end, it follows that $65,000 were disposed of during the year.   The $65,000 therefore represents the cost of the goods sold, and since $100,000 was the total of the selling prices, Honesty made a *Gross Profit* of $35,000.

It should not be assumed, however, that the goods "used up" in the calculation of cost of goods sold are entirely consumed by sale.   Some portion of the goods may have been spoiled during the year, and some portion may have "walked out the door" without being paid for.

The periodic inventory system is far more prevalent than the perpetual inventory system because of the simplicity of its record-keeping requirements.   It has the disadvantage that the enterprise does not know its inventory except when it is physically examined.   Moreover, it is more difficult under the periodic inventory system to determine what portions of the goods were lost to spoilage and theft.   Recent development of computerized accounting systems using "intelligent terminals" at the point of sale has made the perpetual inventory system more feasible, though the necessary manpower and equipment costs generally restrict its use to relatively larger enterprises.

Manufacturing Businesses

The accounting characteristic that distinguishes service businesses from merchandising businesses, as we have seen, is that merchandising businesses maintain inventories. When we shift our attention from businesses that sell goods manufactured by others to businesses that manufacture their own goods, accounting for inventories also changes.

In a merchandising business, there may be several inventories. A department store would likely maintain separate inventories for each department, major appliances, children's clothing, and the like. Indeed, a well designed inventory system might be quite detailed, not only by department but by item.

Manufacturing businesses, too, maintain separate inventories, but there is an additional separation, by degree of completion. Ordinarily, a manufacturing business will maintain separate inventory categories for *Raw Materials*, *Work in Process*, and *Finished Goods*. In the case of a printer, *Raw Materials* might include paper, ink and binding boards; *Work in Process* would likely represent books partially printed or not yet bound; and *Finished Goods* would include finished books ready for shipment to dealers. For an example of balance sheet disclosure of separate inventories, refer to the Times Mirror Company Balance Sheet in Appendix A, and read the detailing of inventories that appears in Note D to the financial statements (page 213).

A Word About Cash Basis Accounting

Accounting without accruals—*Cash Basis Accounting*—is not acceptable under GAAP, and accordingly published financial statements prepared on the cash basis are extremely rare. However, the cash basis is acceptable, with certain limitations, for reporting income for federal income tax purposes for businesses that do not have merchandise inventories. We will examine in Chapter 15 the circumstances under which cash basis tax accounting is acceptable and the situations in which it might be advantageous.

The Connection Between Assets and Expenses

Our examination of the accrual system reveals an intimate connection between assets and expenses. In the following chapters we shall see that many of the assets of a business, as they are utilized in the business activities, *become* expenses. Central among these are inventories, which through sale become part of cost of goods sold, and fixed assets, which become expense through the process of depreciation. Accounting for these assets significantly affects both the balance sheet and the statement of income.

REFERENCES

Official Pronouncements:

Financial Accounting Standards Board, Statement of Financial Accounting Concepts No. 1, Objectives of Financial Reporting by Business Enterprises (1978).

Financial Accounting Standards Board, Statement of Financial Accounting Concepts No. 2, Qualitative Characteristics of Accounting Information (1980).

Financial Accounting Standards Board, Statement of Financial Accounting Concepts No. 3, Elements of Financial Statements of Business Enterprises (1981).

Secondary Sources:

Financial Accounting Standards Board, Conceptual Framework for Financial Accounting and Reporting: Elements of Financial Statements and Their Measurement (Discussion Memorandum, 1976).

Chapter Four

INVENTORIES

Take it from me—he's got the goods.

O. Henry, The Unprofitable Servant

Introduction: The Effects of Inventory Calculations

Inventories, goods held for manufacture or sale in the ordinary course of business, are carried as current assets on the balance sheet. Inventory determinations play a central role in calculation of the gross profit of the business. Therefore, variations in the method of determining inventories may significantly affect the gross profit and may alter the reader's perception of the performance of the enterprise. These effects may be demonstrated in a simple example.

	1982	1983
Sales	$40,000	$50,000
Cost of Goods Sold:		
Beginning Inventory	$10,000	$ 8,000
Plus Purchases	27,000	43,000
Goods Available for Sale	$37,000	$51,000
Less Ending Inventory	8,000	14,000
Cost of Goods Sold	$29,000	$37,000
Gross Profit	$11,000	$13,000

This now familiar gross profit calculation contains an important lesson: the ending inventory for any year becomes the beginning inventory for the following year. The $8,000 ending inventory for 1982 becomes $8,000 of beginning inventory for 1983. It follows that *any change in the calculation of ending inventory will affect the gross profit of two years*.

In the illustration above, the company shows a trend of increasing sales and increasing profits. However, if the ending inventory for 1982 were determined to be $9,000 rather than the $8,000 shown, the gross profit for 1982 would *increase* to $12,000 and the gross profit for 1983 would *decrease* to $12,000. The company would then appear to have level profits despite its increasing sales. If the ending inventory were determined to be

$10,000 in 1982, the profit picture would actually be reversed, with $13,000 profit shown in 1982 and $11,000 in 1983.

Since reported income, and trends in income, are of great importance to investors and others who evaluate a company's performance, the method of inventory determination and valuation must be carefully analyzed in order more fully to understand the significance of reported income figures. A variety of different conventions may be used to determine inventory valuation, and many of these fall within Generally Accepted Accounting Principles. The choice may easily produce variations in results as dramatic as those in the illustration above.

What Is Included in Inventory?

In general, inventory is carried on the books at its cost, which includes all elements of cost necessary to make the inventory salable. Cost will therefore include some items that might otherwise have been viewed as expenses. These include shipping costs paid by the company in connection with acquiring the inventory, called *Freight In*. So, for example, if a company purchases 100 items costing $6.00 each and pays $50 shipping costs to acquire them, the items will be carried at a cost of $650 in its inventory, or a price of $6.50 per unit.

Certain other expenses may have a character similar to freight in. Warehousing costs, for example, are generally an expense and not included in the value of inventory. However, if warehouse aging is necessary to make the goods ready for sale, as in the case of aged whiskey, the warehousing costs would be added to the value of the inventory.

There is an important distinction between categorizing an item as expense and adding it to the cost of inventory. The difference is in timing: expense items are immediate expenses for the year in which they are incurred, whereas inventory costs become expense (by inclusion in the cost of goods sold) only when the inventory items are sold. The items might, of course, be sold in the same year in which they were purchased, but they might also be sold in a subsequent year.

In the case of inventories in a manufacturing enterprise, the timing distinction becomes more dramatic. Suppose a manufacturing company produces 100 wooden folding chairs, and the raw materials (wood, nails, glue) used in the manufacture of the chairs cost a total of $1,000. At what value will the chairs be shown in inventory? The question cannot be answered without more data because the carrying value of the chairs must include not only the cost of raw materials but also the cost of labor directly attributable to their manufacture—*Direct Labor*—and an allocated portion of the overall expense of maintaining the manufacturing facility in which they were made—*Overhead.*

Thus, if the laborers who worked on the chairs were paid $1,500 for their efforts in manufacturing the chairs, that $1,500 becomes part of the inventory value. Moreover, the total overhead expense of maintaining the manufacturing plant—including heat, light, power, rent, supervisory expense, insurance and the like—must be appropriately allocated among all of the items manufactured by the company. If the allocation shows that $200 is applicable to the chairs, it too must be added to their inventory value. The total, $1,000 raw materials + $1,500 direct labor + $200 overhead = $2,700 inventory value for the 100 chairs, or $27 per chair.

At the risk of redundancy, note that neither the direct labor nor the overhead is charged to expense. If the chairs were manufactured in 1982 but not sold until 1983, the money spent on direct labor and overhead would not become expense in 1982. Instead, it would become part of cost of goods sold in 1983.

When Are Items Included in Inventory?

Inventory items constantly move into and out of a business, and questions frequently arise as to whether certain items have entered or left the inventory in a given year. Suppose that a company ordered certain items in December, 1982 for immediate delivery, but that the goods did not arrive and were not paid for until January, 1983. When did they enter the inventory? Ordinarily, one would assume that they entered the inventory in 1983, but that is not always the case. Accountants' rules for so-called *cut-off inventory* determinations are frequently complex, and turn on the terms of the contract. In this illustration, if in 1982 the goods were set aside for the purchaser and the purchaser assumed the risk of shipment and loss, they would be properly included in the 1982 inventory, despite the fact that they arrived later. A similar analysis must be made with respect to year-end sales of inventory items.

We illustrate this problem to show that a multitude of complex questions must be resolved at year-end in order to reflect fairly the inventory values, and therefore the net income, of the business. Moreover, these year-end transactions present opportunities for the cunning, and sometimes unscrupulous, company to alter the reported results for the year. The practice of bringing forward or pushing back year-end transactions for the purpose of improving reported results has earned the descriptive name, *window dressing.*

Inventory Flow and Inventory Flow Conventions

For the analysis that follows, we will indulge in the simplifying assumption that a business has only one type of inventory item—accountants have for generations called that item a "widget"—and that the inventory calculation is concerned only with the cost of the inventory of widgets. If the inventory consists of two or more items, the same calculations will generally be applied *separately* to the inventory of each item.

Remember that inventory is carried on the books at its cost. If every widget purchased by the company were to cost the same price—for example $10—inventory calculations would be greatly simplified. Inventory would be physically counted at year-end, and the number of units would be multiplied by $10 to arrive at a cost figure for the ending inventory. It is rarely that simple. Costs change. Suppose that some widgets were purchased for $10, and some for $11, $12, $13 and $14? Which ones are left at the end of the year?

The actual flow of inventory in most businesses can best be analogized to a pipeline. The first material that enters one end of the pipeline is the first material to emerge from the other end. In accounting terminology, this model would be called *First-In, First-Out*, known by the acronym *FIFO*. Of course, not all inventories flow in this manner. Some might follow the analogy of a parts bin. The items last dumped into the bin would likely be the first to be removed from the top and put to use. This model is known as *Last-In, First-Out*, or *LIFO*. Alternatively, one might envision an inventory flow analogous to a gasoline tank, where withdrawals from the tank represent a mixture of everything that has been put into it. In accounting terms, such an inventory model would be called *Average Cost*. One additional model might be mentioned, though it certainly does not exhaust the possibilities. Inventory might be specifically chosen, item by item, as it is used. Perhaps the best example of this approach, known in accounting as *Specific Identification*, is the inventory of an automobile dealership.

Accounting is generally unconcerned with actual inventory flow, but rather applies one of several generally accepted principles to financial calculations of inventory value. In other words, the accounting inventory flow is a *convention*, not necessarily reflective of the real flow of inventory. Why is this so, and how can it be justified?

To begin, we must note that in many instances inventory items are completely or nearly fungible; one item of inventory is functionally indistinguishable from another. This tends to be true in most manufacturing processes. Iron bought in September is not different, but for price, from iron bought in January. Therefore, the *physical* flow of inventory bears little relevance to the *financial* flow. Indeed, if physical flow were the criterion on which inventory accounting were based, there would be opportunities for financial manipulation based on the choice of which iron (September or January) to use in the manufacturing process.

Therefore, accounting principles allow a variety of inventory flow conventions—all irrespective of actual physical flow—but insist upon consistency in the convention used. We explore below the effects of choice of convention and of change in the convention applied. You may be troubled with the range of choices. We will discuss the advantages and disadvantages of open choice after examining the range of alternatives.

FIFO, LIFO and Weighted Average

Suppose that a wholesaler begins the year 1983 with 10 units of inventory that cost $10 per unit, and that purchases for the year are as follows:

Date		Units	Unit Price	Total
Opening Inventory		10	$10	$100
Purchases:	2/1	15	11	165
	4/15	20	12	240
	7/20	15	13	195
	11/10	10	14	140
Total		70		$840

The year-end physical examination of inventory shows that 20 units remain. What is the value at which the 20 units will be shown on the income statement and balance sheet?

If the *FIFO* convention is followed, it will be assumed for accounting purposes that the earliest items that entered inventory will leave first. In other words, the first items deemed to be sold will be the opening inventory, followed in turn by the purchases of 2/1, 4/15, 7/20 and 11/10, in that order. Therefore, the ending inventory will consist of the last items purchased and not sold. With 20 units remaining, 10 will be from the purchase of 11/10 and the remaining 10 from the purchase of 7/20. Therefore the value of the ending inventory will be:

10 units @ $14 (11/10 purchase) = $140
10 units @ $13 (7/20 purchase)   =   130
Total $270

If instead the *LIFO* convention is followed, it will be assumed for accounting purposes that the last items that entered the inventory will leave first. In other words, the first items deemed to be sold will be the purchases of 11/10, followed by the purchases of 7/20, 4/15 and 2/1 and the opening inventory, in that order. Therefore, the ending inventory will consist of the first items purchased and not sold. With 20 units remaining, 10 will be from the opening inventory and the remaining 10 from the purchase of 2/1. Therefore the value of the ending inventory will be:

10 units @ $10 (opening inventory) = $100
10 units @ $11 (2/1 purchase)   =   110
Total $210

Finally, if the *Weighted Average* convention is followed, it will be assumed for accounting purposes that items leave inventory at the weighted average cost of all inventory items for the year. Since a total of 70 items were available in inventory for the year, and since their total cost was $840, the weighted average equals $840 ÷ 70, or $12 per unit. Similarly, the ending inventory would be calculated as:

20 units @ $12 (weighted average) = $240

All three of these inventory flow conventions fall within Generally Accepted Accounting Principles (GAAP).

The Retail Inventory Method

Inventories generally consist of many different items with different characteristics and different costs. In general, GAAP requires that the costs of different *items* be separately maintained. Thus, an appliance manufacturer could not properly mix the costs of washing machines with the costs of television sets. In some businesses, the multiplicity of inventory items and the need to maintain records of each may produce massive record-keeping problems. In retail businesses, these problems led to the widespread use of an alternative inventory calculation system, known as the *Retail Inventory Method*. In this method, inventories are physically counted at the end of the accounting period and are listed at their *selling prices*, which may be readily determined. Of course, the selling prices do not reflect the *costs* of the inventory items, so an adjustment is made to the selling prices to approximate cost. Suppose that in 1982, Righteous Retailer had the following income statement:

Sales		$100,000
Less Cost of Goods Sold:		
Beginning Inventory	$20,000	
Purchases	70,000	
Goods Available for Sale	$90,000	
Less Ending Inventory	30,000	
Cost of Goods Sold		60,000
Gross Profit on Sales		$40,000
Expenses		20,000
Net Income		$20,000

Righteous is now preparing its 1983 income statement, and has finished the examination of its ending inventory. The value of the inventory at *selling price* is $30,000. At what value should Righteous carry the inventory in its financial statements? From its 1982 income statement, we learn that Righteous earned a gross profit on sales of $40,000 ÷ $100,000, or 40%. Therefore, the selling prices of Righteous' inventory, on the whole, yield a 40% profit. Phrased differently, the *cost* of the Righteous inventory is on the whole equal to 60% of its *selling price*. Therefore the cost of the 1983 ending inventory, assuming that the gross profit percentage for 1982 is maintained in 1983, is calculated as $30,000 × 60% = $18,000. The Retail Inventory Method is acceptable under GAAP.

Why Does GAAP Permit a Choice of Inventory Techniques?

If you will return to the opening paragraphs of this chapter, you will recall that both the balance sheet and the income statement are affected by the choice of inventory technique. We must now examine why GAAP allows a choice, and what the implications of a given choice and of a change in inventory technique are likely to be.

The most convincing argument in favor of variation in inventory techniques is that accounting must accommodate to the varying character of different businesses by allowing the application of a range of principles. This argument is supported by the illustration of the Retail Inventory Method, a technique developed clearly in response to business convenience and necessity. There may be further support for the argument in the case of enterprises whose physical inventory flow can be mirrored in the accounting principles actually applied.

The other arguments for variation turn not on the character of the business, but rather on outside factors affecting the business. The two most widely used techniques, FIFO and LIFO, are generally selected on the basis of their effect on reported and taxable income. During periods of increasing prices, LIFO generally has the effect of reducing reported net income, and similarly of reducing taxable income. You may see this effect by comparing the illustration above, in which ending inventory under FIFO amounts to $270, while ending inventory under LIFO is $210. The $60 difference translates into an increase of $60 in cost of goods sold under LIFO, and therefore a decrease of $60 in gross profit and in net income when that method is used.

Would a company wish to *reduce* its reported income in a period of rising prices? Interestingly, the answer is generally yes. One of the reasons for the affirmative reply is obvious: if a company reduces its taxable income, it pays lower taxes. The other reason is not so obvious. Generally, a company is evaluated by investors and creditors not solely based on the amount of its net income, but also based on its trend. If you will again review the first section of this chapter, you will note that the calculation of one year's ending inventory necessarily affects the income of that year and of the succeeding year. If the income for 1983 is reduced by using LIFO, there will tend to be an increase—though not necessarily in the same amount, since LIFO will also be applied at the end of the next year—in the income for 1984. Viewed another way, one possible effect of LIFO in periods of rising prices is to improve the trend of income by tending to shift income forward to succeeding years. One might therefore expect that in periods of substantial inflation many companies would shift to the LIFO technique, and that expectation is borne out by the facts.

The differences among the permitted inventory techniques cannot be so simply analyzed, however. Prices go up, but they also come down. Inventory techniques affect not only reported income, but, also valuation on the balance sheet. LIFO and FIFO represent the extremes:

FIFO: — Tends to reflect most accurately the actual inventory flow.

— Shows the most current costs for inventory on the balance sheet, generally producing a more realistic balance sheet figure.

— Shows earlier costs as part of cost of goods sold, therefore reflecting price changes more slowly in the calculation of gross profit and net income.

LIFO: — Generally does not reflect actual inventory flow.

— Shows the oldest costs (often many years old) on the balance sheet, often producing an artificially low figure for inventory in periods of increasing prices.

— Shows the most recent costs as part of cost of goods sold, therefore rapidly reflecting price changes in the calculation of gross profit and net income.

Since the current emphasis in financial disclosure is on the income statement, there appears to be a consensus that in periods of changing prices (principally rising prices, or inflation), LIFO produces a more realistic evaluation of the financial status of the business. As we note above, this conclusion is only partially accurate, since an inevitable result of LIFO is to produce unrealistic balance sheet inventory figures. In fact, changing prices present a particularly difficult problem for the accounting process, which in general is based on the notion that the dollar remains constant in value. We discuss the problems of changing prices with respect to inventories and other items in detail in chapter 14.

LIFO poses an interesting technical problem not present in the other inventory techniques: what happens if through oversight or intention the company sells a portion of the inventory that is carried at very early prices? This phenomenon, known as "dipping into the base stock," may be illustrated as follows:

Sales, 50 units @ $60				$3000
Cost of Goods Sold:				
Opening Inventory,	20 units @ $10	=	$ 200	
Purchases,	50 units @ $40	=	2000	
Goods Available for Sale			$2200	
Ending Inventory,	20 units @ $10		200	
Cost of Goods Sold				2000
Gross Profit				$1000

In the situation above, the units were purchased for $40 each and sold for $60 each, a profit of $20 per unit. Since 50 were purchased and 50 were sold, the gross profit is shown as $1000. Suppose, however, that the company had purchased only 40 units, while still selling 50? The income statement would look very different:

Sales, 50 units @ $60				$3000
Cost of Goods Sold:				
Opening Inventory,	20 units @ $10	=	$ 200	
Purchases,	40 units @ $40	=	1600	
Goods Available for Sale			$1800	
Ending Inventory,	10 units @ $10		100	
Cost of Goods Sold				1700
Gross Profit				$1300

Now the gross profit has leaped to $1,300 (which translates to $26 per unit) simply because the company failed to purchase as many units as it sold! The reason: the company sold some of its "base stock" of old price inventory ($10 per unit) at current prices. However, next year the company will have to purchase new inventory at current prices, $40 per unit. The $1300 gross profit figure is unrealistically high. Companies using LIFO generally take great pains to avoid this result, since it also causes payment of substantial additional taxes for the period.

Have we answered the original question why GAAP allows a variety of inventory techniques? Note that there are arguments in favor of each, and that it is difficult if not impossible to choose one definitively over another. *If the technique chosen is fully disclosed in the statements, the reader should be able to evaluate the results in an informed manner.* GAAP therefore makes no choice, but does require disclosure of the choice made by the reporting company.

Change of Inventory Method

If choice of a method of inventory determination can affect reported results, it follows that change from one method to another may affect those results. GAAP allows changes from one method to another, but requires that the change be disclosed on the financial statement and that the effects of the change also be disclosed. As a result, the reader will retain the ability to compare the results of a company's operations from one year to another, even if the inventory method is changed.

For income tax purposes, as we later discuss in Chapter 15, the inventory method used must be the same as the method used for financial accounting. Moreover, a change of inventory method will require prior approval of the Internal Revenue Service.

Lower of Cost or Market

In Chapter 3 we discussed the concepts of realization and recognition, and we noted that GAAP generally does not call for recognition (reflection of an item in the accounting records) until realization (the economic events leading to income or expense) takes place. We now encounter an interesting and controversial variation on the principles of realization and recognition, the principle of *conservatism*. As applied to inventories, the principle of conservatism requires that all losses in the value of inventory be recognized, even if not yet realized; but the principle precludes recognition of gains in inventories until those gains are realized by sale. For example, if an item of inventory cost $10 but is worth $20 at year-end, it must be carried on the books at its original cost of $10. By contrast, if the same item of inventory were worth $8 at year end, it would be carried on the books at the lower value of $8. As applied to inventories, the principle is called *Lower of Cost or Market,* and it is a central element of GAAP.

Application of the principle of lower of cost or market involves some complexity. We have already explored the variations in determination of cost by application of varying inventory flow conventions. Market is determined on a wholly different basis. Market is ordinarily presumed to be *Replacement Value,* the present cost to the business of obtaining comparable units. Once cost and market have been determined, the principle of lower of cost or market is applied to the inventory either by units or by categories of inventory. As an illustration, suppose that a company has four categories of inventory at year-end, as follows:

Category	Cost	Market	LCM
A	$100	$150	$100
B	200	175	175
C	300	250	250
D	350	350	350
Totals	$950	$925	$875

The last column shows the value at which the inventories would be carried on the financial statements. Within each category of inventory (A, B, C and D), the company might apply lower of cost or market either to the category as a whole, as shown above, or item by item.

We should note once again that the effect of reducing inventory value at the end of any year is to reduce income for that year and to increase income for the succeeding year. Therefore, while the principle of lower of cost or market is conservative (or pessimistic) in the sense that it reduces one year's reported income, it tends to produce the appearance of an upward trend of income in the succeeding year. The principle has been widely criticized by scholars and commentators, but remains well entrenched in GAAP.

The complexity in lower of cost or market has to do with determination of market value. Although market is presumed to be replacement cost, it may not exceed *net realizable value.* Nor may it be lower than *net realizable value less normal profit margin.* Net realizable value is the amount of money that is expected to be received for the inventory item less the expected cost of it disposal. For example:

Item A:	Cost	$25
	Replacement Cost	25
	Expected Selling Price	32
	Expected Selling Expense	8

In the illustration, replacement cost is $25, so it would appear at first glance that lower of cost or market is $25, since market is no lower than cost. However, the item is expected to sell for $32, with selling expenses amounting to $8, and therefore the net realizable value ($32 − $8) is $24. The correct market value is therefore $24, and lower of cost or market is also $24. A more complex illustration:

Item B:	Cost	$40
	Replacement Cost	30
	Expected Selling Price	45
	Expected Selling Expense	5
	Normal Profit on Sale	7

In this case, it first appears that market is $30, or replacement cost. However, market may not be lower than net realizable value less normal profit margin. Here, it is expected that the item will sell for $45, less selling expenses of $5, yielding net realizable value of $40. If we further subtract the normal profit margin of $7, the lowest value at which the item may be carried becomes $33. Lower of cost or market is also $33.

The process of calculating lower of cost or market may be somewhat simplified by dividing it into four mechanical steps:

1. Determine cost under the inventory flow convention being used by the business.

2. Determine replacement cost, net realizable value, and net realizable value less normal profit margin.

3. Market equals the median (or middle) figure of the three figures in (2) above.

4. Inventory is carried at the lower of cost (1 above) or market (3 above).

Inventories Stated Above Cost

Only in exceptional cases may inventories properly be stated above cost, since statement above cost has the effect of recognizing income prior to its realization through sale. However, precious metals having a fixed monetary value with no substantial cost of marketing may be stated at their monetary value. Also, inventories representing agricultural, mineral and similar products the units of which are interchangeable and have immediate marketability at quoted prices may be stated at those prices when appropriate costs are difficult to ascertain. When inventories are reported above cost, their value should be reduced by expected costs of disposition, and full disclosure of the valuation method must be made.

REFERENCES

Official Pronouncements:

American Institute of Certified Public Accountants, Committee on Accounting Procedure, Accounting Research Bulletin No. 43 (1953), chapter 4.

Secondary Sources:

Jannis, Poedtke, Carl & Ziegler, Managing and Accounting for Inventories (1980).

Chapter Five

FIXED ASSETS: DEPRECIATION
AND DEPLETION

Continual dropping wears away a stone.

Lucretius, De Rerum Natura

Introduction: The Concept of Fixed Assets as Prepaid Expenses

In the last chapter we examined the process by which the asset, inventory, becomes an expense, cost of goods sold. To the extent that inventory remains on hand at the end of the year, it remains an asset, and to the extent that it is consumed in production or sale, it becomes a part of the expenses of the business. Many other assets flow through the business cycle in a similar manner. These include such items as office supplies and cleaning materials. Other assets, however, are consumed in a somewhat different manner.

Let us examine the use of a truck by Truthful Transporters Co. Over the long run, the truck is "consumed" in a manner not unlike the inventory. Although the truck is not sold to customers and does not become a part of a manufactured item, it is used by Truthful to render services and is ultimately worn out and disposed of as scrap. The principal difference, from a financial viewpoint, between the truck and the inventory is that the truck takes longer to consume. Phrased differently, the useful life of the truck extends over several years or several accounting periods.

Earlier, we identified items like trucks, equipment and buildings as *fixed assets*, assets having lives that extend beyond the current accounting period or, in general, assets having lives in excess of one year. Now we shall examine the process by which accounting allocates the cost of fixed assets to expense over the course of the useful lives of those assets. The process is known by various names, depending upon the nature of the asset involved. With most physical assets—machinery, equipment, vehicles, buildings—the allocation process is known as *depreciation*. A few fixed assets are actually physically consumed in the process of use. These include forests, mines and wells, and as to these the allocation process is known as *depletion*. Some long-term assets are nonphysical in nature, such as patents or long-term leases. The allocation process for these assets is known as *amortization*.

Whatever the name of the process, it is a process of *allocation of cost over time*. We emphasize the point, because it is sometimes erroneously assumed that depreciation accounting is designed to show the actual physical wearing out of the asset or the decline in *value* of the asset, or that it is designed to provide funds to replace the asset. None of these is necessarily true, though in some instances sheer coincidence might result in accounting depreciation satisfying one or another of these propositions.

Problems of Estimation and Evaluation

In the previous chapter, we noted that inventory accounting may follow several different principles, all of which are generally accepted, and that judgment plays an important role in the determination of inventory values. The same may be said about depreciation, and therefore about the accounting valuation of fixed assets. Moreover, depreciation accounting requires that estimates be made of the useful life and expected scrap value of assets, estimates that are necessarily based on judgment.

We may examine these judgments by returning to the example of Truthful Transporters Co. Let us assume that Truthful purchased one truck on January 1, 1983 for $45,000 and that the truck was used in the business for the entire year 1983. What portion of the truck became expense in the form of depreciation? To answer this question, Truthful must first make three determinations:

(1) What is the expected useful life of the truck?

(2) What is the expected scrap value of the truck after its useful life has expired?

(3) What method of depreciation will be applied?

The answers to the first two questions are judgmental. They require estimates of expected future events, which may or may not ultimately prove accurate. Suppose Truthful expects to use the truck for four years, and that its expected scrap value or trade-in value at the end of four years is $5,000. We may now calculate the depreciation for 1983 using a simple formula:

$$Annual\ Depreciation = \frac{Cost - Scrap\ Value}{Useful\ Life}$$

Substituting the numbers in the formula:

$$Annual\ Depreciation = \frac{\$45,000 - \$5,000}{4} = \$10,000$$

Note, however, that the formula we have applied also responded to question 3 above: we have assumed that annual depreciation will be in the same amount for each year of the truck's useful life. This principle, known as *straight line depreciation*, will be examined further below. For the moment, we will examine the first two questions. How are the useful life and scrap value determined? Suppose that the determinations ultimately prove wrong, that the truck lasts three years or five years, or that the scrap value is greater or less than $5,000? As we will see, adjustments may subsequently be made if the initial estimates prove erroneous. However, there is no avoiding the necessity for making the estimates in the first place. Past experience, independent appraisals, published guidelines and income tax regulations, among other sources, serve as a basis for making the estimates.

Disclosure of Depreciation on the Income Statement and the Balance Sheet

If you will refer to Appendix A, you will note that Times Mirror Company discloses on its Consolidated Balance Sheets (page 206) the original cost of buildings, machinery and equipment, and separately deducts from the total an *allowance for depreciation and amortization*. This practice is required by GAAP because it provides more informative disclosure than simply showing the net figure after depreciation. The depreciation figure may be called *allowance for depreciation, accumulated depreciation,* or other similar term. On the December 31, 1983 balance sheet of Truthful Transporters Co., this information would be disclosed as follows:

Truck, at cost $45,000
Less: Accumulated Depreciation   10,000
                                                  $35,000

Times Mirror provides further disclosure in Note A to its consolidated financial statements:

Timberlands. . . . Depletion of timberlands is provided on the unit-of-production method based upon estimated recoverable timber.

Property, Plant and Equipment. Property, plant and equipment are carried on the basis of cost. Generally, depreciation is provided on the straight line method for buildings, machinery and equipment.

Similar disclosure would be required in the financial statements of Truthful.

On the income statement, *depreciation expense* (or depletion or amortization expense, as applicable) appears among the operating expenses for the business. In a manufacturing business, a substantial portion of the depreciation expense (relating to machinery, equipment and plant) will ordinarily be considered manufacturing overhead, and will therefore be included as part of cost of goods sold.

The Effects of Depreciation Calculations

Depreciation methods, like inventory techniques, affect both the income statement and the balance sheet. The determination of depreciation for each year will affect *depreciation expense* on the income statement and will have a corresponding effect on *accumulated depreciation* on the balance sheet. Ordinarily, depreciation will be recorded at the end of the accounting period (usually one year) as part of the adjusting entries prepared before closing the books. In the case of Truthful Transporters, the effects of the entry of $10,000 depreciation on the Fundamental Equation are:

— $10,000 Accumulated Depre-   =   — $10,000 Depreciation Ex-
        ciation, Truck (re-   pense (increase ex-
        duce Assets)   pense, which
                                                           reduces Net Worth)

[*53*]

You will remember that variations in the determination of ending inventory affected the financial statements of two years. Variations in depreciation calculations affect the financial statements over the entire life of the fixed assets in question. Let us expand on the Truthful Transporters illustration and suppose that the truck actually lasts five years rather than four. Compare the results when Truthful uses its original four year depreciation figures with the results using a five-year life for its truck.

Four-Year Life

	1983	1984	1985	1986	1987
Shipping Income	$20,000	$22,000	$24,000	$26,000	$28,000
Less:					
Depreciation (4 years)	$10,000	$10,000	$10,000	$10,000	$ —
Other Expenses	2,000	3,000	4,000	5,000	6,000
Total Expenses	$12,000	$13,000	$14,000	$15,000	$ 6,000
Net Income	$ 8,000	$ 9,000	$10,000	$11,000	$22,000

Five-Year Life

	1983	1984	1985	1986	1987
Shipping Income	$20,000	$22,000	$24,000	$26,000	$28,000
Less:					
Depreciation (5 years)	$ 8,000	$ 8,000	$ 8,000	$ 8,000	$ 8,000
Other Expenses	2,000	3,000	4,000	5,000	6,000
Total Expenses	$10,000	$11,000	$12,000	$13,000	$14,000
Net Income	$10,000	$11,000	$12,000	$13,000	$14,000

The differences are dramatic. Using the five-year life, which turned out to be correct, the company shows a steady increase in income each year. Using the four-year life, the company shows steady increases in income in the first four years, followed by a sudden spurt in income in the fifth. The reason for the substantial increase in the fifth year, of course, is that the fifth year shows no depreciation, since the truck has already been fully depreciated down to its scrap value. Once an asset has been fully depreciated no further depreciation is reflected, even if the asset continues to be used. In the illustration, the truck continued to be useful for a fifth year despite the fact that it had originally been expected to be used for only four.

Comparison of the two sets of income statements shows that the choice of a four-year useful life as compared with a five-year life affected the reported net income for each of the five years. In general, this illustration applies to all depreciation determinations, including estimated life, scrap value and depreciation method.

What Costs Are Included in Fixed Assets?

An enterprise ordinarily acquires many assets during its business cycle. Which of these are treated as fixed assets, which as current assets, and which are charged immediately to expense? As we have already seen, fixed assets are those that are expected to have a useful life beyond one year, and most assets (even current assets like inventory) become expense as they are consumed. These guidelines will generally be sufficient to characterize most asset acquisitions. In some instances, however, practical considerations will call for alternative treatment. For example, small hand tools used in manufacturing may be charged immediately to expense on acquisition, to avoid the need for a multiplicity of depreciation accounts.

All expenditures necessary to acquire an asset and put it to use should be included in the cost of the asset. These include shipping, preparation and installation. In the case of land or a building, the costs of removing undesired structures would be added to the cost of the asset retained. Thus if a company purchased land for $100,000 and spent an additional $25,000 to demolish an existing structure on the land in order to prepare it for subsequent construction, the land would be carried on the company's books at a total cost of $125,000.

Interest expense is generally not considered a part of the cost of the asset. If, for example, a company purchased equipment "on time", paying $200,000 plus $20,000 interest for the equipment over the next 18 months, the equipment would be carried on the books at only $200,000. The additional $20,000 would be shown as interest expense.

An interesting question arises when repairs, improvements or additions are made to fixed assets. Are they to be treated as additions to the asset cost—*capitalized*—or are they to be charged to expense? In general, expenditures that increase the useful life of an asset or improve or extend its utility should be capitalized. By contrast, repairs and general maintenance, which maintain but do not extend the asset's utility, are charged directly to expense. As illustrations, addition of an air conditioning system to a building would be capitalized, whereas painting the building would ordinarily be treated as an expense.

Depreciation Methods

The most common depreciation method used for financial reporting is *straight line depreciation*, as described earlier in this chapter, under which the cost of the fixed asset (less its scrap value) is allocated evenly over the years of its useful life.

Depreciation may also be allocated on a nonlinear basis, with greater depreciation in earlier years. Methods that allocate more depreciation to earlier years are known collectively as *accelerated depreciation.* There may be several reasons for using accelerated depreciation techniques, including the possibility that the assets in fact decline in value more in the earlier years of their use. However, the foremost reason for the use of accelerated depreciation is to obtain income tax savings. For this purpose, net income for tax purposes, *taxable income*, may be calculated differently by a company than net income for reporting purposes under GAAP. If taxable income can be reduced by appropriate accounting techniques, income taxes can also be reduced. The tax reduction may be temporary and may be offset by a later tax increase, but if payment of taxes can thereby be forestalled for several years the company will have the productive use of more money during that time. Accelerated depreciation techniques achieve this result, and they have therefore been widely used in calculating taxable income. Let us return to the illustration of Truthful Transporters to demonstrate the effects of accelerated depreciation. Suppose that Truthful, having determined that the truck has a useful life of four years, uses an accelerated depreciation method. Instead of showing depreciation of $10,000 each year, it records depreciation as follows:

1983:	$16,000
1984:	12,000
1985:	8,000
1986:	4,000

The total depreciation is no greater than straight line, $40,000. However, the first two years show higher depreciation, and therefore lower income. As a result, Truthful pays lower income taxes for those years. If Truthful's tax rate were 20% of taxable income, it would show a tax saving of $1,200 in 1983 and an additional tax saving of $400 in 1984. To be sure, the piper must be paid, and Truthful's taxes would be increased by $400 in 1985 and by $1,200 in 1986. However, Truthful has benefitted by not having to pay the additional taxes until several years later; it has had the equivalent of an interest-free loan from the Internal Revenue Service.

Since there is no requirement that a company follow the same depreciation technique for tax reporting as it follows for financial reporting, it is very common for companies to use accelerated depreciation for tax purposes and straight line depreciation for financial reporting. For an illustration, see Note F to the financial statements of Times Mirror Company, in Appendix A (page 214).

The two most widely used methods of accelerated depreciation have been *declining balance* and *sum-of-the-years' digits.* Both methods are acceptable under GAAP, and until recent changes in the Internal Revenue Code (discussed in Chapter 15), both were acceptable for tax accounting.

You will recall that straight line depreciation applies a uniform rate of depreciation each year. In the Truthful illustration, assuming a four year life for the truck, the rate of depreciation each year was $1/4$, or 25%, of the cost less scrap value ($45,000 − $5,000). This yielded annual depreciation of $10,000. Under declining balance depreciation, the rate is increased, usually to double the straight line rate (*double declining balance*). However, the rate is applied each year to the remaining balance of the asset value. Truthful's truck would be depreciated at a rate of 50% (double the straight line rate of 25%) as follows:

Year	Balance at Beginning of Year	Depreciation at 50% of Balance	Total Depreciation to Date	Balance at End of Year
1983	$45,000	$22,500	$22,500	$22,500
1984	22,500	11,250	33,750	11,250
1985	11,250	5,625	39,375	5,625
1986	5,625	625	40,000	5,000

Notice that while the 50% *rate* remains constant, it is applied to a constantly declining *amount*, with the result that the depreciation in early years is higher than the depreciation in later

[57]

years. Notice also that scrap value is not considered in applying the declining balance method. Nevertheless, it is not permissible to depreciate an asset below its scrap value. Therefore, if the expected scrap value is $5,000, as the example stated originally, the depreciation in 1986 could not bring the net value of the asset below $5,000. Depreciation is therefore limited to $625 in 1986, despite the fact that the formula would indicate a greater amount. Declining balance depreciation has been the most commonly used form of accelerated depreciation.

The sum-of-the-years'-digits method is applied by adding the digits of the years of useful life and creating a separate fraction for each year. It is best explained by illustration. Truthful's truck has an expected useful life of four years. The sum of the years' digits is therefore: $1 + 2 + 3 + 4 = 10$. Depreciation will be calculated by multiplying the cost less scrap value by a fraction for each year as follows:

$$1983: \ 4/10 \times (\$45,000 - \$5,000) = \$16,000$$

$$1984: \ 3/10 \times (\$45,000 - \$5,000) = \ \ 12,000$$

$$1985: \ 2/10 \times (\$45,000 - \$5,000) = \ \ \ \ 8,000$$

$$1986: \ 1/10 \times (\$45,000 - \$5,000) = \ \ \ \ 4,000$$

Occasionally, a company might apply the *units-of-production* method of depreciation, reflecting depreciation based on actual physical use. Thus, if a machine cost $120,000, had an expected scrap value of $20,000, and was expected to be used in production of 50,000 units of goods, the company might record depreciation of $2 for each unit produced, calculated as follows:

$$\frac{\$120,000 - \$20,000}{50,000 \text{ units}} = \$2 \text{ per unit}$$

This method is not widely used, probably because of its requirements of detailed records.

Although a creditable case might be made for greater depreciation in later years (*decelerated* depreciation?), based on more rapid decline in productive capacity as the asset wears out, no such method has gained general acceptance.

[58]

Depreciation methods may be applied on an individual basis separately to each fixed asset, or may be applied on a composite basis to each group of similar assets.

Why Does GAAP Permit a Choice of Depreciation Methods?

As with inventories, we have once again encountered an area of accounting in which the choice of method heavily affects the balance sheet and the income statement. In the case of inventories, we concluded that choice was permitted to allow for variations among businesses and accounting systems, to afford some degree of responsiveness to changing prices, and to allow for the use of accounting methods that may provide tax savings opportunities. The reasons for permitting choice in the case of depreciation are similar. Group and individual methods, as well as methods allowing for immediate expensing of small items, permit companies to tailor their accounting systems to business practices. Tax advantages heavily argue in favor of the use of accelerated depreciation for determination of taxable income.

The tax laws allow the use of accelerated depreciation methods at least in part to stimulate the purchase of plant and equipment. The immediate expensing of a portion of fixed assets purchased may be used to accomplish the same economic effect as rapid depreciation. Both techniques were adopted as part of the Accelerated Cost Recovery System (ACRS) enacted in the Economic Recovery Tax Act of 1981.

There are a few important differences between the alternative methods available for inventories and those available for depreciation. The first is that the Treasury Regulations generally require that the inventory technique chosen for tax purposes be the same as that applied for purposes of financial reporting. No such requirement is applied with respect to depreciation techniques, with the result that many companies use accelerated depreciation for tax purposes but report financial income based on straight line depreciation. This variation in accounting approach led to GAAP requirements concerning disclosure of expected increased taxes in later years. The subject of such *deferred income taxes* is discussed in Chapter 7.

Another difference concerns changing prices. We saw that an argument can be made in favor of LIFO based on its more rapid response to price changes. No such argument can be made for accelerated depreciation, which only changes the timing of cost allocation during the asset's useful life.

You may be tempted to justify choice of a depreciation technique based on its accuracy in reflecting the physical expiration of asset life, or the actual decline in its value. These factors are usually not given weight in accounting determination, since the purpose of depreciation accounting is to *allocate cost*, and not to indicate present value. Consider the case of a building, purchased in 1965 for $200,000 and depreciated $10,000 per year until 1985. The building then is carried on the books at a depreciated cost of $100,000, but may well be worth $500,000! This result does not impugn the basic allocation approach of depreciation, but it does raise questions as to the meaning of the balance sheet. We shall consider those questions in Chapter 14, when we examine the problems of accounting and changing prices.

Changes in Estimates of Useful Life and Scrap Value

During the course of using a fixed asset, a company may determine that the useful life is greater or less than had originally been estimated. Similarly, it may become evident that the scrap or salvage or trade-in value of the asset has changed. These changes might be handled by recalculating depreciation for all of the years in which the asset was used. GAAP does not follow this approach, for several reasons. In the first instance, it is understood that depreciation is based on estimates and that estimates can only approximate actual results. Also, a requirement to recast the financial statements of earlier years to reflect every change of estimate would be expensive and impractical. Indeed, in a business using many assets, it is likely that variations between estimated lives and actual lives will tend to offset each other. Finally, there is some question as to the value to investors and other users of the financial statements of regular recasting of earlier statements to reflect changed estimates.

The approach taken by GAAP is to require that changed estimates be taken into account in current and future financial statements, but not in statements already published. Let us return once again to the well-worn Truthful Transporters Co. illustration to demonstrate how this works. Suppose that Truthful for two years depreciated its truck (using straight line depreciation) on the assumption that it had an expected life of four years and a scrap value of $5,000. Suppose further that in the third year Truthful determined that the truck would in fact last for five years, and that its scrap value would be $7,000. What results?

In years one and two, Truthful provided depreciation of $10,000 per year, using the formula:

$$\text{Annual Depreciation} = \frac{\text{Cost} - \text{Scrap Value}}{\text{Useful Life}}$$

$$\text{Annual Depreciation} = \frac{\$45,000 - \$5,000}{4} = \$10,000$$

No change will be made in the depreciation for those two years. To determine depreciation for the following years, the formula will be as follows:

$$\text{Annual Depreciation} = \frac{\text{Remaining Cost} - \text{Reestimated Scrap Value}}{\text{Remaining Useful Life}}$$

Substituting in the formula, the remaining cost equals $45,000 less the $20,000 of depreciation already recorded; and the remaining useful life is three years:

$$\text{Annual Depreciation} = \frac{\$25,000 - \$7,000}{3} = \$6,000$$

Therefore, for the remaining three years of its useful life, the truck will be depreciated at the rate of $6,000 per year.

GAAP also allows a change from accelerated depreciation to straight line depreciation (but not the other way), in which case the annual depreciation for years after the change is calculated by applying the formula described above.

Sales and Retirements of Fixed Assets

Ultimately, fixed assets are disposed of by retirement, sale or trade-in. Each asset is carried on the books in two separate accounts: cost (reflecting the original cost of the asset) and accumulated depreciation (reflecting the total depreciation recorded with respect to the asset). The difference between the two is the depreciated cost, or *book value,* of the asset. If the amount realized on disposition is greater or less than the book value of the asset, the company recognizes a gain or loss.

Suppose that after five years of use, Truthful shows the truck on its books at $45,000 cost, with accumulated depreciation of $40,000. It disposes of the truck for $2,000. Truthful recognizes a loss on disposition of $3,000, representing the difference between the proceeds on sale ($2,000) and the book value of the truck ($5,000). The loss on disposition is considered an ordinary operating expense of the company. Had there been a gain on disposition, it would be considered a reduction of the ordinary operating expenses.

Trade-ins may be differently handled. The book value of the traded-in asset may be added to the cost of the newly-acquired asset. If, in the illustration above, Truthful traded in its old truck and paid an additional $50,000 for a new truck, no gain or loss would be recognized on the transaction. Instead, the new truck would be carried at a cost of $55,000, representing the remaining book value of ($5,000) of the truck traded in, plus the additional payment for the new truck ($50,000).

Depletion

Fixed assets like machinery and equipment lose their utility over time by virtue of use, physical wear and obsolescence. One category of fixed assets loses utility as a result of being physically consumed. These assets, occasionally known as *wasting assets,* include mines, wells and timberlands. The eventual exhaustion of these assets is reflected in a process similar to depreciation, called *depletion*. As with depreciation, there are a variety of acceptable methods of depletion accounting, the most common of which for accounting purposes is cost depletion per unit.

Suppose that Grateful Gold Co. purchased a producing gold mine for $400,000, estimating that a total of 4,000 ounces of gold were recoverable from the mine. Following unit cost depletion, Grateful should reflect depletion expense of $100 for each ounce of gold recovered, based on the formula:

Cost ÷ Estimated Units = Depletion per Unit

$400,000 ÷ 4,000 ounces = $100 per ounce

If during the first year of operations, Grateful recovered 1,500 ounces of gold, depletion would amount to $150,000 (1,500 ounces × $100 per ounce). Depletion would be reflected on the balance sheet as a reduction of the asset Gold Mine, and on the income statement, depletion would be included as part of cost of goods sold, as an element in the cost of the gold produced and sold.

As with depreciation, accounting and tax rules for depletion differ. The Internal Revenue Code allows so-called *percentage depletion*, which is not based on cost, in certain extractive industries. Percentage depletion is designed to serve fiscal, economic or political objectives, and is not accepted under GAAP.

A Word About Amortization

Depreciation and depletion are two examples of the accounting process of allocation of cost. The general term *amortization* is also used to describe allocation of costs over time in other settings. The concepts underlying all three terms are the same, though the acceptable methods may vary. Amortization of intangible assets is illustrated in the next chapter.

REFERENCES

Official Pronouncements:

American Institute of Certified Public Accountants, Committee on Accounting Procedure, Accounting Research Bulletin No. 43 (1953), chapter 9; Accounting Research Bulletin No. 44 (revised, 1958) (Declining-balance depreciation).

American Institute of Certified Public Accountants, Accounting Principles Board, Opinions No. 1 (1962) (Depreciation guidelines and rules), No. 12 (1967) (Omnibus opinion); No. 20 (1971) (Accounting changes).

Secondary Sources:

Burton, Palmer & Kay, eds., Handbook of Accounting and Auditing (1981), chapter 20.

Lamden, Gerboth, Dale and McRae, Accounting for Depreciable Assets (AICPA Accounting Research Monograph No. 1) (1975).

Chapter Six

OTHER ASSETS

*How little you know about the age you live in if you
fancy that honey is sweeter than cash in hand.*

Ovid, Fasti

Having examined in detail the two categories of assets most
central to a wide variety of mercantile and industrial businesses,
inventories and fixed assets, we can now turn our attention to
the other assets on the Balance Sheet.

Cash and Cash Equivalents

Cash is the first asset item on the balance sheet. Most businesses, other than retailers, do not hold substantial amounts of
coin and currency on their premises. Retail businesses receive
currency daily and must maintain currency on hand to make
change and disbursements for returned merchandise. The currency and coin that most other enterprises hold is generally
known as *Petty Cash*, used to make miscellaneous disbursements for meals, taxicab fares and other small expenditures.
Petty cash is generally maintained in a lock box and accounted
for by means of vouchers presented by employees who receive
cash advances or reimbursements for expenditures. Modern
businesses handle their cash by means of *Demand Deposits*,
generally known as checking accounts. For accounting purposes, these two are categorized as cash.

Cash balances on deposit in banks may be available for un-
restricted use by the business or may be subject to certain restrictions on use. A common form of restriction is the *compensating balance*, required to be maintained under the provisions
of certain loan agreements. For example, if Upright Corp. borrows $100,000 from Ninth National Bank, the bank might re-
quire as a term of the loan that Upright maintain a balance in its
checking account of no less than $20,000. Of course, the effect
of that term is that Upright has the use of only $80,000 (while
paying interest on the entire loan of $100,000), but such terms
are frequently imposed by lenders. Compensating balance requirements and similar restrictions should be distinguished from
the common requirement that a depositor maintain a *minimum
balance* in a checking account, which does not represent a restriction on the use of cash. A depositor may draw its account

below the minimum balance, with the result that service charges will be payable for use of the account. By contrast, violation of a compensating balance restriction may give the bank the right to demand immediate payment of the depositor's loans. If cash is restricted in use, GAAP requires that the restrictions be fully disclosed by notes to the financial statements.

Cash may also be held for designated purposes or otherwise restricted as to use, as in the case of a trust fund or of moneys required to be paid out on a specified date to discharge indebtedness. Cash so restricted must be shown as a separate item on the balance sheet, with full disclosure of the limitations on its use. A common example of designated cash is a *sinking fund* required to be established under the terms of a corporate bond. The fund is set aside to be used for payment of the bond. Sinking funds and other terms of corporate debt instruments are discussed in Chapter 7.

Marketable Securities and Other Investments

Companies that have excess cash on hand often will invest the cash in a variety of short-term investments, ranging from certificates of deposit (interest-bearing obligations issued by banks or savings and loan associations) to Treasury Bills (short-term government obligations, generally with 91 and 182 day maturities) and commercial paper (short-term obligations generally issued by large corporations with good credit ratings). All of these earn interest, and in each case while the money is not immediately available, it is available within the year. Certificates of deposit may be combined with cash on the balance sheet, but the other investments are generally shown separately, at their cost, as current assets. The interest earned on these investments is disclosed as interest income on the statement of income.

A company may also invest in securities that are traded on the open market, whether on one of the national securities exchanges or in the over-the-counter market. With respect to marketable equity securities (stocks, as opposed to bonds) balance sheet values are determined by a variation of the *lower of cost or market* rule, a rule that we last encountered in our discussion of inventories. Marketable securities must be shown on the balance sheet at the lower of their *original* cost or their current market value. Suppose that Upright Corp. invested in a collection, or *portfolio*, of stocks during 1983 with a total cost of $35,000, and that the total portfolio was worth only $30,000 as of December 31, 1983. Upright's December 31, 1983 balance sheet would show a value of $30,000 for the stock portfolio, and Upright would show a loss of $5,000 ($35,000 cost minus $30,000 value) on its 1983 statement of income. However, had the value of the portfolio increased to $40,000, the increase would not be reflected. In that case, the investments would be shown at their original cost of $35,000.

Although conservatism generally prohibits the recognition of unrealized gains, increases in the value of investments may be shown *up to the original cost of the investments*. Suppose that by December 31, 1984, Upright's stock portfolio, having earlier declined in value to $30,000 in 1983, increases in value to $50,000. What will be its balance sheet value? The increased value has not been realized by sale, and ordinarily cannot be reflected on the balance sheet. However, since the portfolio was earlier (in 1983) written down in value below its cost, it may in 1984 be written back up again, but not in excess of its original cost. The December 31, 1984 value will be $35,000, the original cost of the stock portfolio, and Upright will show income of $5,000 on the portfolio for the year. The remainder of the increase in value may not be shown until it is realized by actual sale.

Note that in the Upright illustration we have not examined into the value of individual securities, but rather have applied the valuation based on the entire portfolio. GAAP requires this treatment, which tends to offset the individual price movements of securities within the portfolio. GAAP also requires that marketable securities be divided into two categories, current and noncurrent, and that separate accounts be kept of unrealized gains and losses on each. The Times Mirror Company Balance Sheets treat all marketable securities as current assets. Appendix A (page 206). Note A to the Times Mirror financial statements (page 212) discloses that marketable securities are carried at cost, which approximates market value. Disclosure of both cost and market value of marketable securities, by notes to the financial statements, is required by GAAP.

Nonmarketable securities, those that are not regularly traded on an exchange or in the over-the-counter market, are carried on the books at their cost. Debt securities, such as bonds and debentures, are accounted for on the basis of interest and discount, a subject we examine in detail in the next chapter.

The Equity Method of Accounting for Investments

Holdings of voting common stock of another company may simply represent an investment, but as the percentage of ownership of that stock increases, the investment may change its character. If Upright acquires 30% of the voting common stock of Downright Corp., Upright ceases to be a mere investor and may in fact be capable of exercising an influence in the control of Downright. Accounting requires that this difference in the character of the investment be recognized. If an investment in voting stock gives the investing company the power to exercise significant influence over the operating and financial policies of the company in which the stock is held, GAAP requires that the investment be accounted for on the *Equity Method.*

Under the equity method, the investment is initially recorded at cost. However, it is increased or decreased in carrying value by the investor's proportionate share of income and losses, and such income or losses are reported as a separate item on the investor's statement of income. The equity method is presumed to apply when the investment is 20% or more of a company's voting stock.

Using the equity method, Upright would initially enter the Downright stock in its books at its cost. We shall assume that the stock was purchased on January 1, 1983 for $100,000. If Downright had net income of $20,000 for the year 1983, Upright would record an increase in the value of its investment of $6,000 (30% of $20,000), representing its proportionate share of that income. Upright's income statement would show $6,000 of investment income for the year as a result of holding the Downright stock.

If the investment in voting stock of a company grows beyond 50%, the investor becomes capable of controlling the company in which the investment has been made. Accounting then permits the preparation of *Consolidated Financial Statements,* which report the financial status and results of the two companies on a combined basis. The Times Mirror financial statements in Appendix A are prepared on a consolidated basis. Consolidated statements are discussed further in Chapter 13.

Accounts and Notes Receivable

Accounts receivable are current assets, since by definition they represent amounts expected to be received from trade creditors in the ordinary course of business, generally within 30 to

60 days. Extension of credit involves a financial risk of nonpayment, and it is a rare company that collects fully on all of its accounts. Therefore, provision must be made for the likely uncollectibility of a portion of the accounts receivable. Ordinarily, past experience of the company, or comparative data from other similar companies, will provide a basis for calculating *Estimated Uncollectible Accounts*, or a *Provision for Bad Debts.*

Suppose that Careful Company shows accounts receivable on December 31, 1983 of $200,000, and its past experience has been that approximately 3% of its accounts are never collected. Careful's accountant should establish a provision of $6,000 (3% of $200,000) for estimated uncollectible accounts. The $6,000 represents a reduction of the value of accounts receivable, since Careful does not expect to recover the full $200,000. Refer to the Times Mirror Balance Sheet, Appendix A (page 206), and note that accounts receivable have been reduced by *"allowances for doubtful accounts and returns."* Correspondingly, the reduction of the asset accounts receivable represents an expense for the year 1983: *Bad Debts Expense.* Bad debts expense is part of the cost of doing business on credit.

Bad debts may also be estimated as a percentage of sales or of credit sales. For federal income tax purposes, a company may report as expense an estimate of uncollectible accounts or may alternatively record individual bad debts as they become uncollectible.

More sophisticated methods are often used to estimate uncollectible accounts, the most common of which is known as *aging accounts receivable.* In this process, the collectibility of accounts receivable is analyzed based on how long the accounts have been outstanding. If Careful's accounts were so analyzed, the accounts receivable aging schedule might look like this:

Accounts Receivable		Estimated Uncollectible	
Outstanding	Amount	Percent	Amount
0–60 days	$100,000	1%	$1,000
60–120 days	60,000	2%	1,200
120–180 days	30,000	5%	1,500
beyond 180 days	10,000	15%	1,500
Totals	$200,000		$5,200

The accounts receivable aging schedule not only provides more information upon which an estimate for uncollectibles may be based, but also offers further analysis of the credit and collection performance of the company.

Prepaid Expenses

We encountered the concept of prepaid expenses in our discussion of the accrual method of accounting in Chapter 3. Prepaid expenses are not tangible assets, but they are assets nonetheless since they represent items of continuing value to the company. In most instances prepaid expenses will be current assets, because they avoid the need for the current expenditure of cash and because they are expected to be consumed during the course of business operations within the forthcoming year. Examples include prepaid insurance, prepaid rent, prepaid taxes and prepaid interest. As these assets expire or are used up with the passage of time, adjusting entries are made to reflect the fact that they have become expense. These entries are illustrated in Appendix B, on bookkeeping.

Another category of prepaid expense, called *Deferred Charges*, represents those items of expenditure already made that are expected to have continued utility beyond the current year. In this category are included such items as organizational costs, start-up expenses and relocation costs. These items, unlike rent, interest and insurance, have an uncertain term of future value. Indeed, they may have no continuing value, and for that reason many companies choose to categorize them as expense immediately in the year in which they are incurred. One such group of costs, research and development costs, is required by GAAP to be reflected as expense when incurred. The current charging of such items to expense is consistent with the conservative view of accounting. The tax treatment of deferred charges and intangible assets, which in many instances differs from GAAP, is discussed in Chapter 15.

Intangible Assets

Although prepaid expenses and deferred charges are assets and are intangible, they are separately listed on the balance sheet. Other intangible assets are quite different in character. They include such items as patents, copyrights and trademarks, contract rights of varying kinds, and goodwill. These assets, like other assets of an enterprise, are entered on the books of account at their cost.

Since cost is the basis of accountability, it may take careful reading of the financial statements to understand the worth of a company's intangible assets, and even careful reading may not fully reveal the facts. Moreover, the intangible assets may be the assets of greatest importance to a particular company. Let us illustrate these points.

Suppose that Eager Electronics is a new company whose three employee-shareholders are all scientists. Eager operates in rented facilities, and its only assets are a small cash balance in the bank, a few test instruments and office supplies. After six months of collective effort, the employee-shareholders develop a collection of inventions that will revolutionize solid-state electronic technology. They turn the inventions over to patent attorneys for appropriate filing, and now seek bank financing to obtain funds for production.

What assets will appear on the Eager balance sheet presented to the bank? Only the cash, test instruments and office supplies are shown. The pending patents do not appear on the Balance Sheet, since no cost was incurred in acquiring them. If Eager subsequently incurs expenses of $10,000 to file and obtain the patents, the patents will appear on the balance sheet, but only at $10,000, even if the commercial value of the patents is far greater.

This illustration is of a familiar phenomenon. You already know that the balance sheet does not purport to represent current values. However, there is an important additional point in the case of intangible assets: because they may have cost the company nothing, *they may not appear on the balance sheet at all.* Accordingly, the thoughtful reader of financial statements, as well as the company preparing those statements for use by others, must be alert to the company's possible ownership of assets not reflected on the balance sheet.

One such asset is *Goodwill.* There is persistent confusion in the financial community concerning the meaning of goodwill and the importance to be given to it on the balance sheet. From the financial and business viewpoint, goodwill might be defined as the additional value that a business has, over and above the combined value of its other assets, by virtue of its extra earning power. Suppose that a potential buyer examines into the operations of a well-known local restaurant and finds that the current value of its assets (land, building, fixtures and inventory), less its liabilities, is $760,000. Suppose, however, that the net income of the restaurant averages $200,000 per year, and that the average rate of return in similar businesses is 20%. If the restaurant earned 20% on the value of its assets, its net income would be $152,000 per year (20% of $760,000). Why does this restaurant earn more than the average? The higher earnings may be explained by advertising, customer loyalty, the quality of food and service, efficient management and other similar factors.

The owner of the restaurant is not likely to be unaware of its extra earning power, and will therefore insist that the buyer pay more than the value of its physical assets alone. If, as the facts suggest, other similar businesses earn 20% on their assets, the owner might ask $1 million for his restaurant. An investment of $1 million, earning a 20% return, would average $200,000 net income per year, which is the net income of the restaurant. This illustration of the valuation of a business is obviously simplified, but its important point should now be clear. Most businesses are purchased for *earning power*, not assets, and extra earning power will make the business more valuable than the sum of all of its assets.

Like other intangible assets, goodwill appears on the balance sheet at cost. Therefore, if the buyer pays $1 million for the restaurant, $240,000 (the difference between the $1 million purchase price and the $760,000 value of tangible assets) would be shown on the buyer's balance sheet as goodwill. On the other hand, if instead of purchasing the existing restaurant the buyer were to invest $760,000 in assets and labor for ten years to build its own goodwill, that goodwill would not appear on the balance sheet, just as it did not appear on the balance sheet of the owner of the existing restaurant. Is there an injustice in this result? Not really, for we shall see as we progress through our analysis of the financial statements that excess earning power is evident to the knowledgeable reader. It is not necessary, nor even appropriate, to highlight that earning power by adding a new asset to the balance sheet. However, accounting is designed to account for what has been received and paid, and if a purchaser pays more for assets than they appear to be worth, some explanation is in order. Hence, goodwill appears on the balance sheets only when it has been purchased.

Amortization of Intangibles

The presence of intangible assets on the balance sheet poses a problem. We have seen how most assets (other than cash and land) ultimately become expenses as they are consumed in business operations. Inventory becomes cost of goods sold, fixed assets are depreciated, and prepaid expenses become expense through the processes of accrual accounting. What becomes of intangible assets?

Intangibles with a fixed term expire at the end of that term, so it would seem appropriate to amortize them (write them off to expense) over their term. Thus a patent would be amortized over its legal life of 17 years. Each year, $1/17$ of the cost of the patent would be reflected as expense, and the carrying value of the patent would be reduced accordingly. If, however, the useful life of the patent were less than its legal life, the cost of the patent would be amortized over the shorter period.

Some intangibles have very extended terms. Copyrights continue in effect for the life of the author plus 50 years. Goodwill, in some cases, may have an indefinite life. Under GAAP, all intangible assets must be amortized, and the maximum period of amortization is 40 years. This arbitrary rule has been widely criticized, but remains in effect today. Thus in the case of the restaurant purchased for $1 million, the buyer would be required by GAAP to amortize its purchased goodwill over 40 years resulting in an annual expense of $240,000 \div 40 = \$6,000$. Later, in our examination of goodwill under the tax laws, we will see that amortization of goodwill is not a deductible expense. Therefore, the recording of purchased goodwill usually offers no financial advantage to the purchaser. In Chapter 13, we give further consideration to the problem of goodwill purchased in business acquisitions.

Accounting for Leases

You might assume that the financial effects of a lease would appear only on the lessee's income statement, as rent expense. However, in recent years leases have assumed a wide variety of forms. While some leases retain the typical character of a contract for the use of property, others are indistinguishable from purchases. When a lease is in substance a purchase, GAAP requires that the property which is the subject of the lease appear as an asset on the balance sheet and that the lease obligation appear as a liability.

Leases are characterized either as true leases, called *operating leases*, or as *capital leases*, representing a purchase of the leased property. The determination of the character of the lease pursuant to GAAP is made as of the inception of the lease, on the basis of four factors. If any one or more of the following factors is present, the lease is a capital lease:

(1) Ownership of the property is transferred to the lessee at the end of the term of the lease.

(2) The lease contains a bargain purchase option, a right to purchase the property at a price sufficiently below its expected fair value that the exercise of the option is reasonably assured.

(3) At the inception of the lease, the lease term is substantially equal to the estimated economic life of the leased property. This test is met if the term is 75% or more of the property's estimated economic life.

(4) The present value of the minimum lease payments as of the beginning of the lease term, with certain exclusions, is 90% or more of the fair value of the property at the inception of the lease. Present value is generally determined by applying the lessee's borrowing rate to the stream of required lease payments. (The concept of present valuation is explained and illustrated in Chapter 10.)

The four factors look beyond the form of the lease to characterize its substance. The first two factors apply when the property will in fact be owned by the lessee, or is very likely to be owned by the lessee. The last two factors apply when the practical effect of the lease is that the lessee pays for the use of the property for essentially its entire useful life.

The lessee must show a capital lease on its balance sheet as an asset in an amount equal to the lesser of the fair market value of the property or the present value of the minimum lease payments. Such a lease is a fixed asset, and must therefore be amortized over its estimated economic life, or over the lease term, whichever is applicable.

The lessee shows a corresponding liability, in an amount equal to the value determined for the lease. As payments are made on the lease, a portion of each payment represents a discharge of the liability, and a portion represents interest expense, calculated in accordance with the *interest method*, discussed in Chapter 7. Financial statement disclosure of capital leases must include minimum future lease payments, in total and for the next five years, including the interest rate used for purposes of present valuation.

Leases that do not meet any of the four tests listed above are characterized as operating leases. Such leases are not reported as assets, and no corresponding liability is shown on the balance sheet. Periodic payments under operating leases are reported as rental expense. Financial statement disclosure of operating leases must include minimum future rental payments in total and for the next five years.

Times Mirror Company reports, in Note L to its financial statements, Appendix A (pages 217–218), that capital leases are not significant. The note lists future minimum lease payments on noncancelable operating leases, as required by GAAP.

REFERENCES

Official Pronouncements:

American Institute of Certified Public Accountants, Committee on Accounting Procedure, Accounting Research Bulletin No. 43 (1953), chapter 3A (Current assets and current liabilities).

American Institute of Certified Public Accountants, Accounting Principles Board, Opinion No. 17 (1970) (Intangible assets); Opinion No. 18 (1971) (Equity method of accounting for investments in common stock).

Financial Accounting Standards Board, Statement No. 12 (1975) (Accounting for certain marketable securities).

Financial Accounting Standards Board, Accounting for Leases (FASB Statement No. 13 as amended and interpreted through May 1980) (1980).

Chapter Seven

LIABILITIES

Let us live in as small a circle as we will, we are either debtors or creditors before we have had time to look round.

Goethe, Elective Affinities

Introduction: The Nature of Liabilities

With this chapter, we turn our attention to the right side of the balance sheet, examining in detail the nature of the interests of creditors and owners in the assets of the enterprise. Liabilities, or debts, take a bewildering variety of forms, and part of our objective will be to identify the forms and the differences among them. You will find that it is sometimes difficult to distinguish liabilities (debt) from equity (ownership, or net worth). The difficulties have nothing to do with accounting; rather, they derive from the variety of ways in which businesses raise money and structure their ownership. As you will see, liabilities and net worth are closely connected in this process.

Liabilities, like assets, are listed on the balance sheet in the order of their liquidity, current liabilities (those payable within the year) first, followed by long-term debt.

Current Liabilities

Current liabilities will ordinarily include *Accounts Payable*, which represent trade debts incurred in the usual course of business and payable within one year, as well as short-term notes payable, often representing current bank borrowings. In addition, most businesses will—as of any balance sheet date—owe accrued employee compensation, various accrued expenses (such as utilities, rent and interest), and estimated income taxes. In Chapter 3, we discussed how these liabilities arise and how they are entered on the accounting records.

Once a corporation's board of directors declares a dividend payable by the corporation, the dividend payable becomes a current liability. We will discuss dividends and other corporate distributions in detail in the next chapter.

Before we begin the discussion of long-term liabilities, we should note that not all liabilities that appear to be long-term are in fact long-term. Suppose that Parsimony Corp. borrows $30,000 from a bank, giving its 5-year interest-bearing note in return. Suppose also that the note requires Parsimony to make monthly payments of $500 plus interest, so that at the end of the 5-year period the entire note will be fully paid off (60 months × $500 = $30,000, the amount of the note). How should the note be shown on Parsimony's balance sheet? At any given time, twelve monthly payments on the note, or $6,000 (12 × $500 = $6,000), will be due within the succeeding year. Therefore, of the amount due on the note, $6,000 must be treated as a current liability, while the remainder is a long-term liability. The $6,000 will appear under current liabilities as *current portion of long-term debt*.

For examples of all of these current liabilities, refer to the Balance Sheets of Times Mirror Company, in Appendix A (page 207).

Long-Term Debt: Variations and Financial Statement Disclosure

While current liabilities generally take the form of accounts payable, accrued liabilities and short-term notes, long-term debt can be found in a wide variety of forms. Generally, one who owes long-term debt is obligated to pay not only the *principal* of the debt (the amount borrowed) but also *interest* equal to a stated percentage per year of the unpaid portion of the principal. Long-term debt is invariably evidenced by documents: notes, indentures, loan agreements, mortgages, debentures and bonds. We can analyze the forms of debt and their terms based on four factors: maturity, interest, security and control.

Maturity refers to the required date or dates of payment. Debt may be due in full on a given date, or may be due in several installments. A common form of long-term installment debt is a home mortgage, which usually requires monthly payments of principal and interest throughout its term. The combined monthly payments are calculated to discharge the mortgage debt completely at the end of its term. This type of loan is called *fully amortizing.* Some commercial mortgage loans call for periodic payments, but the payments are not sufficient to discharge the entire loan; a *balloon payment* must be made at the end of the term to pay off the remaining balance of the loan. Bonds, which we discuss below, are not made payable in installments, but may be given *serial maturities.* For example, a corporation might issue $1 million of *serial bonds,* with $100,000 due each year for ten years beginning in 1990. Each bond, normally in the amount of $1,000, will have a stated maturity, but the stated maturities of the bonds will range from 1990 through 1999.

A variation of serial maturity, found in many bond issues, is the provision of a *sinking fund*. A sinking fund is a fund of money required to be set aside by the terms of a debt instrument for the ultimate repayment of the debt. Although sinking funds may sometimes be invested while awaiting the ultimate repayment of a long-term liability, more often they are directly applied to discharge a portion of the liability by early repayment in accordance with the terms of the debt instrument.

Interest is the payment that the borrower makes for the use of the borrowed money. Most long-term debt provides for interest to be paid at a fixed annual rate on the unpaid principal balance. Typically, interest on bonds is payable semi-annually. If Parsimony Corp. issues $100,000 of 12% bonds on March 1, 1983, annual interest of $12,000 (12% × $100,000) would ordinarily be paid in two semi-annual installments of $6,000 each on September 1 and March 1 of each year. During the year 1983, therefore, only $6,000 of interest will actually be paid, on September 1, 1983. But, as you will remember from the discussion of accrual accounting, Parsimony will reflect accrued interest payable as of December 31, 1983 for four months (September 1 through December 31), amounting to $4,000 ($4/12$ × $12,000 annual interest). Again recalling our discussion of accruals, the March 1, 1984 interest payment of $6,000 will therefore represent $4,000 of accrued interest payable from 1983 and $2,000 of interest expense for 1984.

Interest terms may be variable. Some loans, notably those from banks, have interest rates tied to the *prime rate*, the prevailing interest rate charged on short-term loans to the most secure commercial borrowers. Not uncommonly, loans will provide for interest at a stated percentage above the prevailing prime rate from time to time. On these loans, the interest rate therefore changes periodically. Times Mirror disclosed such a loan agreement (interest at 110% of the prime rate) in Note G to its financial statements, in Appendix A (page 215).

Some loans are without interest, or at least appear to be without interest. Normal accounts payable tend not to carry an interest charge, although as prevailing interest rates increase, trade creditors often impose interest charges when payment is not made promptly. Long-term loans that purport to carry no interest contain, as an economic matter, a hidden charge for the use of money. This reality is recognized by GAAP and in tax accounting as well. For example, if Parsimony purchases land from a seller and issues its $100,000 interest-free two-year note in return, Parsimony has in fact paid somewhat less than $100,000 for the land. A portion of the note reflects interest on Parsimony's two-year debt. The calculation of the interest is explained later in this chapter.

Ordinary debts are said to be unsecured, in the sense that if the debtor fails to pay, the creditor has no protection other than to sue for the amount owed. Accounts payable are generally unsecured, as are many notes payable. An example of a secured debt is a mortgage loan; if the debtor fails to pay, the creditor may foreclose on the mortgage and sell the mortgaged property to obtain payment. Full disclosure must be made on the financial statements or in notes thereto indicating the nature of any security interests as well as all other material terms of the company's liabilities. The Times Mirror financial statements show no secured borrowings, but detail the terms of all long-term debt in Note G. Appendix A (pages 215–216).

Long-term debt in the form of publicly issued and transferable securities generally takes the form of *debentures* or *bonds,* both of which are normally issued in denominations of $1,000. Debentures are unsecured, while bonds usually carry some form of security. The security may vary from a general mortgage on business property to a security interest in particular buildings, machinery, airplanes, vehicles or other property.

Upon dissolution, a company's assets must be applied first to the payment of its debts before anything can be distributed to the company's owners. But which debts are paid first if there is not enough to pay all? The answer will depend on the terms of the debt. Secured debt has the first right to the property that serves as its security. All other debt ranks equally, unless it provides otherwise. For example, many companies have in recent years issued *subordinated debentures,* that rank behind certain other creditors in order of payment. Only by examining the debentures and other constituent documents can one determine the exact nature of the subordination, but general disclosure of the terms must be made in the notes to the issuing company's financial statements.

Major creditors seek and often obtain various controls over aspects of the operations of companies that borrow from them. Indeed, the drafting of trust indentures (in connection with issuance of bonds) and loan agreements is a fine art, and those documents are often very complex and lengthy. Examples of controls exercised by creditors include limitations on other borrowing, restrictions on dividends and salary increases, approval requirements for changes in business activities and major personnel, and extensive reporting requirements. The material terms of such loan agreements must be disclosed in notes to the financial statements.

Publicly held companies frequently issue long-term debt with another interesting feature, *convertibility*. A convertible debenture is a debt that may at the option of the holder be converted into stock of the debtor company. Investors may be attracted to convertible debentures since they have some of the desirable characteristics of both bonds and stock. From the accounting viewpoint, convertible debt poses complex disclosure and calculation problems, which we will have an opportunity to examine in our later discussion of earnings per share.

Interest and Discount

Not infrequently, a company will issue its bonds or other long-term debt at a premium or a discount. For example, Parsimony Corp. might issue $100,000 of 10-year 8% debentures for $90,000. The "discount" in this case reflects the fact that the 8% interest is not sufficient to attract investors. Put another way, the $10,000 discount is in fact additional interest, payable over the 10-year life of the debentures. Accounting recognizes the reality of this transaction and treats it in a highly sophisticated manner.

Parsimony is treated as though it originally borrowed $90,000. By application of actuarial tables or formulas, the effective rate of interest is determined on a $90,000 loan, repayable in 10 years in the amount of $100,000, with interest of $8,000 (8% of $100,000) per year. That effective rate, rounded to two decimal places, is 9.60% per year.[1]

Once the effective interest rate is determined, Parsimony is treated as though its loan of $90,000 increased to $100,000 over

---

1. Readers with advanced financial calculators can perform this calculation—though it is not required to understand this material—by entering the following values:

n = number of years = 10

PV = present value of amount borrowed = $90,000

PMT = annual payment = $8,000

FV = future value to be paid = $100,000

Solve for i = effective interest rate = 9.60%

These actuarial concepts are discussed further in Chapter 10.

the ten-year term in an amount sufficient to maintain an effective level rate of interest of 9.60% throughout the entire ten years. This technique, known as the *interest method,* is required by GAAP in reporting the effects of premium and discount on debt. In Parsimony's case, it yields these results:

Year	Debentures Payable 1/1	9.6% Effective Interest	Less Cash Interest	Increased Debentures Payable	Debentures Payable 12/31
1	$90,000	$8,640	$8,000	$ 640	$ 90,640
2	90,640	8,701	8,000	701	91,340
3	91,340	8,769	8,000	769	92,109
4	92,109	8,843	8,000	843	92,952
5	92,952	8,923	8,000	923	93,875
6	93,875	9,012	8,000	1,012	94,887
7	94,887	9,109	8,000	1,109	95,996
8	95,996	9,216	8,000	1,216	97,212
9	97,212	9,332	8,000	1,332	98,544
10	98,544	9,460	8,000	1,460	100,004 [2]

What the table above demonstrates is that while Parsimony pays annually only $8,000 of interest in cash, the original $10,000 discount is treated as additional interest spread over the life of the debt. As that discount is written off, or *amortized,* it is added to the original amount of the debt, so that by the end of the tenth year, the debt is shown as payable in its full amount of $100,000. Each year prior to the tenth year, the debt is shown reduced by the unamortized discount. Thus, at the end of year 7, for example, Parsimony would show on its balance sheet debentures payable of $95,996.

A corresponding set of calculations must be used in the case of debt issued at a premium, except in that case the liability is gradually reduced to its ultimate discharge price. Similarly, companies that purchase debt at a discount or premium, in the form of investments or notes receivable, must amortize the discount or premium using the interest method.

The discounting and amortization process described above must, like all other material items affecting liabilities, be described in notes to the financial statements. An illustration of such a description appears in Note G to the Times Mirror financial statements, in Appendix A (page 215), describing the notes issued in connection with the acquisition of the Denver Post, Inc.

---

2. The correct figure should be $100,000; the $4 error is due to rounding of percentages.

Unearned Income

We discussed the concept of *unearned income* or *deferred income* in the chapter on accrual accounting. Many companies, like Times Mirror, receive advance payment from customers before the related services are rendered or the goods are delivered. You will remember that while receipt of payment increases the company's assets, usually cash, income is not recognized until it is realized by delivery of the goods or performance of the services. Until then, unearned income or deferred income is shown as a liability on the balance sheet. In the case of Times Mirror Company, the unearned income (amounting to $52,038,000 as of December 31, 1981) probably consists substantially of advance subscriptions.

Deferred Income Taxes

The subject of income tax accounting occupies a separate chapter of this book, but it is appropriate here to examine the concept of *deferred income taxes*, an item that usually appears on the balance sheet under the heading of other liabilities. If there were no differences between financial accounting and tax accounting, there would be no need to speak of the concept of deferred income taxes. We have already encountered one major illustration of differences between tax and financial accounting: depreciation. Many companies follow straight-line depreciation for financial purposes while applying accelerated depreciation for determining their income tax liability. That practice creates timing differences in the payment of income taxes that might, without further explanation, be misleading to the readers of the company's financial statements.

Suppose that in 1983 Forthright Enterprises, Inc. purchases for $100,000 certain machinery which is classified as "3-year property" under the Internal Revenue Code. As a result, that property may be depreciated for tax purposes 25% in 1983, 38% in 1984 and 37% in 1985. (These depreciation rates, as well as related provisions of the tax laws are explained in Chapter 15.) If, however, the machinery actually has a useful life of 5 years (and no scrap value), and Forthright applies straight-line depreciation for financial purposes, its financial statements will show depreciation of 20% each year from 1983 through 1987. Assuming Forthright is in the 46% federal corporate tax bracket, this accounting treatment will produce substantial differences in the annual net cost of equipment use:

	1983	1984	1985	1986	1987
Depreciation for Accounting Purposes	$20,000	$20,000	$20,000	$20,000	$20,000
Depreciation for Tax Purposes	$25,000	$38,000	$37,000	$ —	$ —
Tax Saving = 46% of Depreciation	(11,500)	(17,480)	(17,020)	—	—
Reported Net Cost of Equipment Use: Depreciation less Tax Saving	$ 8,500	$ 2,520	$ 2,980	$20,000	$20,000

The schedule above shows that Forthright has high depreciation for tax purposes in the years 1983 to 1985, but no depreciation for tax purposes in the years 1986 and 1987. As a result, Forthright's corporate income taxes are substantially reduced in the first three years, but correspondingly increased in the succeeding two years. Without further disclosure, readers of the financial statements for the years 1983 through 1985 might be unaware that Forthright will have no deductible depreciation in later years, despite the fact that the equipment will continue to be used and to be depreciated for accounting purposes.

Forthright is permitted to use different depreciation methods for tax and accounting purposes. However, GAAP presently requires that the company accrue a liability, *deferred income taxes,* to reflect the future increase in taxes resulting from the decision to take early tax deductions under accelerated depreciation.

Though it is not essential for you to master the calculation of deferred income taxes—and, indeed, the subject is far more complex than this illustration might suggest—we present the calculation here for illustrative purposes. Deferred income taxes will be increased in those years when tax deductions exceed the corresponding financial expenses, and will later be decreased in the years when the tax deductions are less than the financial expenses. In each case, deferred taxes will be calculated by applying the applicable tax rate (46% in the case of Forthright) to the difference between the two figures:

Year	Tax Depreciation	Accounting Depreciation	Excess or (Deficiency)	× 46% = Change in Deferred Income Taxes
1983	$25,000	$20,000	$ 5,000	$2,300 increase
1984	38,000	20,000	18,000	8,280 increase
1985	37,000	20,000	17,000	7,820 increase
1986	—	20,000	(20,000)	9,200 decrease
1987	—	20,000	(20,000)	9,200 decrease

In each year when deferred taxes are increased, the books will reflect an increase in income tax expense; correspondingly, when deferred taxes are decreased, income tax expense will be decreased. The end result on the financial statements of Forthright will be that the reported cost of using the equipment will be "smoothed out", or evenly distributed over its useful life, as follows:

	1983	1984	1985	1986	1987
Reported Net Cost of Equipment Use: Depreciation less Tax Saving	$ 8,500	$ 2,520	$ 2,980	$20,000	$20,000
Deferred Taxes	2,300	8,280	7,820	(9,200)	(9,200)
Adjusted Net Cost of Equipment Use	$10,800	$10,800	$10,800	$10,800	$10,800

As we noted earlier, deferral and allocation of income taxes is much more complex than this illustration might suggest. Tax deferral questions arise in a variety of settings in which estimates, accounting techniques and tax rates cannot be readily determined and are subject to change. Moreover, the concept of deferral of income taxes not currently payable is itself not without controversy. As of this writing, the Financial Accounting Standards Board is reconsidering the entire question of allocation of income taxes. However, reflection of deferred income taxes in the financial statements is now required by GAAP, and this illustration should clarify its purpose: to account for timing differences in the payment of taxes caused by differences in financial and tax accounting methods. A typical example of deferred income tax accounting appears in Note F to the Times Mirror Company financial statements, in Appendix A (page 214).

Loss Contingencies

A loss contingency might be defined as a present set of circumstances involving uncertainty with respect to future loss of assets or incurrence of liabilities. There is, of course, uncertainty with respect to much of accounting: choice of acceptable principles, estimation of the useful life of depreciable assets, determination of the market value of inventories. When we speak of loss contingencies, we are concerned not with problems of estimation and judgment, but rather with uncertainty as to whether a future event will take place. Loss contingencies include potential or pending lawsuits, possible government regulatory proceedings, warranty and product claims, guarantee obligations and similar contingencies. In most instances, these contingencies will not appear on the balance sheet itself, because they have not yet materialized and may never take place. However, we have seen that GAAP requires disclosure by notes or commentary to the financial statements of material items bearing upon the statements.

Loss contingencies are categorized by GAAP at the one extreme as *probable*, likely to occur, and at the other as *remote*, having only a slight chance of occurrence. Between these extremes, the contingencies are categorized as *reasonably possible*. When a loss contingency is probable, and when its amount can reasonably be estimated, the contingency must be reflected on the financial statements for the period. We have already encountered an illustration of such a contingency, provision for estimated uncollectible accounts receivable. That contingency is reflected in the financial statements by reduction of an asset (accounts receivable) and recording of an expense (bad debts expense). Similar treatment would be required of a manufacturer with respect to estimated warranty claims. The manufacturer should show an estimated liability for warranty claims and a corresponding warranty expense.

If a loss contingency is not probable, or if its amount cannot reasonably be estimated, disclosure of the contingency is nevertheless required unless it can be categorized as remote. However, even a remote contingency of loss under a guarantee or financing arrangement would require disclosure. Ordinarily, such disclosure would be in the notes to the financial statements.

Some of the most perplexing disclosure problems arise in connection with *unasserted possible claims*, potential lawsuits or other proceedings against the company that have not yet been—and may never be—initiated. These claims must be disclosed only if it is probable that they will be asserted and there is a reasonable possibility of an unfavorable outcome. Readers of this book who are studying or have studied law will realize the problems inherent in disclosing potential claims against the company before they have been asserted. The disclosure itself may amount to an invitation to bring suit. On the other hand, the auditor must be concerned with full and fair disclosure, lest his opinion with respect to the financial statements be misleading. In Chapter 11 we will discuss the problems that arise when the auditor asks the company's attorney what claims, asserted and unasserted, can be made against the company and what the likely outcome of those claims will be.

Pension Plans

Many companies maintain pension plans that provide for continued payment to employees after their retirement. These plans may be *funded* or *unfunded.* Funded plans require that the employer company make regular contributions into a trust or other fund in amounts designed to be sufficient to pay the pensions required by the plan as employees retire. Unfunded plans are simply contractual promises to pay, and the obligations become current liabilities as employees retire. In addition, some funded plans require that participating employees also make regular contributions into the plan. These are known as *contributory* plans.

The Employee Retirement Income Security Act of 1974, known as ERISA, importantly affects the terms of these plans and their administration. Plans within the coverage of ERISA, including most plans of substantial size, are subject to very detailed requirements concerning such matters as eligibility, coverage, funding and reporting.

Pension plans of various types are very widely used. They afford employees a substantial degree of retirement security and therefore represent an important job perquisite. From the employer's viewpoint, if the plan satisfies the requirements of the Internal Revenue Code, payments by the employer into a trust created to hold the funds of the plan are deductible expenses. Moreover, the income earned by the trust from investment of the funds is generally not taxable. From the employee's viewpoint, however, no income is recognized until the actual pension payments are received upon retirement.

Pension plans fall into two general categories. *Defined benefit plans* specify the benefits to be paid under the plan or the method of calculating those benefits. For example, a plan providing that employees will receive on retirement a pension equal to 50% of their final year's salary would be a defined benefit plan. *Defined contribution plans* specify the amount of the contribution to the plan to be made by the employer, and benefits are based on the amount contributed to each employee's account. Such a plan might provide that the employer will contribute annually 10% of each employee's salary to the plan. An account is kept for each employee, including the contributions made and the income earned thereon. At retirement, the pension paid to each employee is actuarially calculated based on the total amount in that employee's account, the life expectancy of the employee, and the expected income of the pension trust fund.

The accounting profession has struggled for years with the question of how the employer company must disclose its potential liabilities under pension plans. As of this writing, the Financial Accounting Standards Board is reexamining the subject of pension plan disclosure. Generally Accepted Accounting Principles presently require that the annual cost of the pension plan be calculated on an actuarial basis and be accrued as a liability and recorded as an expense. If all or a portion of the cost so calculated has actually been paid into a pension trust under the plan, a smaller liability or no liability will be shown. GAAP gives some leeway in the actuarial calculation of annual cost, but sets upper and lower limits based on normal costs, costs of funding benefits based on prior employee service, and costs of providing for vested benefits (benefits that under the terms of the plan are not forfeitable by the employee).

Disclosure must be made in notes to the financial statements of the existence of any pension plans, their coverage, and the company's accounting and funding policies. The company must disclose the amount provided for pension costs for the period. In addition, disclosure must be made of any excess of actuarially calculated vested benefits over the funds in the pension plan and the pension plan accrued liabilities as shown on the balance sheet. Times Mirror Company made these disclosures in Note K to their financial statements, Appendix A (page 217).

REFERENCES

Official Pronouncements:

American Institute of Certified Public Accountants, Committee on Accounting Procedure, Accounting Research Bulletin No. 43 (1953), chapter 3A (Current assets and current liabilities).

American Institute of Certified Public Accountants, Accounting Principles Board, Opinion No. 8 (1966) (Accounting for the cost of pension plans); Opinion No. 11 (1967) (Accounting for income taxes); Opinion No. 14 (1969) (Accounting for convertible debt); Opinion No. 21 (1971) (Interest on receivables and payables).

Financial Accounting Standards Board, Statement No. 5 (1975) (Accounting for contingencies); Statement No. 36 (1980) (Disclosure of pension information, an amendment of APB Opinion No. 8); Interpretation No. 3 (1974) (Pension plans subject to ERISA).

Secondary Sources:

American Institute of Certified Public Accountants, Illustrations of Accounting for Debt Under FASB Pronouncements (1978).

Financial Accounting Standards Board, Employers' Accounting for Pensions and Other Postemployment Benefits (Discussion Memorandum, 1981).

Pomeranz, Ramsey & Steinberg, Pensions; An Accounting and Management Guide (1976).

Chapter Eight

CAPITAL ACCOUNTS: PARTNERSHIPS AND CORPORATIONS

*They cry out loudly against all banks and corpora-
tions, and a means by which small capitalists become
united in order to produce important and beneficial results. . . . They would choke the fountain of industry and dry all streams.*

John C. Calhoun before the United States Senate

Introduction: Capital Accounts

When we first discussed the Fundamental Equation, we examined the operations of a proprietorship, a business owned by a
single individual. In a proprietorship there is a single capital
account representing the ownership interest of the proprietor.
When the proprietor retires, dies or sells his business, another
owner takes his place or the business is terminated. However,
when an enterprise has more than one owner a single capital
account will no longer suffice. Different owners contribute different amounts to the business and may be entitled to varying
shares of the profits or losses from its operations. When one
owner dies, retires or sells his interest in the business, the business may continue under the ownership of the others or with the
addition of a new owner. Accounting mirrors the complexity of
the enterprise; more owners mean more—and different—capital
accounts.

Partnership Capital: Contributions, Loans and Draw-ings

A proprietorship has one owner; a partnership has two or
more. A partnership exists when two or more persons are co-
owners of a business for profit. Partners generally enter into a
partnership agreement defining their respective rights, but a
partnership may exist even without a formal agreement. If the
partners do not define their relative rights, the Uniform Partnership Act (the UPA)—which is the law in almost all states—supplies the definitions.

Let us suppose that Yetta and Zeke agree to do business as
the YZ Partnership. Yetta contributes $60,000 cash to the new

business and Zeke contributes furniture and fixtures worth $40,000. They agree to divide profits and losses 60% to Yetta and 40% to Zeke. Their opening balance sheet will be:

YZ Partnership
Balance Sheet
As of _____

Assets		Liabilities and Net Worth	
Cash	$ 60,000	Net Worth:	
		Yetta, Capital	$ 60,000
Furniture and fixtures	40,000	Zeke, Capital	40,000
		Total Liabilities and	
Total Assets	$100,000	Net Worth	$100,000

The only difference in form between the balance sheet for YZ and the balance sheet for a proprietorship is the appearance of a separate capital account for each partner. At the end of the year when the books are closed, the net income or loss of YZ will be added to or subtracted from the respective capital accounts in the ratio of 60% to Yetta and 40% to Zeke.

In addition to making capital contributions, partners may also lend money to the partnership. For accounting purposes, loans by partners are treated like any other liabilities, but they are separately identified on the balance sheet. If Zeke lent $30,000 cash to YZ Partnership, the asset cash would increase to $90,000 and the liability *Loan Payable to Partner* would be added to the right side of the balance sheet, in the amount of $30,000. The loan would not be combined with Zeke's capital account since the money was lent to the partnership and not contributed to its capital.

Remember that payment of the liabilities of a business takes priority over return of the capital; if the assets are insufficient to pay both, the liabilities must be discharged before any payment is made on capital. Thus, Zeke's loan stands on a different footing from his capital contribution. If the assets of the YZ Partnership are ultimately insufficient to pay off its liabilities and capital, the liabilities—including Zeke's loan—will be paid first.

With that said, we must now point out that Zeke's loan, even though it is a true liability, is treated differently from liabilities payable to non-partners. The UPA establishes a priority order of payment in the event that assets are not sufficient to pay all liabilities and capital. Outside creditors are paid first, followed by loans made by partners, and finally followed by partners' capital accounts. Since loans by partners therefore have a different legal status from other liabilities, they must be shown separately on the balance sheet.

When a successful proprietor wishes to withdraw from his business a portion of its profits, he causes it to distribute assets (usually cash) to himself and reduces its capital account by the amount of the distribution. A parallel procedure is followed in the case of a partnership, and such distributions to partners are known as *drawings*. Partnerships commonly maintain separate drawings accounts for each partner. Suppose A, B, C, D and E on January 1, 1983 form a partnership to practice law, and they agree to divide and distribute their profits equally, $1/5$ each. Until the end of 1983, they cannot know what the profits for the year will be. However, during 1983 each of them will withdraw money from the partnership to provide for personal living expenses. If a separate drawings account is maintained for each of the partners, the total profits may be fairly divided at the end of the year despite variations in each partner's drawings. If the profits for the year amounted to $200,000, each partner would be entitled to $40,000. If A has taken drawings of $40,000, he is entitled to no further distribution of profits, whereas if B has taken drawings of only $35,000, he is entitled to an additional $5,000.

Division of Profits and Losses, Salaries and Special Allocations

If the partners make no agreement concerning division of profits and losses, the UPA provides that they will be divided equally. The partners may, however, divide profits and losses by any formula acceptable to them. A few variations include the following:

(a) Division by percentages: A, B and C divide profits and losses 50%, 30% and 20% respectively.

(b) Division by "units": In larger partnerships, such as accounting and law firms, admission of a new partner or retirement of an old partner requires that all the profit percentages be recalculated. This process is somewhat simplified if each partner is assigned a stated number of units. The profit share is based on the total of the units. Suppose that A, B, C, D, and E are assigned respectively 10, 10, 8, 6 and 4 units, a total of 38 units. Therefore A's share is $10/38$, C's share is $8/38$, etc. If F is added as a new partner and assigned 2 units, the total now becomes 40 units. A's share automatically becomes $10/40$, C's share becomes $8/40$ and F's share is $2/40$.

(c) Payment of salaries or interest: In an economic sense, as well as under the UPA, partners do not receive salaries or wages for their work. As co-owners of the business, their compensation is a portion of the profits. It is not uncommon, however, for partners to agree that they will first receive stated salaries and that the profits remaining after those salaries will be divided in certain ratios. A, B and C might agree that they will receive annual salaries of $30,000, $20,000 and $10,000, respectively, after which remaining profits will be divided equally. This formula recognizes the additional efforts exerted in the partnership business by certain partners, while ultimately still allowing for even division of the profits. Similar arrangements can be made for "interest" to be paid on capital contributions when the capital contributions of the partners differ.

(d) Profits and losses divided in proportion to capital account balances: A, B and C contribute $60,000, $30,000 and $10,000 respectively to the capital of their new partnership. They agree to divide profits and losses in proportion to their capital accounts. Profits and losses will be divided 60%, 30% and 10%. As the capital accounts change, the profit and loss percentages will similarly change.

Any number of other formulas may be used, tailored to the particular needs of the partners. Some of the most complex profit and loss sharing formulas can be found in contemporary "tax shelter" partnerships. These entities, usually limited partnerships formed in accordance with the Uniform Limited Partnership Act, have as one major purpose the realization of certain tax benefits (usually tax losses and credits) by their partners. It is common to provide detailed "special allocations" of items of income, deductions and credits in order to achieve the desired tax results. For example, losses might be allocated by one formula, operating profits by another, and profits on sale of property by yet a third.

After determining the profit or loss for the year, the accountant will apply the formula or formulas of the partnership agreement in allocating that profit or loss among the partners' individual capital accounts.

Partnership Dissolution and Winding Up

The UPA distinguishes between the concepts of *dissolution* and *winding up*. Dissolution refers only to the change in relationships among the partners caused by any partner ceasing to be a partner, whether by retirement, death or other causes. Dissolution does not mean that the partnership will cease to do business. A dissolution may therefore take place without a winding up, and the remaining partners may continue to carry on the partnership business. When this happens, the partnership must pay off the capital account of the withdrawing partner. The terms of payment ordinarily will appear in the partnership agreement.

A winding up takes place when, by agreement or otherwise, the partnership business is terminated. In that case, the assets of the partnership are sold, the liabilities of the partnership are discharged, and whatever assets remain are distributed to the partners in accordance with their agreement. Suppose that the simplified balance sheet of the ABC Partnership is as follows, just prior to winding up:

ABC Partnership
Balance Sheet
As of _____

Assets		Liabilities and Net Worth	
Cash	$ 20,000	Liabilities	$ 50,000
		Net Worth:	
		A, Capital	40,000
		B, Capital	20,000
Machinery & Equipment	100,000	C, Capital	10,000
		Total Liabilities and	
Total Assets	$120,000	Net Worth	$120,000

Assume that A, B and C share profits and losses equally. Winding up will involve sale of all the assets, payment of the liabilities, and distribution of the remaining assets to the partners. If the machinery & equipment are sold for exactly $100,000, ABC Partnership will be left with $120,000 cash, of which $50,000 will be used to discharge the liabilities and the remaining $70,000 distributed to A, B and C in the amounts of their capital accounts: $40,000, $20,000 and $10,000. Why isn't the $70,000 divided equally among A, B and C? The partners have agreed to divide *profits and losses* equally, but the capital accounts represent their relative *ownership* interests. As the capital accounts show, the partners' ownership interests are unequal. A has invested more than B, and B more than C; accordingly when the partnership is wound up, each will receive his or her appropriate portion of the invested capital.

Suppose, however, that the machinery & equipment are sold for $130,000? If that happened, there would be a profit on sale

[92]

of $30,000 ($130,000 selling price — $100,000 book value), and the profit would be divided equally in accordance with the partnership agreement. Each partner's capital would be increased by $10,000 (⅓ of $30,000), and A, B and C would receive in the winding up $50,000, $30,000 and $20,000 respectively.

Correspondingly, if the machinery & equipment are sold at a loss, the loss is first divided among the partners in accordance with their agreement. Suppose that the proceeds of sale are only $40,000, representing a $60,000 loss from the book value of $100,000. The loss is divided equally, $20,000 to each partner. This leaves A with capital of $20,000, B with capital of zero, and C with capital of minus $10,000. And it brings us face to face with a disturbing aspect of partnership law: a partner is *personally* liable on the debts of a partnership, including the partnership's liability to pay off the capital of other partners. This means that C must pay $10,000 out of his personal funds into the partnership so that A can be repaid what remains of his capital. Indeed, if the loss had been greater, A and B might also have been required to pay money into the partnership so that the liabilities could be fully discharged. Suppose one or another of the partners doesn't have personal funds to pay into the partnership? The remaining partners must pay in that partner's share.

There is much more to say about partners and their liabilities, but this is not a text on partnership law. We have carried the discussion this far, however, to point out the close connection between accounting determinations and reports and the laws of business associations. You may wish to refer to one of the references at the end of this chapter for further discussion of this subject.

A Word About Limited Partnerships

It is not an attractive prospect to an investor in a partnership that he or she may become personally liable on the debts of the partnership. An alternative business form, the *Limited Partnership*, may be established by complying with the requirements of the Uniform Limited Partnership Act (the ULPA), which in one of several versions is the law in every state. In a limited partnership, at least one partner must be a *general partner*, ultimately personally liable for the debts of the partnership. The remaining partners may be *limited partners*, whose personal obligations do not exceed the amount they agreed to contribute as capital. For accounting purposes, limited partnerships are not treated any differently from other partnerships, which are often called *General Partnerships,* in order to distinguish the two.

Corporations: Introduction

The subject of corporate accounting is complex, and it requires an introduction to some fundamental aspects of corporate law and corporate finance. The references at the end of this chapter pursue these subjects in greater depth. Corporations are creatures of the law and may only be formed by filing *Articles of Incorporation* in accordance with state corporation statutes. Unlike the partnership laws, however, corporation statutes vary considerably from state to state. A corporation is formed, or *incorporated,* in a single state, but may do business and be recognized as a corporation nationwide. Ordinarily, the corporation law of the state of incorporation governs the internal affairs of a corporation.

While a proprietorship is managed by its proprietor and a partnership is managed by agreement among its partners, a corporation is an organization of delegated management, run by a *board of directors* elected by its owners. A corporation may have a virtually unlimited number of owners, each of whom may own one or more *shares of stock* of the corporation. Division of the ownership interest into shares allows the owner-investors, called *stockholders* or *shareholders,* to invest varying amounts in the corporation, to exercise varying degrees of control over its operations, and to transfer their ownership interests to others. With rare exceptions stockholders, unlike partners in a partnership, are not personally responsible for the liabilities of their corporation. Therefore the extent of their financial exposure is limited to their investment in the corporation's stock.

Corporate Stock

Corporate stock, like the capital of a proprietorship or partnership, represents the equity or ownership in the corporation. It may take several different forms, called *classes* of stock. The terms that may be varied in a particular class of stock include voting rights, rights to income, and priority of repayment of investment upon dissolution, among others.

Common Stock is the residuary equity interest in a corporation: it is entitled to receive whatever is left after the claims of creditors and all other classes of stock have been discharged. Generally, each share of common stock is entitled to one vote in the election of the board of directors and in other matters on which a vote is required. Distributions of income, called *dividends*, are made ratably to the shares of common stock as determined in the discretion of the corporation's board of directors.

Preferred Stock is so named because it has a preference or priority over common stock with respect to dividends or in the distribution of assets on dissolution of the corporation. A typical share of preferred stock might be issued by the corporation for a par or stated value (discussed below) of $100, and be entitled to a 10% preferred annual dividend and a liquidation preference of par value. The dividend on that stock, equal to $10 per share annually (10% of $100) must first be paid before any dividend is paid on the common stock. Furthermore, upon dissolution of the corporation, after payment of all liabilities, the preferred stock would be paid its $100 per share first, and thereafter any remainder would be payable to the common stock.

The dividend on preferred stock, as on other stock, is not a liability of the corporation until it has been declared by the board of directors. Of course, if the board decides not to declare a dividend on the preferred stock, no dividend may be paid on the common stock either. But suppose that the board intentionally fails for ten years to declare a dividend on the preferred stock described above, and then declares the required dividend of $10 per share and also declares a very large dividend on the common stock. Preferred stockholders will not be pleased, having gone many years without a dividend only to see a large dividend paid to the common stockholders. This eventuality is generally prevented by making the preferred stock *cumulative;* if dividends for a given year are not paid, they accumulate as *arrearages*. Before any dividend can be paid on the common stock, all arrearages as well as the current dividend must be paid to the preferred. In the illustration above, therefore, the preferred stock would be entitled to ten years of dividends—$100 per share—before any dividend could be paid to the common stock. Cumulative preferred stock also generally provides that upon dissolution of the corporation the stock shall be paid its par value plus all arrearages before any payment is made to the common stock.

Ordinarily, preferred stock does not vote, but it can be issued with voting rights on all matters or on some matters. Usually, preferred stock provides that it shall become voting if its dividend has not been paid for a stated period.

It might appear at first glance that preferred stock is the favorite child of the corporation, but this is not necessarily so.

Although preferred stock usually has preferences in the income and assets, the preferences also represent limitations. In our illustration above, the preferred stock has a $10 preferred cumulative dividend, but no more. Once the dividend has been paid on the preferred stock, the board of directors is free to pay no dividend on the common stock or—if the corporate operations have been successful—to pay a much larger dividend on the common stock. Similarly, on dissolution the preferred stock receives its $100 per share first. There may be little or nothing left for the common, but if the corporation has prospered the common stock may receive much more than $100 per share. We may summarize the differences by saying that preferred stock generally has lower risk and lower potential return than common stock.

As with most areas of corporate law, however, our generalizations are subject to exception. Preferred stock may be made *participating;* it may by its terms share in additional dividends with the common stock. Preferred stock is often made *convertible* into common stock, on the basis of a stated conversion ratio. In the illustration above, the preferred stock might be convertible in the ratio of four shares of common stock for each share of preferred stock. When, and if, the common stock becomes worth $25 a share or more, the conversion privilege will be of considerable value to the preferred shareholders.

The rights, preferences and privileges of each class of shares significantly affect the value of those shares, and must be disclosed on the corporation's financial statements or in notes thereto.

Issuance of Shares: Par Value and Legal Consideration

The creditors of corporations do not have access to the personal assets of the shareholders, so the early corporation laws attempted to protect those creditors by assuring that every corporation had at least a minimum of assets available to pay its creditors. Early corporation laws required that a corporation be organized with minimum capital of a certain number of dollars, but those requirements have in most instances been repealed. It is now possible to organize a corporation in most states with capital of a dollar or less. Two other concepts intended to protect creditors have not quite disappeared, however. Accountants must still be concerned with *par value* and *legal consideration.*

Par value is an arbitrary dollar figure representing the lowest price at which a share of stock may be issued by a corporation. Stock with a par value of $100 may be issued for $100 or more, but not less. If the stock is issued for less than $100, it is deemed to be *watered stock*, and the purchaser may be held liable to the corporation for the deficiency. The original reasoning behind this concept was that creditors looked to the *stated capital* of a corporation for their ultimate payment; it was sometimes said that the stated capital was a trust fund for the protection of creditors. Stated capital meant, and still means, the total par value of all shares issued by the corporation. We now know that this concept is erroneous, and that creditors seek their protection in the earning power and the total business condition of a corporate creditor. Rather than looking to stated capital, creditors evaluate the entire statement of income and balance sheet. But par value remains on the statute books.

If corporate stock could be sold today for no less than $100 per share, many corporations would experience difficulty in raising capital from investors. It was not long before corporate laws allowed par values to be lowered, even to less than one dollar per share. Today, all corporate statutes also permit corporations to issue *no par stock*, which may be issued at any price determined by the board of directors. Currently there is a movement to eliminate the concept of par value entirely, but as of this writing only one state, California, has done so. Par value remains important because issuance of stock below par is one the few ways in which shareholders may become liable in excess of their original investment.

Par value, however, relates only to the original issuance of stock by a corporation. Once stock has been issued at or above its par value, it may later be traded or sold at any price. Indeed, we may accurately declare that par value bears no necessary relationship whatever to the true value of corporate stock.

The concept of legal consideration for shares was also intended to protect creditors. To this day, most corporation laws require that a corporation receive cash or other assets for the issuance of its stock. The issuance of stock for promissory notes of the purchaser, or in return for the promise of future services, is specifically prohibited. Therefore, if stock is to be issued in return for future payment, a corporation must enter into a *subscription agreement* with the buyer, and the shares may not be issued until the payment for them is actually received.

Stated Capital, Capital in Excess of Par, and Retained Earnings

The capital accounts of a corporation are divided into three major headings. *Stated Capital* consists of the par value of the shares times the number of shares issued and outstanding. If the shares were issued for more than their par value, the additional amount is separately disclosed as *Capital in Excess of Par Value* or *Additional Paid in Capital.* The accumulated income of the corporation, to the extent that it is not paid out to the shareholders in the form of dividends, is separately identified in the account *Retained Earnings.* Refer to the Times Mirror Balance Sheets, in Appendix A (page 207), and note that as of December 31, 1981 that company had stated capital (listed under the heading of Common Stock) of nearly $33 million and additional paid in capital of more than $43 million. In other words, Times Mirror had issued its stock for somewhat in excess of $75 million, the sum of these two figures. However, more than $838 million of its capital was in retained earnings, illustrating that a successful corporation generally builds through internal growth.

The difference between stated capital and capital in excess of par is largely meaningless in economic terms. Indeed, if a corporation issues only no par stock, the entire issue price will generally appear under the stated capital heading, and there will be no account for capital in excess of par. Still, the two accounts are maintained because the law gives separate significance to them.

The difference between retained earnings and the other capital accounts is central to accounting: it is the difference between capital that has been *contributed* by stockholders and capital that has been *earned* through operations.

Corporate Dividends and Distributions

Owners of corporate stock, like proprietors and partners, invest in the enterprise with the expectation of earning income on their investment. We have seen how profits are distributed in proprietorships and partnerships by distributions of capital or drawings. When a partnership or proprietorship makes a capital distribution, it is ordinarily not separately identified—for financial accounting purposes—as either a distribution of profits or a return of original investment. Corporations, by law, must operate very differently.

The corporation statutes of every state limit the ability of a corporation to distribute dividends. The statutes rely heavily on accounting concepts. However, as with tax law, financial accounting concepts and corporate law concepts are not necessarily the same. With few exceptions the corporation laws have not embodied either Generally Accepted Accounting Principles or contemporary accounting terminology. The California Corporations Code requires application of GAAP in all of its accounting determinations, and the corporation laws of Michigan and a few other states refer indirectly to GAAP. The other state laws are silent on this point. Indeed, most statutes still refer to "Earned Surplus" and "Capital Surplus" instead of the contemporary terms retained earnings and capital in excess of par, even though the earlier terminology was officially abandoned by the accounting profession more than 30 years ago. Apart from mere terminology, there may be other differences between GAAP and the accounting rules applied in a given state's corporation laws, and local lawyers and corporate officers must be familiar with these differences.

Although the statutes vary considerably, most of them provide that a corporation may pay dividends only to the extent of its "Earned Surplus" or retained earnings. Since retained earnings represent the accumulated and undistributed earnings of a corporation, this statutory limitation in effect allows a corporation to distribute only its *income,* and prohibits distribution of its *contributed capital.* This limitation is consistent with the theory that we discussed above, that the contributed capital of a corporation must be maintained intact to protect its creditors. If a corporation makes a dividend distribution in excess of the amount permitted by the statute, the directors or shareholders may be personally liable to return the amount illegally distributed.

Retained earnings may be appropriated or restricted for specific purposes by agreement, by law or by action of the corporation's board of directors. Restricted or appropriated retained earnings are separately disclosed on the balance sheet and are generally not available for dividend distributions.

Many statutes also allow corporate distributions of "Capital Surplus" (capital paid in excess of par), probably based on the original theory that it is the par value of the corporation's stock that serves to protect creditors. In some states, a shareholder vote is required to authorize "Capital Surplus" distributions. In Delaware, however, a corporation may make distributions to the full extent of its entire "Surplus" without seeking shareholder approval.

For accounting purposes, a distribution not in excess of the corporation's retained earnings is treated as a dividend. To the extent that a distribution exceeds retained earnings, however, it is treated as a return of contributed capital. Thus, while Delaware and other states permit the return of the shareholders' contributed capital under the guise of dividends, GAAP would require that the true nature of such distributions be fully disclosed in the financial statements.

Every state imposes an additional restriction on dividend distributions: the corporation must not be *insolvent* at the time of the distribution or be rendered insolvent as a result of the distribution. As used in the statutes, insolvency refers to the inability of a corporation to pay its debts as they become due.

Recently, some legislatures and commentators have adopted the position that the statutory limitations on dividends are rooted in archaic concepts, a position that our earlier discussion indicated may be well justified. In California, the revised Corporations Code now provides for several alternative tests in determining the legality of corporate distributions. Basically, that statute allows a corporation to make distributions to the extent of its retained earnings. However, if retained earnings are insufficient the distribution may nevertheless be made so long as the corporation's total assets exceed its total liabilities, and its current assets exceed its current liabilities, by specified percentages subsequent to the distribution. A variation of the California approach was adopted in a recent revision of the Model Business Corporation Act, which serves as a drafting model for many states.

There are many other state to state variations in the dividend rules. Some allow assets to be written up to their current values, others prohibit write-ups, and most are confusingly silent on the subject. Some states have special dividend rules for coal mines, oil wells and other "wasting asset companies." A few states permit a corporation to pay a dividend in a profitable year, even if it has as a result of earlier losses accumulated a negative balance in retained earnings. Mastery of these variations is the job of the local corporate lawyer; you should simply be alert to the fact that the variations exist.

Accounting for Cash and Stock Dividends

When a corporation pays a cash dividend, an asset (usually cash) is reduced and the net worth of the corporation (retained earnings) is also reduced. A corporation may also declare and distribute a dividend consisting of its own stock, a *stock dividend*. From the corporation's viewpoint, the advantage of such a distribution is that it does not require the reduction of any of the corporation's assets. The effect of a stock dividend is that one capital account is reduced (retained earnings) while another is increased (capital stock) to reflect the issuance of new shares. Since stock dividends do not result in distribution of corporate assets, they are treated differently from cash dividends for both corporate law and tax accounting purposes. The corporate law limitations on dividend distributions described above generally do not apply to stock dividends, since creditors are unaffected by such dividends. For tax purposes, the recipient of a cash dividend reports the dividend as ordinary income, while the receipt of a stock dividend ordinarily does not result in reportable income. Instead, in general the stockholder is required to reallocate the purchase price of his stock (his *basis*) over the original shares plus the new shares received as a dividend. Suppose a stockholder purchased 500 shares of N Corporation stock for $12 per share, paying a total of $6,000. If N Corporation pays a 10% stock dividend, the stockholder will receive an additional 50 shares. His basis of $6,000 will not change, but will be spread over all 550 shares, giving him a basis of $10.91 per share ($6,000 ÷ 550 shares).

Occasionally, a corporation will carry out a *stock split*, in which it divides its outstanding stock. Assume that X Corporation has outstanding 100,000 shares of common stock, which are trading at $80 per share. To widen the market for its shares, X causes a two-for-one stock split, with the result that each shareholder receives two shares in the place of each share held. After the split, X Corporation has outstanding 200,000 shares of common stock, which should trade at about $40 per share. In a stock split, no accounting entry is made: there is no transfer of retained earnings to the capital stock account. Instead, the balance sheet after the split simply shows the increased number of shares outstanding. The line between a substantial stock dividend and a small stock split may be difficult to draw, since their appearance is similar. As a rule of thumb, a stock distribution in excess of 20%–25% should be treated as a stock split, rather than as a stock dividend.

During the course of the year, the net worth, or *Stockholders' Equity*, section of a corporation's balance sheet may change as the result of issuance or repurchase of stock, distribution of cash and stock dividends, and income or loss. These changes are reflected in a separate Statement of Stockholders' Equity. The Times Mirror Statement of Stockholders' Equity appears in Appendix A (page 209).

Repurchases and Redemptions of Shares

A corporation may reacquire its own shares of stock. Reacquisition of shares may be undertaken for the purpose of later issuance, to eliminate or reduce an undesirable outstanding class of stock (such as preferred stock which pays a high dividend), or for a variety of other purposes. Perhaps the most common purpose is to buy out the shares of a retired or deceased shareholder.

Although the corporation's shares are assets in the hands of others, they are treated in the hands of the corporation itself as a reduction of capital. In effect, by repurchasing its own shares a corporation returns a portion of its contributed capital to its shareholders. Moreover, though shareholders generally incur profits and losses on buying and selling stock, a corporation does not recognize gain or loss in transactions in its own stock. Finally, a corporation may not pay dividends on shares of its own stock that it holds. These rules apply not only for financial accounting purposes, but also for tax purposes.

The legal limitations on reacquisition of shares are nearly identical to those for dividend distributions. Thus a corporation will ordinarily be able to reacquire its own shares only to the extent of its retained earnings.

If the reacquired shares are not cancelled, but held for possible later resale, they are known as *Treasury Stock*. Treasury stock is shown on the balance sheet at its cost, as a *reduction* of net worth. Remember, the corporation's own reacquired stock is not an asset, but is instead a reduction of capital. If the treasury stock is later sold, the proceeds are an asset and the reduction of capital is removed. If instead the treasury stock is cancelled, it is removed from the outstanding stock. During the entire time that treasury stock is held by a corporation prior to its cancellation or resale, the retained earnings of the corporation are restricted in an amount equal to its purchase price. As we noted earlier, restricted retained earnings are not available for dividends or other distributions.

Balance Sheet Disclosure of Stockholders' Equity

A comprehensive example of balance sheet disclosure of stockholders' equity is as follows:

Example Corporation
Balance Sheet
December 31, 19___

Assets	Liabilities and Stockholders' Equity		
Assets $5,700,000	Liabilities		$2,000,000
	Stockholders' Equity: 10% Preferred Stock, $100 par, 7,500 shares outstanding		$ 750,000
	Common Stock, $40 par, 50,000 shares issued	$2,000,000	
	Less Treasury Stock, 2,000 shares, at cost	100,000	
	Common Stock Ousanding		1,900,000
	Capital Contributed in Excess of Par Value of Common Stock		250,000
	Retained Earnings (of which $100,000 is restricted as a result of Treasury Stock)		800,000
	Total Stockholders' Equity		$3,700,000
Total Assets $5,700,000	Total Liabilities and Stockholders' Equity		$5,700,000

REFERENCES

Official Pronouncements:

American Institute of Certified Public Accountants, Committee on Accounting Procedure, Accounting Research Bulletin No. 43 (1953), chapters 1, 7.

American Institute of Certified Public Accountants, Accounting Principles Board, Opinion 10 (1966), paragraphs 10, 11; Opinion 12 (1967), paragraphs 9, 10.

Uniform Partnership Act (1914)

Uniform Limited Partnership Act (1916)

Revised Uniform Limited Partnership Act (1976)

Model Business Corporation Act (as amended, 1981)

Secondary Sources:

Conard, Knauss & Siegel, Enterprise Organization (3d ed. 1982).
Bromberg, Crane and Bromberg on Partnerships (1968).
Manning, Legal Capital (2d ed. 1981).

Chapter Nine

ANALYSIS OF FINANCIAL
STATEMENTS

Never ask of money spent
Where the spender thinks it went.
Nobody was ever meant
To remember or invent
What he did with every cent.

Robert Frost, The Hardship of Accounting

The Need for Analysis

The statement of income and the balance sheet present much of the basic information needed by management, creditors, investors and other readers. However, when considered individually many items appearing in the financial statements have limited significance. It is necessary to analyze the relationships among these items and to establish meaningful benchmarks and comparisons in order to evaluate the financial condition of the enterprise and the results of its operations as presented in the financial statements. Creditors look to the financial statements to evaluate their likelihood of being repaid. How do the statements answer their inquiry? Potential investors seek to determine from the statements whether the company will grow or decline. How does the information therein assist in this evaluation? Management looks to the financial statements to establish product pricing policy, credit limitations, cash needs and other operating arrangements. What analytical tools may be applied to the statements to assist in this process?

A wide variety of comparisons, trends, ratios and calculations are employed to interpret and explain solvency, stability, growth, profitability and other aspects of the enterprise. This chapter introduces only the most commonly used of these analytical tools.

Comparative Financial Statements

Annual reports filed with the United States Securities and Exchange Commission (the SEC) must contain balance sheets as of the end of the two most recent years and statements of income for the three most recent years. Companies not required to file with the SEC frequently provide such information to their shareholders on a voluntary basis. The Times Mirror financial statements in Appendix A illustrate the columnar presentation of these statements. Referring to the Statements of Income (page 208), you will note that while revenues increased steadily from 1978 through 1981, net income declined from 1979 to 1980 and increased in 1981. Overall performance has improved, but it will take further analysis to see why. These comparisons are, of course, only with earlier years' operations for Times Mirror Company; they give no basis for comparative evaluation with other similar companies.

By referring to the comparative Balance Sheets of Times Mirror (pages 206–207), we can see that nearly every category of assets increased from 1980 to 1981, as did most liabilities. The most important comparison, however, is shareholders' equity, which shows a considerable increase, demonstrating that the value of the ownership interest of the stockholders has increased.

Further annual comparative data are generally available in schedules published with the annual report. Times Mirror provides a ten-year comparative summary of selected financial data (pages 192–193) which offers the reader an extended view of the overall financial performance and condition of the company.

Also included with SEC-filed financial statements is a commentary by management that should assist the reader in evaluating the year-to-year performance. The Times Mirror financial statements are accompanied by *Management's Discussion and Analysis of Financial Condition and Results of Operations*, (pages 196–205) which under a series of headings explains the company's performance by major product and service categories. For example, the detailed information concerning book publishing explains the increase in revenues on the basis of facts that are not available in the financial statements themselves. Since the management discussion is required by SEC rules and not by GAAP, companies not required to file statements with the SEC often will not include this information with their financial statements. Nevertheless, major creditors or potential investors who are familiar with the nature of the information ordinarily provided in the management discussion may seek this information by direct inquiry of company officers.

[*106*]

Balance Sheet Analysis: Working Capital

Current liabilities must be discharged within the year, and most are ordinarily paid within 30 to 120 days of being incurred. They are paid, of course, with cash, and cash flows into the company primarily through liquidation of its current assets: sales of inventory and payments of accounts receivable. Effective carrying on of business activities requires that the company have an adequate excess of current assets over current liabilities, called *working capital*. In the absence of adequate working capital, even a profitable company will be unable to finance its operations and to pay its debts as they become due. Consider this example of two companies:

	Company A	Company B
Assets		
Cash	$ 12,000	$ 4,000
Accounts Receivable	58,000	26,000
Inventories	30,000	20,000
Plant & Equipment, less Depreciation	100,000	150,000
Total Assets	$200,000	$200,000
Liabilities & Net Worth		
Accounts Payable	$ 50,000	$ 50,000
Common Stock	90,000	90,000
Retained Earnings	60,000	60,000
Total Liabilities & Net Worth	$200,000	$200,000

The companies have the same net worth, and both appear to be successful, since they show substantial retained earnings. Company A has current assets (cash, accounts receivable and inventories) of $100,000, and current liabilities (accounts payable) of $50,000. Its working capital (current assets — current liabilities) is therefore $50,000. However, Company B has current assets of $50,000 and current liabilities of $50,000, leaving a working capital balance of zero. Company B is in a dangerous financial position, since it may not be able to produce in time the cash required to pay its current liabilities of $50,000. Indeed, even if it collects all of its accounts receivable promptly, there will still be insufficient cash to pay its accounts payable. Company B is, in fact, a classic illustration of a company on the brink of *insolvency*, inability to pay its debts as they come due.

Working capital represents, in a sense, the company's financial cushion, its surplus of funds readily available to pay creditors. Why, then, don't companies maintain large cash reserves and maximize working capital?   Investors seek income, and if too large a portion of the company's assets consists of working capital, the company's income will be inadequate.   Consider the extreme case of a company whose only asset is cash, in a substantial amount.   While it is ordinarily desirable to own money— particularly a substantial amount of it—a company that owns only money obviously cannot generate income.   The money must be put to use.

Working capital must therefore be maintained at an optimal level, sufficient to assure adequate funds for regular operations, but not so great that investable funds lie idle.   The most widely used tests to evaluate the adequacy of working capital are the *Current Ratio* and the *Quick Ratio* or *Acid-Test Ratio.*   The current ratio is the ratio of current assets to current liabilities. In Company A, that ratio is 2 to 1 ($100,000 ÷ $50,000), which is viewed by many analysts as the optimal figure.   In Company B, the current ratio is 1 to 1, a figure well into the danger zone. The quick ratio is a more severe test, based on the fact that inventories require time to be converted into cash under normal operating conditions.   *Quick Assets* are cash, marketable securities, and accounts and current notes receivable.   Inventories and prepaid expenses are excluded.   The ratio of quick assets to current liabilities is the quick ratio.   Company A's quick ratio is therefore 1.4 to 1 ($70,000 ÷ $50,000); a ratio of 1 to 1 or more is generally satisfactory.   Company B has a quick ratio of 0.6 to 1 ($30,000 ÷ $50,000), showing further evidence of forthcoming inability to pay its debts.

Debt Ratios

Existing or potential creditors wishing to evaluate the security of their loans frequently look to the ratio of debt to capital or debt to equity.   These ratios may be calculated by literally a dozen different formulas, but their underlying theory is that a creditor has substantial security when the ratio of debt to contributed capital is low.   The ratios are generally calculated as follows:

$$\text{Debt to Equity Ratio} = \text{Total Debt} \div \text{Stockholders' Equity}$$

$$\text{Debt to Capital Ratio} = \frac{\text{Long-Term Debt}}{\text{Long-Term Debt} + \text{Stockholders' Equity}}$$

As used in the debt to capital ratio, "capital" refers to the concept of long-term investments often used in the financial world, a concept that unlike the accounting definition of capital includes long-term debt.

Applying these ratios to the 1981 balance sheet of Times-Mirror Company, we obtain these results:

$$\text{Debt-Equity} = \frac{\$328,706 + \$478,273 + \$195,030}{\$915,203} = 1.09 \text{ to } 1$$

$$\text{Debt-Capital} = \frac{\$478,273}{\$478,273 + \$915,203} = 0.34 \text{ to } 1$$

In both cases, the ratios indicate substantial protection for creditors, the debt-equity ratio demonstrating that for every dollar of total debt the company has nearly one dollar of capital invested by stockholders, and the debt-capital ratio showing that long-term debt amounts to only one-third of total long-term investments in the company.

Turnover of Accounts Receivable and Fixed Assets

The "turnover" of accounts receivable is a useful test of the effectiveness of the company's credit and collection policy. It is calculated by dividing the net sales for the year by the average of the accounts receivable for the year, as follows:

	1982	1983
Net Sales	$750,000	$870,000
Average Accounts Receivable	75,000	113,000
Accounts Receivable Turnover:		
Number of Times	10	7.7

The average accounts receivable may be calculated by averaging the beginning and ending balances, or preferably by averaging the monthly balances in order to take account of seasonal variations. Carrying the calculation one step further, we can determine the average number of days it took to collect the accounts, by dividing a 360 day year by the turnover. In 1982, it took an average of 36 days (360 ÷ 10) to collect the accounts, but by 1983 the average collection time had increased to 47 days (360 ÷ 7.7). If sales were made on 30-day credit, the collection department did a satisfactory job in 1982 and an unsatisfactory job in 1983. Accounts receivable should be examined to determine the reason for the slowdown in collections.

A similar turnover calculation may be made with respect to fixed assets, to provide a comparative view of the utilization of fixed assets in improving sales. When a company undertakes major fixed asset acquisitions, this ratio is useful in determining whether the additional investments have produced proportional increases in sales. Generally, the ratio is based on total fixed assets without reduction for accumulated depreciation, since the depreciation figure often is not reflective of actual decline in value due to wear or obsolescence.

	1982	1983
Net Sales	$870,000	$950,000
Fixed Assets Before Depreciation	150,000	200,000
Fixed Asset Turnover:		
Number of Times	5.8	4.8

It appears that the purchase of additional fixed assets resulted in a decline in the turnover ratio, a disappointing result. The decline may be explained by a general economic downturn, by startup problems with the new machinery, or by other factors. As with all ratio evaluation, the calculations are only the beginning of the analysis.

Book Value Per Share

Stockholders generally wish to analyze the company not only as a totality, but also in terms of their individual investment. Publicly traded stock is, of course, regularly evaluated by the market, and trading prices usually represent the best guide to the inherent value of the stock. There are, however, more corporations whose stock is not traded than there are corporations with publicly traded stock. Moreover, even when a market price is available, further analysis of stock value may be appropriate.

The beginning point for such analysis is the book value per share of common stock. In a company that has only common stock outstanding, this calculation is as follows:

$$\text{Book Value per Share} = \frac{\text{Total Assets} - \text{Total Liabilities}}{\text{Number of Shares Outstanding}}$$

The Times Mirror financial statements do not disclose the number of shares outstanding, but the book value per share is listed in the ten-year Summary of Selected Consolidated Financial Data and Other Information (page 192). As of the end of 1981, the book value per share of common stock was $26.81. Note that the market value of the common stock ranged from $39.75 to $58.50 during the year, well in excess of book value. The discussion of intangible assets and goodwill in Chapter 6 explained why a successful business is generally worth more than the figures represented on the books. In Chapter 14 we will explore another reason for the divergence between book value and market price, inflation.

Book value is generally calculated for common stock only, since preferred stock is ordinarily entitled to receive only its liquidation preference. If preferred stock is outstanding, its liquidation preference must first be subtracted from net assets before the book value of the common stock may be determined.

Income Statement Analysis: Percentages and Trends

Percentage analysis of the income statement often provides important insights into the company's performance and the trend of its operations. The percentages are usually based on sales, as in the following example:

	1982		1983	
	$	%	$	%
Sales	100,000	100.0	120,000	100.0
Cost of Goods Sold	62,000	62.0	76,000	63.3
Gross Profit	38,000	38.0	44,000	36.7
Operating Expenses	22,000	22.0	26,000	21.7
Net Income	16,000	16.0	18,000	15.0

The percentage analysis reveals that while sales and net income have increased, the relative profitability of the company has in fact declined. The cost of goods sold increased by more than 1%, although operating expenses decreased slightly. Net income as a percentage of sales decreased from 16% to 15%; had the previous year's percentages remained unchanged, net income for 1983 would have been $19,200. These figures need further examination. They might show that the company's 1983 selling prices were too low, or on the other hand they might confirm that aggressive marketing in 1983 produced an increase in net income at the cost of a decline in the profit margin. Here, as with earlier examples of statement analysis, the numbers only begin to tell the story. Well managed companies will generally establish guideline or budgeted percentages at the beginning of each operating period and will analyze the variation between budgeted and actual results at the end of the period.

[*111*]

The percentage of gross profit, often referred to as the *Gross Profit Margin*, declined from 38% to 36.7% in the illustration above. Merchants often attempt to maintain a predetermined gross profit margin which is calculated to cover operating expenses and produce a desirable net income. This practice provides a basis for evaluating actual results, and has the incidental advantage of permitting the use of the *Retail Inventory Method*, discussed in Chapter 4.

Calculation of the percentages of change in key income statement items from year to year provides a basis for examining trends in the business operations. These calculations may be made from one year to the next, or may be made over a longer period, using one year as a base year. Consider the following trends of sales and cost of goods sold, using 1980 as the base year:

	Sales		Cost of Goods Sold	
	$	Trend %	$	Trend %
1980	275,000	100	200,000	100
1981	316,250	115	240,000	120
1982	261,250	95	210,000	105
1983	220,000	80	190,000	95

The percentages for each year after 1980 are calculated based on 1980. Thus, for sales, $316,250 is 115% of $275,000; $261,250 is 95% of $275,000; and $220,000 is 80% of $275,000.

These figures indicate an unsatisfactory trend. When sales increased in 1981 to an index percentage of 115, cost of goods sold increased to a greater index percentage of 120. In 1982 and 1983, when sales declined to index percentages of 95 and 80, cost of goods sold did not decrease proportionately. This trend should alert management to problems with respect to sales prices, costs, or both.

Inventory Turnover

Efficient utilization of inventory can spell the difference between profits and losses. An efficient company will try to convert its inventories into cash by means of sale as rapidly as possible. An index to the company's effectiveness in disposition of its inventory is *Inventory Turnover*, which is calculated by dividing cost of goods sold by the average inventory for the year. The following is a simplified example of the calculation:

Cost of Goods Sold:

Inventory, January 1	$ 75,000
Purchases	310,000
Goods Available for Sale	$385,000
Less: Inventory, December 31	90,000
Cost of Goods Sold	$295,000

Average Inventory = (Opening Inv. + Closing Inv.) ÷ 2

($75,000 + $90,000) ÷ 2 = $ 82,500

Inventory Turnover = Cost of Goods Sold ÷ Average Inventory

$295,000 ÷ $82,500 =   3.6 times

Inventory turnover varies from industry to industry. Food markets have a high turnover, perhaps 20 or more times per year. Furniture stores have much lower turnovers, perhaps 2 to 6 times per year. Inventory turnover figures for various businesses, as well as other financial ratios, may be found in the annual statistics compiled by Dun & Bradstreet. The higher the turnover, the less money a company must maintain invested in inventories to achieve a given level of sales. The desire for a high rate of inventory turnover must, however, be balanced against the need to maintain an adequate stock of merchandise to make available to customers. In addition, the company must take into account the desirability of purchasing or manufacturing inventory in economic lot sizes, and of maintaining relatively steady production operations.

Business Segment Information

Companies that file annual reports with the SEC are required to provide information concerning revenues, profits, assets, depreciation and capital expenditures with respect to major segments of their business operations. An example of this disclosure appears in the *Five-Year Summary of Business Segment Information* accompanying the financial statements of Times Mirror Company, in Appendix A (pages 194–195). The information is extremely important in analyzing the results of operations. For example, note that in 1980 and 1981, newspaper and forest products produced a loss for Times Mirror, while in the same years many other operations showed increased profits. These results are further explained in *Management's Discussion and Analysis of Financial Conditions and Results of Operations* (pages 196–205).

Analysis of Operations: Earnings Per Share

Perhaps the single most widely used figure on the financial statements is *Earnings Per Share* (EPS), which is required by GAAP to be calculated and disclosed on the financial statements of public enterprises. Nonpublic enterprises—those whose securities are not publicly traded and that do not file financial statements with the SEC—are not required to disclose EPS, but are likely to do so in most instances. Earnings per share represents the net income of the company allocable to each share of common stock. Therefore the EPS figure is understandably relied upon heavily by investors and others in determining the value of a company's common stock. In a company with a simple capital structure, the calculation of EPS poses no difficulty:

$$\text{Earnings Per Share} = \frac{\text{Net Income After Taxes}}{\text{Weighted Average of Shares Outstanding}}$$

Thus if Profitable Products, Inc. had net income of $300,000 for 1983, and during all of 1983 had outstanding 150,000 shares of common stock, earnings per share would be $2.00. If Profitable Products issued or repurchased common stock during the year, the number of shares outstanding would be determined by calculating a weighted average, generally on a monthly basis.

If a company had extraordinary items of gain or loss during the year, EPS must be calculated both before and after the extraordinary items, and generally should be shown also for the extraordinary items themselves. Suppose that profitable Products' net income consisted of $450,000 net income from operations, and $150,000 extraordinary loss on destruction of a plant that was uninsured. Profitable's EPS disclosure would be as follows:

Earnings per share:	
Before extraordinary loss	$3.00
Extraordinary loss	1.00
After extraordinary loss	$2.00

When a company has a capital structure that includes preferred stock, convertible securities or options, the EPS calculation becomes more complex. Suppose that Extraordinary Enterprises Corp. had net income of $500,000 in 1983, and that it had outstanding 20,000 shares of preferred stock with a $10 annual dividend and 50,000 shares of common stock. The calculation of EPS is as follows:

Net income	$500,000
Less: preferred stock dividend (20,000 × $10)	200,000
Income attributable to common stock	$300,000
$300,000 ÷ 50,000 shares	$6.00 EPS

The calculation is the same whether or not the preferred dividend is paid, since the preferred is entitled to receive the dividend prior to any distribution to the common stock.

Suppose, however, that the Extraordinary Enterprises preferred stock is convertible into common stock, in the ratio of 2 shares of common stock for each share of preferred. If the preferred stock were all converted at the beginning of the year, the EPS calculation would change:

Net income	$500,000
Less: preferred stock dividend	0
Income attributable to common stock	$500,000
Common stock outstanding: 50,000 + (2 × 20,000)	90,000 shares
$500,000 ÷ 90,000 shares	$5.56 EPS

This is an illustration of *dilution*, reduction of the effective earnings per share of the common stock by conversion of the preferred stock. Dilution may also occur upon conversion into common stock of convertible bonds, upon the exercise of stock options or warrants, or upon the issuance of contingent shares. In the case of Extraordinary Enterprises, which is the "correct" EPS figure, $6.00 or $5.56? To this question there is no easy answer.

The effects of dilution on EPS must be disclosed. GAAP requires that companies with complex capital structures calculate and disclose *primary earnings per share*, and if appropriate *fully diluted earnings per share*. Some securities are categorized as *common stock equivalents*, sufficiently close to common stock that their dilutive effects must be included in calculating even primary earnings per share. Stock options and warrants fall into this category, as do certain convertible securities. When primary earnings per share are calculated, these options and warrants must be assumed to have been exercised and the convertible securities must be assumed to have been converted. The actual calculations of the effects of the exercise and conversions are quite complex, and need not concern you as a reader of the financial statements. If, however, you wish to understand the calculations, explanations may be found in the references at the end of this chapter.

Convertible securities are categorized as common stock equivalents on the basis of their characteristics as of issuance; basically if such securities as of issuance carry a cash yield of less than ⅔ the average yield of corporate bonds with a high rating (Aa) of security, they are deemed common stock equivalents. Remember that common stock equivalents are treated as though they are converted in calculating primary earnings per share. All other convertible securities are treated as converted in calculating a second EPS figure, fully diluted earnings per share.

You may by now have concluded, correctly, that a complex company may be required to disclose *four* EPS figures, primary and fully diluted for earnings both before and after extraordinary items. We may now refine our initial question: is one of the four the "correct" figure? The answer should now be obvious. All four provide useful insights into the performance of the company, and no one figure would be entirely satisfactory.

Despite the complexity of calculation, and the frequent requirement of multiple calculations, investors tend to give great weight to the EPS figure. A further refinement of the EPS calculation, also in wide use, is the *Price Earnings Ratio*, also known as the P–E Ratio. The price earnings ratio is calculated on a daily basis by dividing the current market price of a share of common stock by the most recent figure for EPS. Newspapers publish the P–E ratio daily in the stock quotation columns. A stock transaction page near the end of 1982 showed the following closing market prices and price earnings ratios of shares of common stock of selected major corporations:

	Market Price	P–E Ratio
Amer. Tel. & Tel.	60¼	7
General Tel. & Elect.	40½	9
Exxon	27⅞	6
Gulf Oil	28⅛	6
IBM	88¼	14
Xerox	38⅞	8

The price earnings ratio is a reflection of many factors, including the market's evaluation of the relative risk of the company's operations and expectations with respect to future income. As with all the calculated data discussed in this chapter, the price earnings ratio can be understood only after careful analysis of the underlying financial and other data with respect to the company.

REFERENCES

Official Pronouncements:

American Institute of Certified Public Accountants, Accounting Principles Board, Opinion No. 9 (1966) (Reporting the results of operations); Opinion No. 15 (1969) (Earnings per share).

Secondary Sources:

Bernstein, Financial Statement Analysis: Theory, Application and Interpretation (1974).

Graham, Dodd & Cottle, Security Analysis: Principles and Techniques (4th ed. 1962).

Gibson, Financial Ratios in Annual Reports, The CPA Journal, Sept. 1982, p. 18.

Chapter Ten

CASH FLOW AND FUNDS FLOW: THE STATEMENT OF CHANGES IN FINANCIAL POSITION

O money, money, money, I'm not necessarily one of those who think thee holy,

But I often stop to wonder how thou canst go out so fast when thou comest in so slowly.

Ogden Nash, Hymn to the Thing That Makes the Wolf Go

Net Income and Cash Flow

To this point, we have discussed the operations of the enterprise in terms of accrual accounting; we have dealt with recognition of income and expense independently of the timing of cash payments and receipts. We now return to a more basic but increasingly important concept: cash flow. Indeed, in the view of some analysts cash flow has begun to supplant income as the key measure of enterprise performance.

Cash flow, in its most direct sense, refers to the receipts and disbursements of cash by the enterprise. An enterprise is said to have positive cash flow in any period in which more cash is received than paid out. Correspondingly, negative cash flow refers to an excess of cash payments over cash receipts. Net income is a source of cash flow, but net income and cash flow are rarely equal. For example, a company may earn $300,000 of fee income during the year, but if the company extends credit, it will have positive cash flow only to the extent that the accounts receivable for fee income are actually collected. In some instances, cash flow exceeds net income. For example, a building may show rental receipts of $100,000 and depreciation expense of $80,000, producing net income of $20,000. The rentals produce positive cash flow of $100,000, but the depreciation expense involves no negative cash flow, since it represents only the writing off of an asset that was purchased earlier. Therefore, although net income from the building is $20,000, its positive cash flow is $100,000.

Furthermore, positive and negative cash flows occur in transactions having nothing to do with income and expense. If a company buys land for cash, cash has flowed out of the business. If the company sells a building for cash, it has positive cash flow whether or not it recognizes income on the sale.

Cash flow is vitally important in both the short-run and long-run operations of the enterprise. Despite substantial net income, a company with continued negative cash flow may face bankruptcy, since it may be incapable of paying its creditors on time. At the other end of the spectrum, a company with substantial losses may be able to continue in business long enough to return to profitable operations provided it has adequate cash flow.

Discounted Cash Flow, Present Values and Related Concepts

An understanding of the timing of cash flows and of the concept of present valuation of future cash flows is important in appreciating contemporary accounting theory as well as other related financial concepts.

Money and other assets have time value. A dollar today is worth more than the same dollar a year from now, even ignoring the effects of inflation. If you go to the bank and ask for a dollar today, with your promise to repay it one year from now, the bank will insist on being paid *interest*, which represents compensation to the bank for providing you with the use of one dollar for one year. Therefore, the bank will require repayment of perhaps $1.15 one year from now, representing the dollar plus 15% interest. The $1.15 is known as the *compound amount* of one dollar for one year at 15%. If, instead of borrowing the dollar for one year, you borrow it for two, an additional 15% interest would be payable for the second year. However, during the second year you would effectively be borrowing $1.15, the original dollar plus the 15 cents unpaid interest for the first year. Therefore, interest in the second year would be 15% of $1.15, or 17 cents. In this situation, the interest is said to be *compounded*. Repayment at the end of the second year would therefore require a compound amount of $1.32. This compounding process would continue for every year in which no payment was made. At the end of ten years, the compound amount payable would be $4.05, more than four times the original loan!

The compound amount calculation is important to accountants because it demonstrates the extent to which invested money will grow at a given rate of return. Thus, if a company regularly earns a 15% return on its invested capital, and if it continues to do so, it can expect that over a ten-year period its invested capital will quadruple.

A variation of the compound amount calculation is particularly important in accounting and financial planning. What is the value today of one dollar to be received one year from today? Using the same concept of time value of money, a dollar one year from now is obviously worth less than a dollar today. At 15% interest, a dollar one year from now is worth 87 cents today. Phrased differently, 87 cents invested today at 15% interest would amount to one dollar a year from now. The 87 cents is known as the *discounted value* or *present value* of one dollar at 15% for one year. Just as interest is compounded on unpaid loans, the present value of future payments is calculated using compound interest. The present value of one dollar ten years from now at 15% interest is slightly less than 25 cents. The formulas for calculating compound amount and present value need not concern you, though they are reproduced at the end of this chapter for interested readers. These calculations may be performed by using readily available compound interest tables, or by using an electronic calculator with financial functions.

We may illustrate the importance of discounting future cash flows with a few simple examples. Suppose that a company is considering the purchase today of a tract of land that it expects it will be able to sell for $100,000 ten years from now. What is the *present value* of that land? In terms of cash flow, the land is the equivalent of a single payment of $100,000 in ten years. The present value of that payment, discounted at 15%, is $24,718. In other words, if the company ordinarily earns 15% on its capital, an investment of $24,718 will grow in value to $100,000 in ten years.

Since enterprises invest their funds with the expectation of earning a return, and since the return is ultimately cash, it is appropriate to evaluate potential investments—and entire companies—on the basis of their expected cash flows. Of course, most investments produce more than a single cash payment; generally, an investment will produce a stream of payments. In actuarial terms, a stream of payments is known as an *annuity*. Calculation of the present value of a stream of future payments is only a mathematical variation of calculating the present value of a single payment. Tables and calculators provide solutions to this problem as well, and one basic formula, the present value of an annuity, is shown at the end of this chapter for your reference. Suppose that a company is contemplating the purchase of a machine for $150,000 which is expected to increase the company's revenues by $20,000 annually for the next 12 years. Is the investment worthwhile, assuming that the company generally earns 15% on its investments? The present value of a twelve-year annuity of $20,000 per year, discounted at 15%, is approximately $108,400. Therefore, if the company's predictions are accurate the machine represents a bad investment. Using a financial calculator, one could determine that the actual rate of return on this investment would be slightly over 8%, well below the company's normal return on invested funds.

Even if the expected cash flows are not conveniently even in amount, they may be reduced to a single present value figure for analysis. This calculation, known as *Net Present Value*, can only be done with advanced financial calculators or with computers. For example, assume that a real estate company has the opportunity to buy an office building for $2,000,000, which it expects to operate for four years and sell at the end of that time for $2,800,000. Suppose that the expected cash flows for the four years of ownership are:

Purchase	($2,000,000)	Cash paid out on purchase
Year one	(100,000)	Negative cash from operations
Year two	(50,000)	Negative cash from operations
Year three	150,000	Cash from operations
Year four	200,000	Cash from operations
Year four	2,800,000	Cash from sale of building

The company ordinarily earns 12% on its investments. Is the building a good investment? The net present value of these positive and negative cash flows, discounted at 12%, is ($115,824), a negative figure. The building is a bad investment. In fact, the *Internal Rate of Return*, the effective average interest rate earned on the building, is only 10.39%.

These calculations are complex, and there is ordinarily no need for the reader of financial statements to perform them. Furthermore, though the calculations have the appearance of precision, many judgment factors can affect the results. However, the concept underlying the calculations is fundamental: flows of cash may be discounted to determine an effective rate of return. Even more fundamental than the discounting process is our emphasis on *cash*, rather than the accounting concept of net income. Have we now abandoned all of the accounting concepts that we so carefully studied in earlier chapters?

[*121*]

Accounting Theory and Cash Flow

It remains the basic function of accounting to provide to investors, creditors and other users information that is useful in making rational decisions concerning investment, extension of credit and other matters involving the enterprise. A central element of this information is the determination of the amounts, timing and uncertainty of prospective cash receipts from dividends, interest, loan repayments, sale of stock, and the like. Ultimately, the investor or creditor seeks to receive a return of cash from an original investment of cash.

Since the cash return to the investor or creditor is related to the cash flows of the enterprise itself, accounting should provide information to assist readers of financial reports in assessing the cash flows of the enterprise. This includes information on enterprise resources and the claims against those resources (the balance sheet) and on the effects of enterprise operations (the income statement and the statement of changes in financial position, discussed below). Thus, analysis of cash flow does not supplant traditional balance sheet and income statement data, but rather serves as an important supplement to that data. It is important to note, however, that contemporary accounting theory has moved substantially toward recognizing cash flow, rather than net income, as the crucial test of enterprise performance.

Accounting for Cash Flow and Funds Flow

An effectively managed company will prepare a cash budget, predicting expected inflows and outflows of cash. Such a budget will allow the company to plan short-term or long-term financing, through borrowing or stock sales, to provide necessary cash not otherwise generated through operations. The budget indicates *planned* cash flows, but an additional financial statement is needed to report on *actual* cash flows. That statement, which originated more than fifty years ago, is the *Statement of Changes in Financial Position*, sometimes known as the Statement of Source and Application of Funds. The statement is required by GAAP. The statement may be prepared on the basis of cash flow, but most companies report on the broader basis of flows of *funds*. The concept of funds generally is the same as that of working capital: all current assets less all current liabilities. Some companies, however, report on funds flow more narrowly, limiting funds to cash, accounts receivable and short-term investments. The Times Mirror Company *Statement of Consol-idated Changes in Financial Position,* in Appendix A (pages 210–211), is based on the broad concept of funds. It reports sources and applications of funds and indicates changes in work-ing capital.

The Statement of Changes in Financial Position

The statement of changes in financial position reports on three major areas for the period covered (usually one year):

1. The amount of working capital generated and consumed by the operations of the enterprise.

2. The financing and investing activities of the enterprise, whether for cash or otherwise.

3. The net changes in each element of working capital.

Working capital, you will remember, is the excess of current assets over current liabilities. The statement is prepared by de-termining the increases and decreases of working capital and other accounts between the balance sheet at the beginning of the period and the balance sheet at the end of the period. These figures, together with the figures for net income and noncash expenses, are arranged in an order designed to satisfy the three major objectives listed above.

We may illustrate in simplified form the preparation of the statement of changes in financial position for Pecuniary, Inc., whose balance sheets for the years ended December 31, 1982 and 1983 are listed in the first two columns of the schedule on the following page. The balance sheets are based on the as-sumptions that Pecuniary's net income for 1983 was $120,000 (which was added to retained earnings) and that Pecuniary had depreciation expense of $30,000 for 1983 (which was added to accumulated depreciation). The two columns following the bal-ance sheets reflect the increases and decreases in each item that occurred from the end of the first year to the end of the second. (Following the Fundamental Equation, increases in assets are shown on the left side, and increases in liabilities and net worth are shown on the right side). These columns simply represent the arithmetic differences between the two balance sheets.

[*123*]

Pecuniary, Inc.
Worksheet for Statement of Changes in Financial Position
Balance Sheets as of 12/31   Net Change

	1982	1983	Increase	Decrease
Cash	$120,000	$ 90,000		$ 30,000
Accounts Receivable	180,000	270,000	$ 90,000	
Inventories	285,000	360,000	75,000	
Machinery & Equipment	100,000	355,000	255,000	
Building	—	150,000	150,000	
Less: Accumulated Depreciation	(70,000)	(100,000)		30,000
Total Assets	$615,000	$1,125,000		

	1982	1983	Decrease	Increase
Accounts Payable	$225,000	$ 195,000	30,000	
Notes Payable—Current	15,000	60,000		45,000
Bonds Payable—Long-Term		150,000		150,000
Common Stock	300,000	525,000		225,000
Retained Earnings	75,000	195,000		120,000
Total Liabilities & Net Worth	$615,000	$1,125,000		
Total Changes			$600,000	$600,000

The increases and decreases may now be summarized in a two-part statement. The top section will list the sources of funds and the applications of funds, and the bottom section will detail the changes in working capital. Phrased another way, the top section shows *where* the working capital came from and went to, while the bottom section shows what *items* of working capital changed in amount. Although the items on the statement are drawn directly from the worksheet, a few of them need explanation.

Net income is a source of funds because it results in an increase in the net assets of the company. In calculating net income, as we learned earlier, the expenses for the period are subtracted from the revenues. One type of expense reduces net income but does not reduce funds provided by operations: depreciation. This is so because depreciation does not require the outflow of funds, since it represents an allocation to expense of the cost of assets that were paid for earlier. Therefore, in determining the funds provided by operations, depreciation is added back to net income.

Just as some expenses do not require the application of funds, many applications of funds do not involve expense. Pecuniary's purchases of equipment and building (as revealed by the increases in these items from 1982 to 1983) represented an application of funds. Where did the funds come from to buy these additional fixed assets? Funds were provided not only by operations, but also by increases in the corporation's outstanding stock and bonds.

All of these changes are reflected in the statement of changes in financial position, developed from the worksheet above:

Pecuniary, Inc.
Statement of Changes in Financial Position
For the year ended December 31, 1983

Funds were provided by:		
Operations: Net income		$120,000
Add expense items not requiring outlay of		
funds: depreciation		30,000
Total funds provided by operations		$150,000
Issuance of bonds		150,000
Issuance of stock		225,000
Total funds provided		$525,000
Funds were applied to:		
Purchase of equipment	$255,000	
Purchase of Building	150,000	
Total funds applied		405,000
Net increase in working capital		$120,000
Working capital was increased by:		
Increase in accounts receivable		$ 90,000
Increase in inventories		75,000
Decrease in accounts payable		30,000
Total increases in working capital		$195,000
Working capital was decreased by:		
Decrease in cash	$ 30,000	
Increase in notes payable	45,000	
Total decreases in working capital		75,000
Net increase in working capital		$120,000

[*125*]

Analysis of the Statement of Changes in Financial Position.

The Times Mirror Statement of Consolidated Changes in Financial Position, in Appendix A (pages 210–211), follows a similar form. The statement is in the same two parts, separately listing sources and applications of funds and changes in working capital. Under the heading sources of funds, the principal source was net income from operations, amounting to over $150 million in 1981. To this are added expense items that did not require the outlay of funds: depreciation, amortization and depletion of $90 million and noncurrent deferred taxes of $25 million. Although these expenses reduced the net income of Times Mirror to $150 million, the company's operations actually provided nearly $266 million of funds.

Funds were also provided by a nearly $52 million increase in long-term debt. Remember that funds and working capital are defined in terms of net *current* assets. If a company borrows money by issuing long-term debt, its *net* assets do not increase, but its working capital (*current* assets—*current* liabilities) does increase. Similarly, an increase in other (noncurrent) liabilities provided some $8 million of funds. Finally, sale of fixed assets increased funds by almost $4 million. In that case, total assets remained unchanged, but current assets increased through conversion of property, plant and equipment into cash.

The largest application of funds was the purchase of more than $188 million of fixed assets. Here again, total assets remain unchanged, but the purchase resulted either in reduction of cash (decrease in current assets) or increase in accounts payable (increase in current liabilities). In either case, working capital was reduced. Additions to timberland similarly represented an application of some $27 million of funds. Decrease in long-term debt is shown reducing funds by nearly $22 million. How does payment of a debt reduce funds? Remember that long-term liabilities do not enter into the calculation of working capital. Therefore, when cash is used to discharge those liabilities, a current asset (cash) declines but no current liability is reduced. As a result, discharge of long-term debt reduces working capital. Dividends of some $61 million also reduced working capital, since cash was distributed to stockholders and no assets were received in return.

Times Mirror ended the year 1981 with working capital more than $16 million greater than 1980. The lower section of its statement of changes in financial position lists the particular changes that comprised this increase of $16 million. Some of the changes represented increases in working capital; for example, cash increased by some $4 million, accounts receivable increased by more than $24 million, and income taxes payable (a current liability) decreased by $1.5 million. Some of the changes represented decreases in working capital; for example accounts payable increased by some $10 million, and employee compensation payable increased by more than $4 million. The net effect of all of these changes was an increase in working capital of $16,394,000.

Although the statement of changes in financial position contains little information not already present in the company's balance sheets and income statements, the form of presentation highlights different operational results. The focus is not on status and not on income, but on the flow of current assets and current liabilities. When the statement is prepared on the cash basis, the focus is then directly on the inflows and outflows of cash. As the discussion earlier in this chapter demonstrates, cash and funds flow appear destined to occupy an increasingly important role in accounting and financial analysis.

Afterword: Actuarial Formulas

The basic formulas used in calculating compounded and discounted amounts are reproduced below. All of the formulas are based on an amount of one dollar; to obtain results for different amounts, simply multiply the formula answer by the number of dollars involved. In all formulas, the following notation is used:

i = compound interest rate per period

FV = future value, or compound amount

PV = present value, or discounted amount

n = number of periods

Compound amount of one: $FV = (1 + i)^n$

Present value of one: $PV = \dfrac{1}{(1 + i)^n}$

Compound amount of annuity of one paid at the end of each period:
$$FV = \frac{(1 + i)^n - 1}{i}$$

Present value of annuity of one paid at the end of each period:
$$PV = \frac{1 - (1 + i)^{-n}}{i}$$

REFERENCES

Official Pronouncements:

American Institute of Certified Public Accountants, Accounting Principles Board, Opinion No. 19 (1971) (Reporting changes in financial position).

Financial Accounting Standards Board, Statement of Financial Accounting Concepts No. 1, Objectives of Financial Reporting by Business Enterprises (1980).

Secondary Sources:

Mason, Cash Flow Analysis and the Funds Statement (AICPA Accounting Research Study No. 2) (1961).

Thorndike, The Thorndike Encyclopedia of Banking and Financial Tables (1980).

Chapter Eleven

AUDITING

Then how, when nature calls thee to be gone,
What acceptable audit canst thou leave?

Shakespeare, Sonnet IV

The Need for Auditing of Financial Statements

The function of auditing can be traced back to the late 19th century, when dramatic growth in industry and commerce led to the need for reliable financial information. What assurance can be given to investors, creditors and management that they can rely upon the financial statements of the company? Assets and income can be readily overstated, and liabilities and expenses understated or omitted from the financial records. These errors or intentional misstatements can exaggerate the net worth of the enterprise and mislead those who deal with it. The informed buyer of an expensive gemstone will insist that the stone be examined by a competent independent appraiser, who will give an opinion on its value. Independent audit serves a similar function: the auditor collects information, conducts inquiries and other procedures, and expresses an opinion concerning the fairness of presentation of the financial statements of the company. You may refer to the last page of Appendix A (page 223) for an example of such an opinion, rendered by Ernst & Whinney, CPA's on the financial statements of Times Mirror Company.

Responsibilities of Management

The management of the company has the direct responsibility for assuring the fairness of the representations made through the financial statements, and only management is in a position to adopt the accounting policies and internal systems to achieve this result. The auditor may make recommendations concerning the company's policies and practices, but cannot implement those recommendations. The auditor is responsible only for the auditor's report. A concise and informative delineation of management and auditor responsibility appears on the first page of the Times Mirror Company financial statements, in Appendix A (page 191).

Materiality

A pervasive quality of financial statements, one that significantly affects the audit function, is *materiality*. Materiality refers to the magnitude of omission or misstatement of accounting information that, under the circumstances, might change or influence the judgment of a reasonable person relying on the information. In all matters affecting accounting, immaterial items generally are not considered. The concept of materiality is based on professional judgment. Large variations in amount are always material: for example, it is often said that a 10% variation in any balance sheet or income statement item is material. However, it does not follow that smaller errors or omissions are immaterial. For example, an illegal payment of even a small amount is usually material. Similarly, the auditor's discovery of a small shortage of cash may be indicative of a larger defalcation. The legal concept of materiality in financial information, as applied under the federal securities laws, is similar to the accounting concept. In both, there are no fixed guidelines; informed professional judgment is the ultimate test.

The Auditor

Today, the audit function is generally performed by licensed professional auditors, known in the United States as *Certified Public Accountants (CPA's)*, and in other nations as Chartered Accountants, Licensed Accountants or similar titles. Certified Public Accountants are licensed to practice by each state, based on meeting certain education and experience requirements and passing the Uniform CPA Examination prepared by the American Institute of Certified Public Accountants (AICPA). CPA's are regulated by state boards of accountancy and are subject to the ethical and professional standards of the AICPA and the accounting principles promulgated by the AICPA and the Financial Accounting Standards Board (FASB), many of which we have already examined under the heading of GAAP. CPA's who audit financial statements filed with the SEC are also subject to accounting principles and professional standards disseminated by the SEC, and CPA's involved in preparation of federal tax returns and related matters are subject to the practice requirements of the Internal Revenue Service. CPA's may practice individually or in firms. Interestingly, although many smaller CPA firms are organized as professional corporations, the largest firms are organized as partnerships. The largest of these firms are international partnerships with professional staffs numbering in the thousands and with offices in dozens of countries. You may occasionally hear reference to the "big eight", the eight largest CPA firms.

The unique character of the CPA, which distinguishes the CPA from other professionals, is the requirement of independence. While the attorney, physician, architect or engineer *represents* a client or patient, the CPA is *engaged* by an enterprise to audit its financial statements. The role of the CPA is not to represent the company, but rather to provide *independent* review of its financial statements for the benefit of its shareholders, creditors, management and others.

Generally Accepted Auditing Standards

The auditor must comply with *Generally Accepted Auditing Standards (GAAS)*, and the auditor's report, or opinion, indicates this compliance in standardized language as follows:

> Our examinations were made in accordance with generally accepted auditing standards and, accordingly, included such tests of the accounting records and such other auditing procedures as we considered necessary in the circumstances.

Unlike GAAP, which we earlier discovered consists of no single identifiable body of definitive pronouncements, GAAS can be readily identified. Generally Accepted Auditing Standards are promulgated in the form of Statements on Auditing Standards by the Auditing Standards Board of the AICPA. These, together with related statements (on such matters as ethics, tax practice, review services and management advisory services) are published and compiled periodically. AICPA members, who constitute the overwhelming majority of independent auditors, are ethically bound to observe the requirements of these statements or to justify their departure from them.

There are ten basic standards in GAAS, under three categories:

General Standards: (1) The auditor must have adequate technical training and must be proficient in auditing.

(2) The auditor must be independent.

(3) The auditor must exercise due professional care in the conduct of the audit, including the preparation of the audit report.

Standards of Field Work: (1) The audit must be adequately planned and supervised.

(2) The audit must include a study and evaluation of the company's system of internal control.

(3) The auditor's opinion must be based on sufficient competent evidential matter.

Standards of Reporting: (1) The report must state whether the financial statements are presented in accordance with Generally Accepted Accounting Principles.

(2) The report must state whether GAAP has been applied on a consistent basis.

(3) If informative disclosures in the financial statements are not reasonably adequate, reference to disclosure must be made in the auditor's report.

(4) The auditor must express an opinion on the financial statements or state the reasons why an opinion cannot be expressed.

These standards are explained and interpreted in the Statements on Auditing Standards. The first and third of the general standards, which require training and due care, are similar to standards in every other profession. We have already noted that the second standard, independence, is unique. The AICPA Code of Professional Ethics prohibits the CPA or any firm of which he is a partner from expressing an opinion on financial statements unless he and his firm are independent with respect to the enterprise. For example, independence is considered impaired if the CPA has any direct or material indirect financial interest in the enterprise (such as ownership of stock), is a party to any loans to or from the enterprise, or holds any officership or similar position in the enterprise. A CPA may indeed serve as a director or officer of a corporation, or own substantial stock in a corporation, or be a partner in a business partnership; but in those cases, the CPA is forbidden to audit the financial statements of the enterprise.

The standards of field work are designed to assure that the CPA accumulates sufficient evidence to express an opinion on the financial statements and that the audit procedures are adequately documented. The first standard of field work requires that an *audit program* be developed, indicating the steps that will be taken during the course of the audit. The audit of any major company is a substantial undertaking, involving the efforts of many accountants over the course of many weeks. It is not unusual for the audit staff to consist of one or two partners of the CPA firm plus a dozen or more junior and senior accountants. Audit procedures will be conducted both before and after the end of the year. Therefore, it is essential that the audit be conducted pursuant to a detailed audit program, and that the completion of each audit procedure be appropriately documented.

Internal Control

The second standard of field work requires an examination of the company's system of *internal control*. Internal control refers to the plan of organization and the measures adopted by a company to safeguard its assets, check the accuracy and reliability of its accounting records, promote efficiency, and assure adherence to management policies. An adequate system of internal control will include policies and procedures to carry out the following major objectives:

(a) All transactions should be appropriately authorized by specific or general procedures. For example, issuance of checks, determination of prices and granting of credit should be carried out only under procedures requiring advance authorization.

(b) All transactions should be validly recorded at the correct amounts and prices, and procedures should be implemented to prevent recording of spurious transactions.

(c) Transactions should be properly classified in the records. For example, assets should not be recorded as expenses.

(d) Transactions must be recorded in the proper period. Our discussion in earlier chapters demonstrated that the timing of transactions can affect the financial statements of several years.

(e) Transactions should be accurately and fully summarized in the financial records. An "error" in summarizing cash receipts, for example, can hide an employee fraud.

The process of auditing is one of sampling, of examining selected records and transactions in order to determine the reliability of the financial statements as a whole. To accomplish this, a system of internal control that assures overall reliability of the records is a necessity.

In recent years, particular problems of internal control have been created by the widespread use of electronic data processing and the emergence of "computer fraud". Special standards have been developed for internal control and audit procedures in a computer environment. Recently, as well, national attention was focussed on bribery and illicit foreign payments by major corporations. Many senior corporate officials claimed to be unaware of such activities, allegedly carried on by junior personnel of the companies involved. The response of Congress was to pass the Foreign Corrupt Practices Act of 1977, applicable to companies that file financial statements with the SEC. That Act not only imposes fines and penalties against corporations and individuals that violate its provisions, but also specifically requires that every company within its coverage devise and maintain a system of internal control. That system must provide reasonable assurance that transactions are executed in accordance with management's authorization and that access to assets is permitted only in accordance with management's authorization. In addition, the system of internal control must provide reasonable assurance that transactions are recorded to permit accountability of assets and the preparation of financial statements in accordance with GAAP, and must provide for periodic comparison of the actual assets with the recorded figures for those assets.

We may illustrate the operation of a system of internal control by examining one key element, separation of duties between those who have custody of assets and those who must account for them. Two or more people should always be involved in the receipt or disposition of assets, with the result that fraud, theft and violation of company policies and procedures are rendered more difficult. For example:

(1) In a restaurant, the waiter or waitress prepares the bill (accountability), but the cashier receives payment of cash from the customer (custody of assets).

(2) A bill is submitted to a company by a supplier. A clerk prepares a written *voucher* (request for payment) with the bill attached (accountability); a second clerk prepares a check to the supplier (accountability); an assistant treasurer signs the check (custody of assets); and a bookkeeper prepares the journal entry reflecting payment (accountability).

(3) In a bank, cash is received for deposit by a teller, who records the deposit on an electronic terminal (custody of assets and accountability). The deposit slips and the electronic record are each checked by different individuals (accountability). The cash in the teller's deposit drawer at the end of the day is physically counted by a different teller (accountability).

Internal control is frequently augmented by internal audit, regular examination of transactions by internal personnel of the company. Of course, no system of internal control is foolproof, and occasional spectacular frauds demonstrate that concerted activity by those intent on wrongdoing can—for a time, at least—subvert the company's safeguards. However, a well designed internal control system, coupled with annual independent audit, remains the most effective method of assuring efficient and honest operations consistent with management policies.

Audit Procedures: Collection of Evidential Matter

The third standard of field work requires that sufficient evidential matter be collected. Audit procedures are designed to carry out this standard. Modern audits very rarely involve examination of all of the transactions of a company. The volume of transactions would render the costs of such an audit prohibitive. Instead, the auditor examines a sample of all relevant transactions, selected either statistically or on the basis of professional judgment. Every element of the financial statements must be examined, however, and the audit procedures must be tailored to each element and to the company being examined. We shall examine a few illustrative audit procedures to convey a sense of the process.

Accounts receivable are usually examined by tracing a sample of accounts back to the sales in which they originated, and by examining the actual sales invoices to assure that sales were made, the goods were delivered and the amounts recorded were correct. At the same time, this audit procedure serves as a verification of sales. In addition, the sales and accounts receivable transactions are examined for the period prior to and after the year-end to determine whether the transactions were recorded in the proper period. This examination, known as a *cut-off examination*, is generally performed for all items affecting determination of income. Finally, accounts receivable must be confirmed, on a test basis, by direct communication with customers, who will be asked to respond directly to the auditor indicating any disagreement with the amounts shown on the company's records.

Inventories must actually be physically examined by the auditor. In businesses where the inventory is counted annually, the auditor should be present to verify the count. In other businesses, a test examination of the inventory, by physical inspection, may be appropriate. The importance of physical inventory examination is periodically highlighted by well-publicized inventory frauds. Among the most famous of these were the McKesson Robbins case, in which a purported Canadian inventory of rare spices in fact was nonexistent, and the more recent salad oil scandal, also involving nonexistent inventories. A variation on this theme involved manipulation of computer records by employees of Equity Funding, documenting purported assets of the company (reinsurance policies) that did not exist. In addition to physical examination, audit of inventories includes review of inventory records to verify the accuracy of entries adding to and subtracting from inventory. Where appropriate, inquiry is made of other professionals to determine questions of title and valuation of inventories.

Accounts payable are traced, on a sample basis, to the transactions giving rise to liability. The auditor will examine the invoices for the related purchases or expenses, verifying amounts and timing, and checking that the goods or services were actually received by the company. In addition, a sample of actual payments is examined to verify that an appropriate voucher was prepared, that the check was properly authorized and signed, and that it was in fact endorsed by the payee. In addition, a sample of accounts payable may be verified by direct contact with creditors.

Liabilities and Loss Contingencies: The Auditor's Inquiry Letter

The auditor must collect sufficient evidential matter not only concerning what appears on the financial statements, but also with respect to what does not appear. Fair presentation of the company's financial condition and results of operations can be impaired or destroyed by the presence of undisclosed liabilities or claims. The auditor examines for unrecorded *existing* liabilities by tracing the company's purchases of inventory, other goods and services to verify that the associated liabilities or payments have been properly recorded. For example, if examination reveals that the company received in December an order of $60,000 of merchandise but recorded no account payable or cash payment for the order, the auditor must inquire further. Further examination may show not only an unrecorded liability (account payable) of $60,000 for that particular order, but also unrecorded liabilities for other purchases.

Earlier, in Chapter 7, we discussed *loss contingencies*, including present or possible lawsuits or claims against the company that might give rise to liability. Ordinarily, the auditor is not equipped either to discover these contingencies or to evaluate the likelihood that they will mature into actual liabilities of the company. Nevertheless, the auditor must obtain assurance that all material loss contingencies have been adequately disclosed. Auditors have for many years requested that company management make inquiry of the company's attorneys concerning pending litigation and other contingent claims. Attorneys occasionally face a problem in responding to these inquiries, since the attorney-client privilege is waived with respect to information disclosed to the auditors. Therefore, attorneys have generally been unwilling to reveal anything beyond the existence of actual lawsuits. As a result, some tension developed between the professions: attorneys believed that auditors' inquiry letters were overly broad, while auditors were of the view that attorneys' responses were inadequate.

In 1975, the AICPA and the American Bar Association adopted a *Statement of Policy Regarding Lawyers' Responses to Auditors' Requests for Information,* which details what inquiries and what responses are appropriate. The policy statement identifies the loss contingencies about which inquiry is to be made under three categories:

(1) Overtly threatened or pending litigation, whether or not specified by the company.

(2) Contractually assumed obligations which the company has specifically identified and upon which the company has requested that the attorney comment to the auditor.

(3) Unasserted possible claims or assessments which the company has specifically identified and upon which the company has requested that the attorney comment to the auditor.

Although attorneys are not required to respond in accordance with the policy statement, their failure to respond adequately might lead to the rendering of a qualified opinion by the auditor on the company's financial statements. The effects of a qualified opinion, as discussed later in this chapter, are often so damaging that the company, its attorneys and its auditor are likely to reach agreement on satisfactory disclosure.

The request for information will be prepared by the company and sent to its attorneys, with the request that the attorneys respond directly to the auditors. It will ordinarily describe the lawsuits, claims and other contingencies affecting the company and ask the attorneys to indicate any additional items, changes or further description or explanation the attorneys consider necessary. The attorneys may limit their responses to matters with respect to which they have been engaged by the company and to which they have devoted substantive attention. The inquiry letter is limited to material items, and the letter often indicates a dollar standard of materiality.

Finally, the inquiry letter will contain a paraphrase of the lawyer's professional responsibility concerning disclosure, as stated in the policy statement:

> The auditor may properly assume that whenever, in the course of performing legal services for the client with respect to a matter recognized to involve an unasserted possible claim or assessment which may call for a financial statement disclosure, the lawyer has formed a professional conclusion that the client must disclose or consider disclosure concerning such possible claim or assessment, the lawyer, as a matter of professional responsibility to the client, will so advise the client and will consult with the client concerning the question of such disclosure and the applicable requirements of Statement of Financial Accounting Standards No. 5.

In practice, material pending lawsuits or claims will be disclosed in notes to the financial statements. Except in the relatively few instances in which an unfavorable outcome can be described as either probable or remote, the attorney will not evaluate the likely outcome of the claim. Therefore, disclosure will ordinarily consist only of a description of the lawsuit or claim, accompanied by a statement that the company is pursuing its defense. Unasserted claims—such as possible antitrust action by the Justice Department, or possible products liability claims by injured consumers—are not usually disclosed. Their disclosure alone might be an invitation to a lawsuit, and nondisclosure may often be justified on the ground that the matter is not material until a claim is actually made. The problem of disclosure is particularly troublesome to the attorney, who represents the company and who is generally forbidden to make disclosure of privileged matters without the consent of the company. The policy statement addresses this problem by stating that the attorney must advise the company with respect to disclosure, but in the difficult cases where the company refuses to permit disclosure, the problem remains.

The Audit Report: Restrictions on the Scope of the Audit

The auditor's report usually consists of two paragraphs of standardized language, as follows:

March 10, 19__

To the Shareholders and Board of Directors of _____

We have examined the balance sheet of _____ as of December 31, 19__, and the related statements of income, shareholders' equity, and changes in financial position for the year then ended. Our examinations were made in accordance with generally accepted auditing standards and, accordingly, included such tests of the accounting records and such other auditing procedures as we considered necessary in the circumstances.

In our opinion, the financial statements referred to above present fairly the financial position of _____ at December 31, 19__, and the results of their operations and changes in financial position for the year then ended, in conformity with generally accepted accounting principles applied on a consistent basis.

_____

Certified Public
Accountants

The first paragraph describes the scope of the examination, and the second expresses the auditor's opinion concerning the presentation of information in the financial statements. There may be situations in which the auditor is not able to perform all the necessary audit procedures. Restrictions imposed by the company or by external factors may result in a *limitation of the scope* of the audit. Often, limits on the scope may be dealt with by alternative audit procedures. Where they cannot, the scope limitation must be disclosed in the first paragraph of the auditor's report, and generally will prevent the auditor from expressing an opinion on the financial statements.

The Audit Report: GAAP

The first standard of reporting requires that the report state whether the financial statements are presented in accordance with GAAP. Note that the report says that the financial statements *"present fairly* . . . in conformity with generally accepted accounting principles." Fair presentation and conformity with GAAP are generally considered to be part of a single concept, meaning conformity in all material respects with GAAP. The courts have not always accepted this view however. In a few actions against auditors based on misrepresentation, fair presentation has been held to be a separate concept from GAAP, with the result that the court was able to hold the auditor liable despite the fact that the financial statements conformed with GAAP. The issue of legal liability of accountants and auditors is discussed in the next chapter.

If the auditor's examination reveals that the financial statements do not comply with GAAP, the auditor will ordinarily discuss with company management the adjustments that must be made in the statements to bring them within GAAP. In the unusual situation where management refuses to make the required changes, or where the company's accounting system is such that the changes cannot practicably be made, the auditor must issue a *qualified report*. An additional paragraph is added to the standard language explaining the departure from GAAP and indicating the dollar effects thereof, and the last paragraph is modified to reflect the exception to the opinion. For example:

> The company has reported as income certain cash receipts for which the related services have not yet been rendered. In our opinion, these receipts should have been reported as deferred income, with the result that liabilities as of December 31 would be increased by $———, and net income and earnings per share for the year ended December 31 would be reduced by $——— and $——— respectively.

> In our opinion, *except for the effects of reporting as income certain cash receipts as discussed in the preceding paragraph*, the financial statements referred to above present fairly . . . .

The effect of the additional language is, of course, to make the disclosure that the company refused to make. Remember that the financial statements are the statements of management. Only the auditor's report is the statement of the auditor. If the departure from GAAP is very substantial, it may be necessary for the auditor to issue an adverse opinion. The departure from GAAP would be disclosed in an additional paragraph, but the last paragraph would be modified as follows:

> In our opinion, for the reasons discussed in the preceding paragraph, the financial statements referred to above *do not present fairly* . . . .

The effects of qualification of the auditor's report are often very serious. Many banks will not extend loans to a company based on a qualified report. A qualified report is generally not acceptable for filing by companies required to file financial statements with the SEC. Moreover, a qualified report may alert the investment and credit community to financial or management problems within the company. Management will usually take all necessary steps to assure that the auditor's report is issued without qualifications.

The Audit Report: Consistency

The second reporting standard requires that the report state whether GAAP has been consistently applied. Several times in earlier chapters we noted that a change in accounting principles may change the reported financial results of the company. For example, a change of inventory methods from FIFO to LIFO—both being acceptable under GAAP—generally produces a drop in reported income in the year of change. Any such material change must be disclosed in the auditor's report. The auditor will require that the company disclose the change in accounting principles in notes to the financial statements, indicating in those notes the dollar effects of the change on assets, liabilities, and net income. The audit report will contain an exception for consistency, as follows:

> In our opinion, the financial statements referred to above present fairly the financial position of _____ at December 31, 19___ and the results of their operations and changes in financial position for the year then ended, in conformity with generally accepted accounting principles applied on a consistent basis *except for the change, with which we concur, in the method of valuing inventories as described in Note X to the financial statements.*

The exception for consistency does not impair the utility of the financial statements or reflect adversely on the company. However, the auditor must be satisfied that the change is to a principle within GAAP and that management's justification of the change is acceptable. If these conditions are not satisfied, the auditor must issue a qualified or adverse report.

The Audit Report: Informative Disclosures and Opinion

The third reporting standard requires the auditor to make reference in the audit report to inadequate disclosures in the financial statements. We have illustrated above some examples of disclosure in the audit report. Even disclosure in the audit report may not be adequate if the financial statements are rendered misleading by the omission of material information. In such a case, the auditor must issue an adverse opinion.

The last of the reporting standards requires that the auditor express an opinion on the financial statements or state why an opinion cannot be expressed. This standard is designed to clarify the degree of responsibility undertaken by the auditor whose name is associated in any way with the financial statements. For example, when an accountant has been associated with the preparation of financial statements but has not audited or reviewed them, the following report would be issued:

> The accompanying balance sheet of _____ as of December 31, 19__, and the related statements of income, retained earnings, and changes in financial position for the year then ended were not audited by us and, accordingly, we do not express an opinion on them.

Review of Interim Financial Reports

Companies subject to the reporting requirements of the SEC must file and distribute quarterly reports to their shareholders. These reports are not audited because the full audit process is too expensive and time consuming to be followed more than once a year. However, the independent accountants for the company usually review such statements before they are released. The review involves procedures far short of an audit, but nevertheless justifies a greater association than the disclaimer illustrated above. The Auditing Standards Board of the AICPA has promulgated standards for review of interim financial information. The review report accompanying the unaudited quarterly financial statements would read essentially as follows:

> We have made a review of the balance sheet of _____ as of March 31, 19__, and the related statement of income for the three-month period then ended, in accordance with standards established by the American Institute of Certified Public Accountants.
>
> A review of interim financial information consists principally of obtaining an understanding of the system for the preparation of interim financial information, applying analytical review procedures to financial data, and making inquiries of persons responsible for financial and accounting matters. It is substantially less in scope than an examination in accor-

dance with generally accepted auditing standards, the objective of which is the expression of an opinion regarding the financial statements taken as a whole. Accordingly, we do not express such an opinion.

Based on our review, we are not aware of any material modifications that should be made to the accompanying financial statements for them to be in conformity with generally accepted accounting principles.

REFERENCES

Official Pronouncements:

American Institute of Certified Public Accountants, Codification of Statements on Auditing Standards, Numbers 1–39 (1982). Codification of Generally Accepted Auditing Standards.

American Institute of Certified Public Accountants, Statements on Auditing Standards, Numbers 40–41 (1982).

Financial Accounting Standards Board, Statement No. 5 (1975) (Accounting for contingencies).

American Bar Association, Statement of Policy Regarding Lawyers' Responses to Auditors' Requests for Information, 31 Bus. Lawyer 1709 (1976).

American Institute of Certified Public Accountants, Information for CPA Candidates (1983). A description of the preparation and content of the Uniform CPA Examination and the licensure procedures for certified public accountants.

Secondary Sources:

Defliese, Johnson & McLeod, Montgomery's Auditing (9th ed. 1975).

Burton, Palmer & Kay, eds., Handbook of Accounting and Auditing (1981, supp. 1982), chapters 9–16.

Chapter Twelve

ACCOUNTANTS' LIABILITIES: THE ACCOUNTANT AND THE SEC

Don't tell me of facts, I never believe facts; you know Canning said nothing was so fallacious as facts, except figures.

Sydney Smith, Lady Holland's Memoir

Introduction: Who Sues the Accountant?

The principal function of independent accountants, and the one that gives rise most often to suits against them, is auditing. The auditor's opinion is a representation with respect to the fairness of presentation of the company's financial statements. If those statements prove false or misleading, the auditor is a natural target of lawsuits by those who relied on the statements. The principal users of the financial statements are investors and creditors, and most of the litigation concerning accountants' liabilities has been instituted by unpaid creditors or disappointed investors. However, the company itself uses the financial statements, and occasional lawsuits have been brought by company management against the auditor.

An important area of accounting practice, directly related to auditing, involves examination of financial statements and preparation of supplementary information for filing with the Securities and Exchange Commission (SEC). This area is examined in detail later in this chapter, since it involves an additional body of accounting principles and special statutory liabilities of accountants.

Accountants also perform other functions, including tax planning and preparation and filing of tax returns, preparation of financial records, financial planning and management advisory services. Of these, tax work is the area of greatest exposure to liability, not only to the company but also for criminal and civil penalties.

Accountants' Liabilities Under Common Law

Accountants have been held liable on a non-statutory, or *common law*, basis to both clients and other users of financial statements. The auditor's liability to the company for which the audit was performed (the client) may be based on breach of contract, negligence, fraud or all three. Such actions have usually been brought because the audit failed to uncover a fraud being committed against the company by its employees or others. In general, the auditor is held liable in such cases only on the basis of negligence, failure to observe due care in the conduct of the audit. The audit cannot be expected to unearth the most sophisticated and collusive fraudulent schemes. Substantial compliance with GAAS ordinarily has been considered evidence of due care, but as discussed below, the courts have not always held that adherence to the standards of the profession will avoid liability. Moreover, if the auditor is engaged for the specific purpose of investigating for a suspected fraud, compliance with GAAS without carrying out appropriate additional procedures may constitute negligence. Accountants sued by their clients have often defended on the basis of *contributory negligence*, failure of the client to exercise due care in supervision of its employees, operation of its accounting system or implementation of its system of internal control. This defense has rarely avoided liability on the part of the accountant.

Most actions brought against accountants have been by creditors, investors and other outsiders, claiming damages for losses they incurred by relying on erroneous financial statements audited by the accountant. Traditional common law analysis holds that the auditor's report is prepared primarily for the benefit of the company, and only incidentally for the benefit of outsiders to whom the financial statements might be submitted. The courts draw a connection between the extent of the auditor's fault and his exposure to liability to these third parties. In general, the courts have held that mere negligence (failure to exercise due care in the audit) does not give rise to liability other than to the client itself. However, where the auditor has committed fraud (intentional deception or knowing misstatement), liability is extended to the foreseeable third party users of the financial statements. The leading case is Ultramares Corp. v. Touche, 255 N.Y. 170, 174 N.E. 441 (1931), in which Judge Cardozo stated:

> If the liability for negligence exists, a thoughtless slip or blunder, the failure to detect a theft or forgery beneath the cover of deceptive entries, may expose accountants to a liability in an indeterminate amount for an indeterminate time to an indeterminate class. The hazards of a business conducted on these terms are so extreme as to enkindle doubt whether a flaw may not exist in the implication of a duty that exposes to these consequences.

A second, more expansive, common law rule originated with a decision of the English House of Lords concerning the liability of bankers who negligently gave erroneous credit information, upon which a third party relied to its detriment. The case of Hedley Byrne & Co., Ltd. v. Heller and Partners, Ltd., [1963] 2 All E.R. 575, held that certain special or proximate relationships could give rise to the duty of care even in the absence of a contract between the person supplying the information and the person relying upon it. This approach has been adopted in the American Law Institute's *Restatement (Second) of Torts*, which extends the liability of professionals for negligent misrepresentation to the persons and classes foreseen as users of the information. The approach of *Hedley Byrne* and the *Restatement (Second)* expands the class of persons who may recover from auditors for negligence, but the extent of the expansion is not clear. Are all creditors included in the foreseen group of users, or only creditors known to the auditor as of the time of the audit? Are all potential investors able to recover for negligence?

The courts are widely divided in their views. In some states, including New York, the primary benefit rule of *Ultramares* has been reaffirmed. In others, variations of the *Restatement* rule have been followed, extending liability to directly foreseen users of the financial statements in some instances, and to a broader class of possible users in other cases. This development may ultimately extend the potential common law liability of the auditor, but more significant changes in the accountants' legal and regulatory environment have already been wrought by the federal securities laws. We turn now to a discussion of these laws, which ultimately will return us to the subject of accountants' liabilities.

The Federal Securities Laws and the Securities and Exchange Commission

The Federal securities laws and the regulations issued pursuant to them by the Securities and Exchange Commission significantly affect the role of the accountant and the liabilities to which the accountant is exposed. The Securities Act of 1933 (the Securities Act) regulates principally the initial issuance of securities—including stocks, bonds, limited partnership interests and investment contracts of all kinds—by corporations, partnerships and other issuers. The companion Securities Exchange Act of 1934 (the Exchange Act) broadly regulates trading and exchange of securities, as well as continuing disclosure by companies to their owners. These two acts, administered and implemented by the SEC, form the core of United States securities regulation. These acts have been amended and augmented by other acts from time to time, including the Trust Indenture Act of 1939, the Investment Company Act of 1940 and the Foreign Corrupt Practices Act of 1977.

The Securities Act and the Exchange Act are designed to assure financial and other disclosure by companies subject to their provisions. The Securities Act prohibits the distribution of securities by an issuer unless a *Registration Statement* is filed with the SEC and a *Prospectus* is distributed to offerees of the securities. Exemptions within the Securities Act and in the regulations of the SEC allow issuance of securities without registration or with simplified filing when the offering is made solely within a single state, when the offering is to a limited number of investors, when the offering is under certain dollar amounts, and under other prescribed circumstances. The Registration Statement filed with the SEC is an elaborate document, rarely less than 50 pages long, containing audited financial statements and a detailed description of the business of the company, its personnel, and the uses to which it will put the money raised by the issuance. The Prospectus distributed to potential investors contains most of the information in the Registration Statement.

The filing required by the Securities Act takes place once, upon issuance of securities. Of course, if a company subsequently issues more securities, an additional filing will be required. However, the Securities Act does not require annual or other periodic reporting by companies. That requirement is imposed by the Exchange Act. The filing requirements of the Exchange Act apply to all companies with $1 million or more in assets and 500 or more owners of an equity security, such as common stock. Such companies must file an annual report with the SEC on Form 10–K, as well as quarterly reports on Form 10–Q and periodic reports of material events on Form 8–K. In addition, companies subject to the filing requirements of the Exchange Act must comply with the *proxy regulations* concerning dissemination of information and proxies to shareholders for voting at annual and special meetings of shareholders.

The annual report on Form 10–K contains much of the information that is required in a Prospectus under the Securities Act. It includes audited financial statements, a detailed description of the company, its management and its business, management's discussion and analysis of financial condition and results of operations, and numerous detailed disclosures of such matters as loans, leases, transactions with management, legal proceedings and security ownership. The quarterly report on Form 10–Q contains principally unaudited interim financial information for the preceding three months.

The proxy regulations issued under the Exchange Act provide that a company may not solicit proxies without providing its shareholders with an annual report and a proxy statement in the required form. The financial information provided by Times Mirror Company to its shareholders, as shown in Appendix A, complies with the annual report requirements. The proxy statement of Times Mirror must also include further information about the directors and officers of the company and their remuneration, and about matters to be voted on by the shareholders at their annual meeting.

Many of the requirements of these acts are primarily the concern of attorneys, and a substantial amount of law practice has developed in the area of securities regulation. However, since the principal elements of disclosure under the securities laws are financial statements and related schedules and commentary, these laws have heavily affected accounting practice.

The Securities Act and the Exchange Act grant to the SEC specific statutory authority to prescribe accounting and reporting principles. Despite this broad authority, however, the SEC has generally left the development of accounting principles and auditing standards to the accounting profession. Indeed, the SEC has formally stated that it will look to the private sector for leadership in establishing and improving accounting principles and standards through the Financial Accounting Standards Board. However, the SEC has continued to scrutinize accounting and auditing practices, and has issued extensive regulations governing the form and content of documents to be filed with it. Moreover, the SEC has periodically prodded the accounting profession to adopt standards when it has considered the private standard-setting procedures inadequate.

The SEC's principal accounting regulation is *Regulation S–X*. Until recently the SEC promulgated amendments to Regulation S–X, as well as other statements concerning financial reporting, in *Accounting Series Releases (ASRs)*. The ASRs also included public releases of enforcement actions against accountants and others in connection with financial reporting. In 1982, the SEC codified existing Accounting Series Releases relating to financial reporting in *Financial Reporting Release (FRR) No. 1*, and future releases will be under the title of FRRs. The Accounting Series Releases related to enforcement were collected in *Accounting and Auditing Enforcement Release (AAER) No. 1.*

Filings with the SEC must be made in compliance with *Regulation S–K.* This regulation details the disclosures that must be included in reports under the Securities Act and the Exchange Act.

Since most major companies are subject to the filing requirements of the federal securities laws, Regulations S–X and S–K and the FRRs are applicable to their financial statements and other disclosures to their shareholders. And since most of the disclosure is financial information in the form of financial statements and schedules, the SEC ultimately exercises a significant regulatory effect on accounting principles and the accounting profession. Contemporary financial statements and related disclosure are far more detailed and extensive than those of one or two decades ago. The changes are attributable in no small part to the activities of the SEC.

Accountants' Liabilities Under the Securities Act of 1933

The federal securities laws do more than simply mandate disclosure. They also impose civil and criminal penalties and liabilities upon those who file or distribute false or misleading information. The liabilities of accountants under these acts are based, as they are under the common law, on the accountants' opinion concerning the fairness of presentation of the financial statements. However, the statutory liabilities under the securities laws extend more broadly than common law claims.

The principal civil damage provision of the Securities Act is Section 11, which creates a private right of action with respect to a registration statement that contains an untrue statement of a material fact or a material omission of facts. The damage action extends far more broadly than common law rights, to any person acquiring a security, unless it is proved that the person knew of the misstatement or omission at the time of acquisition. It need not be proven that there was reliance on the registration statement, unless the acquisition of the security took place after the issuance by the company of an income statement covering the 12 months subsequent to the effective date of the registration statement. The purchaser of the security can, of course, sue the issuing company for damages. However, when the misstatement or omission has misrepresented the company's financial position, it is not unlikely that by the time the misstatement or omission is discovered, the company will have failed. In most Section 11 cases, the purchaser also sues the accountants, attorneys and other experts involved in the preparation of the registration statement. Section 11 applies to those individuals and imposes liability for the portions of the registration statement made on their authority as experts. Thus, the accountants would be liable for their opinion on the fairness of presentation of the financial statements. As a result, any material error or omission in the financial statements might be the basis for Section 11 liability of the accountants. The potential liability of the accountants is literally enormous.

The defense of a Section 11 action is difficult. Accountants and other experts may avoid liability only by proving that they had, after reasonable investigation, no reasonable ground to believe, and did not believe, that the portion of the registration statement made on their authority as experts contained a material misstatement or omission. Section 11 therefore imposes on the accountant the burden of proving due diligence; by contrast the traditional common law actions impose on the person seeking damages the burden of proving the accountant's lack of due care. Moreover, the decided cases offer no assurance that compliance with Generally Accepted Auditing Standards will be held to satisfy the Section 11 standard of due diligence. One natural result of the operation of this section is that accountants tend to extend their audit procedures and exercise additional care when examining financial statements that will be included in registration statements filed under the Securities Act. In addition, accounting firms generally obtain insurance coverage against these liabilities, lest a single lawsuit threaten the bankruptcy of the accounting firm.

Accountants' Liabilities Under the Securities Exchange Act of 1934

Accountants have less exposure to liability under the Exchange Act. Section 18 establishes civil liability for materially false or misleading statements filed under that Act, but it requires that the person claiming damages demonstrate that they were in fact caused by reliance on the false statement. Moreover, it is a defense to such an action that the person making the statement acted in good faith and had no *knowledge* that the statement was false or misleading. Accountants would therefore be unlikely to have any exposure under Section 18 in the absence of an intentional misstatement.

A second basis of accountant liability under the Exchange Act is Rule 10b–5, promulgated by the SEC pursuant to Section 10 of the Act. The rule prohibits the following conduct in connection with the purchase or sale of any security:

(1) employment of any device, scheme or artifice to defraud.

(2) misstatement of a material fact or omission to state a material fact necessary to make the statements made not misleading.

(3) engaging in any act, practice or course of business constituting a fraud or deceit upon any person.

Rule 10b–5, including its application to accountants, has assumed great importance in the private enforcement of the securities laws and has been heavily interpreted by the courts. It has been held to create an implied remedy for damages against one who violates its prohibitions and in favor of the damaged party or parties. Furthermore, Rule 10b–5 is not limited to securities or transactions registered with the SEC. Its application extends to all purchases and sales of securities subject to federal jurisdiction. Therefore, any purchase or sale of securities involving interstate commerce or the mails is within its ambit.

Actions brought against accountants under Rule 10b–5 have sought damages based on aiding and abetting, or participating in, material misstatements of fact in the audited financial statements. Until 1976, it was unclear what standard of liability was applicable to accountants in Rule 10b–5 actions, whether accountants could be held liable for mere negligent misstatement to any purchaser or seller of securities, or whether a greater degree of culpability was necessary. With the United States Supreme Court decision in Ernst & Ernst v. Hochfelder, 425 U.S. 185, 96 S.Ct. 1375, 47 L.Ed.2d 668 (1976), the accounting profession breathed a collective sigh of relief. The Court held that a private action for damages under Rule 10b–5 requires more than negligence, that the language of the Exchange Act requires that the party seeking damages prove some element of *scienter* on the part of the defendant. The term scienter carries no fixed meaning, and has been interpreted to mean anything from gross negligence through deliberate intent to defraud. Most of the decisions by lower courts subsequent to *Hochfelder* have held that the accountants may not be found liable in the absence of reckless conduct, an extreme departure from the ordinary standards of due care. These holdings in many of these cases are therefore similar to those of the traditional common law cases, such as *Ultramares*.

Accountants may be held liable for violation of the proxy rules under Section 14 of the Exchange Act, since proxy solicitations almost invariably involve distribution of audited financial statements to shareholders. The likely standard of culpability, as under Rule 10b–5, involves scienter, some evidence of reckless or knowledgeable assistance in disseminating misleading financial information. In recent years, one of the most notorious cases involving auditor misconduct under the proxy rules involved the proxy statement for the merger of National Student Marketing Corp. Ultimately, members of the accounting firm consented to an injunction, and one partner was convicted of criminal violations of the Exchange Act.

Investors have attempted to obtain damages from accountants and others based on implied remedies in other sections of the Exchange Act or other federal securities laws. However, the Supreme Court and many lower courts have in recent years applied stringent criteria to recognition of such implied remedies. For example, an attempt to establish an implied remedy against accountants for violation of a section of the Exchange Act regulating broker/dealer filings was rebuffed in Touche Ross & Co. v. Redington, 442 U.S. 560, 99 S.Ct. 2479, 61 L.Ed.2d 82 (1979).

GAAS, GAAP, and the Accountants' Standard of Care

Whenever action is brought against accountants, the accountants may be expected to rest their defense on compliance with the standards of the profession, which include observance of Generally Accepted Auditing Standards and reporting in compliance with Generally Accepted Accounting Principles. There is no assurance that compliance with GAAS will be considered by the courts as satisfaction of the applicable standard of due care or due diligence, or that reporting in conformity with GAAP will avoid a claim based on misleading financial statements. The trend of recent decisions has been to hold GAAP and GAAS determinative, but some important earlier cases held that compliance with these standards is no absolute defense.

Disciplinary Proceedings

The SEC has available to it a wide variety of enforcement proceedings to deal with violation of the federal securities laws. These include investigations, actions for injunctive relief or penalties, and referral to the Department of Justice for criminal proceedings. In addition, the SEC may initiate administrative disciplinary proceedings under its Rules of Practice. Rule 2(e) provides for permanent or temporary disqualification from practice before the SEC of any person who is found after a hearing:

(a) Not to have the required qualifications to represent others,

(b) To be lacking in character or integrity or to have engaged in improper conduct, or

(c) To have willfully violated any provisions of the federal securities laws or regulations, or willfully aided and abetted any such violation.

The potential sanctions against accountants and other professionals, censure or suspension from practice, are very severe. They are tantamount to termination, or substantial curtailment, of a professional career.

Recently, the SEC has aggressively pursued disciplinary proceedings under Rule 2(e) against accountants and other professionals, notably lawyers. In many instances, the firms subject to Rule 2(e) proceedings have consented to alternative sanctions, such as continuing education programs, peer reviews by other professionals, and temporary restrictions on new engagements involving SEC practice. Proceedings under Rule 2(e) have provoked considerable controversy among professionals practicing before the SEC, many of whom believe that the SEC's actions are inappropriate. The proceedings have, however, been held to be within the rule-making authority of the SEC, though the question of the extent of permissible sanctions has not been resolved. See Touche Ross & Co. v. SEC, 609 F.2d 570 (2d Cir. 1979).

REFERENCES

Official Pronouncements:

Securities Act of 1933; Securities Exchange Act of 1934; General Rules and Regulations Under the Securities Act of 1933 and the Securities Exchange Act of 1934; SEC Rules of Practice, reprinted in:

Jennings & Marsh, eds., Selected Statutes, Rules and Forms Under the Federal Securities Laws (1982).

Secondary Sources:

Gormley, The Law of Accountants and Auditors: Rights, Duties and Liabilities (1981).

Causey, Duties and Liabilities of Public Accountants (Rev. ed. 1982).

Chapter Thirteen

CORPORATE ACQUISITIONS AND COMBINATIONS: CONSOLIDATED STATEMENTS

A power has risen up in the government greater than the people themselves, consisting of many and various and powerful interests, combined into one mass, and held together by the cohesive power of the vast surplus in the banks.

John C. Calhoun

Introduction: Business Growth

A business may expand by issuing more stock or bonds, by internal growth through retention and reinvestment of its income, or by acquiring or combining with another business. The first approach is often followed in the early stages of a company's development, before it has developed a track record of profitability. Retention and reinvestment of income remains the most widely used and important method of growth among corporations in the United States. In both instances, sale of securities and retention of income, the business grows by investing the new funds in additional assets for the existing business or by acquiring assets for a new business.

Growth by business acquisition or combination is a variation of the first two approaches. Funds accumulated through retention of income may be used to purchase an entire existing business, rather than the assets to expand. Alternatively, the corporation may issue its stock or bonds to acquire or combine with another company, rather than selling them for cash. A business acquisition may take any of a bewildering variety of forms, and variations in accounting for the acquisition may confuse the uninitiated reader of the financial statements. In this chapter, following a brief description of the forms, we will analyze the effects on corporate financial statements of business acquisitions and combinations.

Forms of Business Acquisition and Combination

One corporation, which we will call the *acquiring corporation*, may acquire the business of another, which we will call the *target corporation*, in a variety of ways. The acquiring corporation may purchase all or part of the assets, and undertake to pay (assume) all or part of the liabilities of the target corporation. Alternatively, the acquiring corporation may purchase the stock of the target corporation from its stockholders. Finally, the acquiring corporation may combine with the target corporation in a *statutory merger*, in accordance with the provisions of the applicable state corporation laws. In any of these forms, the acquiring corporation may pay in cash or notes, may issue its stock or bonds to carry out the acquisition or combination, or may use a combination of these forms of consideration.

These forms are widely referred to as *corporate reorganizations*, under the terminology used in Section 368(a) of the Internal Revenue Code, as follows:

"A" Reorganization. A statutory merger or consolidation carried out pursuant to the terms of state law.

"B" Reorganization. Acquisition by the acquiring corporation of a controlling interest in the stock (for tax purposes, 80% of each class) of the target corporation, by exchanging its own shares with the target corporation's stockholders.

"C" Reorganization. Acquisition by the acquiring corporation of substantially all of the assets of the target corporation, by issuing its own shares to the target corporation.

Note that in the "A" and "C" reorganizations, only the acquiring corporation survives the acquisition, and all of the assets of both corporations are combined in the acquiring corporation. By contrast, in the "B" reorganization, the acquiring corporation obtains the *stock* of the target corporation, and the target corporation may be kept intact as a majority or wholly-owned subsidiary of the acquiring corporation. There may be considerable business and legal advantages to keeping the target corporation alive as a subsidiary. Among these are that the liabilities of the target corporation may not be asserted against the acquiring corporation. In some instances tax and business planning objectives may also be facilitated by maintaining the separate corporations.

Our decriptions of the reorganization forms do not reflect the complexities or subtleties required to determine "reorganization" status under the Internal Revenue Code. Details of that subject may be found in a text on corporate taxation, as noted in the references at the end of this chapter. It is necessary, however, to be aware of these basic forms, since they often affect the accounting treatment of business acquisitions and combinations. It is also important to appreciate that qualification of the transaction as a "reorganization" generally produces the result that the transaction gives rise to no tax liability on the part of either of the corporations involved or their shareholders.

In all three forms illustrated above, the acquiring corporation issues stock as part of the reorganization. A combination of stock and bonds or other consideration may be used in some forms of reorganization without changing the basic tax character of the transaction, although the use of the additional consideration may give rise to recognition of some taxable gain in the transaction. One major variation on these forms is for the acquisition to be made entirely with notes or cash, thereby disqualifying the transaction for reorganization treatment under the Internal Revenue Code with the result that taxable gains or losses will be recognizable by the parties involved.

Another variation of these forms, widely used in recent years, is the so-called *triangular reorganization*, in which the acquiring corporation establishes a new corporation to carry out the acquisition. The target corporation is merged into the new corporation, which is wholly owned by the acquiring corporation; or alternatively, the new corporation is merged into the target. Either way, when the merger is concluded the business of the target corporation is owned by a wholly-owned subsidiary of the acquiring corporation.

We have assumed in all of the situations above that there was agreement on the transaction by all the parties involved. In some instances, the acquisition may be agreeable, but the value to be given for the acquisition may be open to dispute. Suppose, for example that the target corporation is the defendant in a major lawsuit; if the lawsuit is lost, the value of the corporation will be substantially reduced. Or suppose that the target corporation has developed a new, but untested, product that may be very valuable or may be useless. How can the parties agree on a value for the target corporation? They might agree to a base value, whether in stock, bonds, cash or other consideration, subject to adjustment after the event in question has been resolved.

The acquisition is based, in other words, on *contingent pricing*. When the contingent pricing involves the possible issuance of additional shares of stock at a later date, the transaction is commonly known as a *contingent stock* acquisition.

Occasionally, the acquisition is not friendly. The acquiring corporation quietly purchases shares of the target corporation from major stockholders or through the stock market until it obtains a substantial block of shares. It may then propose an acquisition to the target corporation management, but if the acquisition talks do not produce agreement, the acquiring corporation may seek to obtain a controlling block of shares by publicly approaching the remaining stockholders of the target corporation. The result is a *tender offer*, in which the acquiring corporation offers to buy, on stated terms, shares tendered to it by shareholders of the target corporation. If the tender offer is successful, the target corporation becomes a controlled subsidiary of the acquiring corporation.

Accounting for Acquisitions and Combinations: Form and Substance

There are important differences in the forms of acquisition or combination. The choice of form will be based on financial and tax considerations, requirements of state corporation law, and the often diverse interests of the managements and shareholders of the corporations involved. Although the form of the transaction may therefore be vitally important for tax, legal or managerial purposes, from the accounting viewpoint the form of the transaction is usually irrelevant. The financial substance of the transaction must be reflected in the books and financial statements. Generally Accepted Accounting Principles distinguish between acquisitions and combinations under the two headings of *purchase* and *pooling of interests*. A purchase is the acquisition by one corporation of another, whereas a pooling of interests is the uniting of the ownership interests of two or more corporations by the exchange of equity securities, such as common stock. The differences between the two methods may be examined by comparing their application to a hypothetical acquisition. In the illustration below, A Corp. and T Corp. will undertake a statutory merger in which A Corp. will be the surviving corporation. The former shareholders of T Corp. will receive 200,000 new shares of A Corp., with a fair market value of $800,000.

A Corp.
Balance Sheet
As of _____

Assets		Liabilities & Net Worth	
Cash	$ 200,000	Accounts Payable	$ 400,000
Accounts Receivable	300,000	Capital Stock, $1 par,	
Inventories	400,000	400,000 shares	400,000
Fixed Assets	500,000	Retained Earnings	600,000
		Total Liabilities &	
Total Assets	$1,400,000	Net Worth	$1,400,000

T Corp.
Balance Sheet
As of _____

Assets		Liabilities & Net Worth	
Cash	$100,000	Accounts Payable	$200,000
Accounts Receivable	200,000	Capital Stock, $1 par,	
Inventories	100,000	200,000 shares	200,000
Fixed Assets	300,000	Retained Earnings	300,000
		Total Liabilities &	
Total Assets	$700.000	Net Worth	$700,000

Pooling of Interests

When a transaction is characterized as a pooling of interests, GAAP requires that the existing values for assets and liabilities carried on the books of the acquiring corporation and the target corporation be combined. The theoretical basis for simply combining existing book values is that a pooling represents the continuation of both corporations in combined form. For the same reason, the retained earnings of the two corporations are combined. The resulting balance sheet of the surviving corporation, A Corp., is constructed by adding each item of the individual balance sheets just prior to the pooling. Moreover, since the theory of pooling is that there has been no purchase, the fair market value of the 200,000 shares issued by A Corp. in the acquisition is not entered on the balance sheet. The resulting balance sheet of the combined corporations under pooling of interests is as follows:

A Corp.
Balance Sheet
As of _____

Assets		Liabilities & Net Worth	
Cash	$ 300,000	Accounts Payable	$ 600,000
Accounts Receivable	500,000	Capital Stock, $1 par,	
Inventories	500,000	600,000 shares	600,000
Fixed Assets	800,000	Retained Earnings	900,000
		Total Liabilities &	
Total Assets	$2,100,000	Net Worth	$2,100,000

Under pooling of interests, the results of operations of the combined corporations are presented as though they had been combined as of the beginning of the accounting period. Subsequent multi-year summaries of operations are also presented on a combined basis.

Purchase of Assets

When the transaction is characterized as a purchase, it is treated for accounting purposes like all other purchases. Assets purchased are entered on the books at their cost. If the assets are purchased for cash, cost is readily determinable. If, however, they are acquired by the issuance of stock or bonds, the purchase price is the fair market value of the stock or bonds issued, which in the example was assumed to be $800,000.

Why would A Corp. be willing to issue stock worth $800,000 to acquire T Corp., which shows a net worth (capital stock + retained earnings) of only $500,000? Remember that the net worth of a corporation is based on *book value*, the values shown on the accounting records based on original cost reduced by depreciation and amortization. The current value of some assets may be greater than book value. Furthermore, a successful company is generally worth more than the total current value of its assets, and the additional value (representing extra earning power) is usually categorized as the intangible asset, *goodwill*. You may wish to review the discussion of goodwill in Chapter 6.

Under purchase accounting the $800,000 total purchase price for T Corp. must be allocated among all of the assets and liabilities acquired, and these must then be added to the existing book values of A Corp. The book values of the assets of A Corp. are not changed, since only T Corp. was purchased. The purchase price of T Corp. was $800,000 in new stock plus the assumption by A Corp. of $200,000 of T Corp. liabilities; the total price was therefore $1 million. The book value of the T Corp. assets is only $700,000. Let us assume, however, that the fixed assets are actually worth $400,000, rather than the $300,000 shown on the books. This leaves $200,000 that was paid above and beyond the fair market value of the assets. The $200,000 will be reflected as purchased goodwill. To summarize, the following items will be added to the assets and liabilities of A Corp. as a result of the purchase:

Cash	$100,000
Accounts Receivable	200,000
Inventories	100,000
Fixed Assets	400,000
Goodwill	200,000
Accounts Payable (liabilities)	(200,000)
Total (equals purchase price)	$800,000

If the acquiring corporation pays *less* for the assets of the target corporation than the book value of those assets, the purchase price must similarly be allocated among the assets. In that case, however, the noncurrent assets are written down in proportion to their fair market values. In some very unusual situations, the purchase may be at so low a price that even when the noncurrent assets are valued at zero the purchase price is below the book value of the remaining assets. Companies undertaking such purchases have in some instances recorded *negative goodwill*, representing the equivalent of a bargain purchase of assets, which is then amortized as an income item, generally over a short period of years.

In a purchase, the retained earnings of the target corporation are not added to the existing retained earnings of the acquiring corporation, since the acquisition is viewed as a purchase of assets rather than the continuation of the business of the target corporation. The retained earnings account of T Corp. disappears, and the entire fair market value of the stock issued in the acquisition ($800,000) is considered as contributed capital. Since the stock issued by A Corp. has a par value, the capital stock account is increased by the par value and the remainder is added to the account *capital contributed in excess of par*. Thus,

$200,000 of the purchase price (representing 200,000 shares at $1 par) would be added to the capital stock account, and the remaining $600,000 would be classified as capital contributed in excess of par. (You may find it helpful at this point to review the discussion of capital accounts in Chapter 8.) The resulting balance sheet using purchase accounting is as follows:

A Corp.
Balance Sheet
As of _____

Assets		Liabilities & Net Worth	
Cash	$ 300,000	Accounts Payable	$ 600,000
Accounts Receivable	500,000	Capital Stock, $1 par,	
Inventories	500,000	600,000 shares	600,000
Fixed Assets	900,000	Capital Contributed	
		in Excess of Par	600,000
Goodwill	200,000	Retained Earnings	600,000
		Total Liabilities &	
Total Assets	$2,400,000	Net Worth	$2,400,000

The differences between the two methods of accounting are important. Since most business acquisitions are at a value greater than book value, purchase accounting reflects in the financial statements the higher value of assets acquired. Therefore, your first reaction might be to consider the purchase method more desirable. Careful analysis will reveal the flaw in this conclusion. The increased balance sheet values produced by the purchase method are not generally given great weight by investors and creditors. Goodwill is considered a "soft" asset, not likely to provide protection to creditors when they need it. Furthermore, more sophisticated investors and creditors seek information about the current values of assets, even when those current values are not reflected on the balance sheet.

The increased balance sheet values generally required by purchase accounting usually have an unfortunate effect on the income statement. The company must show greater depreciation and amortization expenses on its income statement. In the example, if the fixed assets have an average useful life of 10 years, the increase of $100,000 required by purchase accounting will cause an increase of $10,000 per year in depreciation expense, using straight-line depreciation. In addition, since goodwill must be amortized over a period not in excess of 40 years, the $200,000 of goodwill will create an annual amortization expense of $5,000. The goodwill amortization will not provide a tax deduction, and in many instances the additional depreciation expense will also not be usable for tax purposes. Since the actual revenues of the combined companies are unaffected by the method of accounting for the combination, it is generally undesirable to apply a method that *reports* lower income.

For these reasons, businesses show a strong preference for application of pooling of interests accounting to business acquisitions and combinations. In the view of many financial analysts, the generally higher net income shown by the pooling approach should result in greater investor interest and higher stock prices than the purchase method. However, several controlled studies have concluded that the choice between purchase and pooling accounting has no measurable effect on stock prices, and that the market apparently adjusts for the variation in reported results. These studies to the contrary notwithstanding, the financial community maintains its aversion to the purchase method.

Criteria for Application of Purchase and Pooling

The rules governing accounting for business combinations were originally promulgated by the Accounting Principles Board in 1970, and have been very heavily interpreted since then. The rules have also been sharply criticized on many grounds, including arbitrariness. As of this writing, however, they are not being reexamined by the Financial Accounting Standards Board, and they remain fully in effect.

Given the heavy preference for pooling of interests accounting, GAAP imposes a series of requirements before that method may be applied. Unless all of the requirements are met, purchase accounting is required. The requirements are under three headings: combining companies, combining interests and absence of certain planned transactions. Under the heading of combining companies, it is required that each of the companies be autonomous and not have been a subsidiary or division of another corporation within the two years prior to initiation of the plan of combination. Moreover, each of the companies must be independent of the others; no more than a 10% intercompany investment in common stock is permitted prior to initiation of the plan of combination. These tests basically exclude from pooling accounting transactions involving "creeping control", in which the acquiring corporation gradually buys up stock of the target corporation and subsequently carries out a merger.

The test of combining interests involves a series of related criteria. Pooling requires that the combination be carried out in a single transaction or be completed according to a plan within one year. The acquiring corporation must issue to at least 90% of the holders of voting common stock of the target corporation only its own common stock having rights identical to those of a majority of its own common stockholders. The theory behind this requirement is that pooling requires continuity of ownership interest, and such continuity can only be assured if the previous voting common stockholders of the target corporation become voting common stockholders of the acquiring corporation. Note, however, that there is no requirement that the target shareholders receive any specified percentage of the *total* voting common stock of the acquiring corporation, only that they receive voting common stock in return for the voting common stock they give up. Therefore, it is possible to have a pooling of interests even when the former stockholders of the target corporation receive only 1% or less of the voting common stock of the acquiring corporation. This result has been criticized by some commentators, who take the view that when the target shareholders receive only a small percentage of the voting common stock of the acquiring corporation the overall effect of the transaction is equivalent to a purchase.

The combining interests tests include several criteria designed to preclude use of pooling when the capital structure of the companies involved has been changed in contemplation of the combination. Pooling may not be used unless the ownership ratios of common stockholders within each corporation remain unchanged and their voting rights remain exercisable after the combination. Finally, pooling is not available unless the combination is resolved at the date the plan is consummated. This requirement ordinarily requires that combinations and acquisitions with open pricing terms be treated as purchases. However, an adjustment of price for the resolution of a contingency (such as a contingent liability) will not disqualify the transaction from pooling treatment.

Three categories of planned transactions, all of which suggest an intent not to continue combined operations or ownership, will prevent the companies from applying pooling accounting. The first is agreement to retire or reacquire part of the common stock issued in the combination. Also prohibited are financial arrangements for former stockholders that negate the effect of the exchange of equity securities, such as guaranteeing loans secured by the stock issued in the combination. Finally, the combined company must not plan to dispose of a significant part of the combined assets within two years after the acquisition.

All of these criteria are relatively easy to meet when the transaction takes the form of a merger solely for voting common stock. However, tender offers, acquisitions for nonvoting stock and bonds, and "creeping control" acquisitions will almost invariably be treated as purchases.

A Comment on Certain Federal Tax Aspects of Business Acquisitions and Combinations

You may be tempted to assume that the tax treatment of business acquisitions and combinations parallels the accounting treatment. Make no such assumption. The area of corporate reorganizations—which encompasses acquisitions, combinations and other transactions—is among the most complex in all of federal taxation, and its rules bear very little relation to those of accounting. In very general and necessarily oversimplified terms, if an acquisition qualifies as a *reorganization*, no gain or loss is recognized by the corporations that are parties to the reorganization or by the shareholders who exchange their shares in connection with the reorganization. In addition, the acquired assets generally take a *carryover basis*. In other words, their basis for tax purposes, including depreciation, remains the same in the hands of the acquiring corporation as it was in the hands of the target corporation. If the acquisition does not qualify as a reorganization, the transaction is treated for tax purposes as a *sale or exchange*, with the general result that gain or loss will be recognized by the parties to the transaction and, in addition, the acquired assets take a basis equal to their fair market value.

Qualification as a reorganization for tax purposes bears no relationship to application of purchase or pooling accounting. Therefore, a particular acquisition might result in carryover basis for tax purposes, but an increase in value for accounting purposes, or vice versa. You may pursue this subject further in a course on corporate taxation or in a text on that subject, one of which we have identified in the references at the end of this chapter.

Consolidated Financial Statements

Many corporations, like Times Mirror Company, conduct their operations in whole or in part through the ownership of other corporations, or *subsidiaries*. These subsidiaries may be wholly or partially owned. The purpose of consolidated financial statements, as illustrated by those of Times Mirror in Appendix A, is to present the financial position and results of operations of the corporation (the *parent*) and its subsidiaries on a combined basis, as though they were one company. Generally Accepted Accounting Principles concerning consolidated financial statements were promulgated in 1959, and have remained essentially unchanged since then.

Consolidated statements are permitted only when the parent has a controlling financial interest in the subsidiary or subsidiaries. It is extremely rare that ownership of less than 50% of the voting shares will meet this criterion, and in most cases ownership of over 50% will justify consolidation. There is a general presumption that consolidated statements are more meaningful than separate statements. Most corporations prepare consolidated financial statements including all subsidiaries, although some industrial companies do not consolidate the financial statements of subsidiaries in unrelated businesses, such as banking, credit and insurance.

The process of preparing consolidated financial statements involves relatively straightforward theoretical concepts, but often is quite complex in practice. Basically, the financial statements of the consolidated corporations are combined. However, *intercompany transactions*—such as sales from one subsidiary to another, or from the parent to the subsidiary—and intercompany receivables and payables, must be eliminated in the combination. Similarly, profits or losses recorded on intercompany transactions must be eliminated unless they have been recognized by ultimate sale to third parties.

Frequently, the parent owns less than all of the stock of a subsidiary. For purposes of consolidated statements, the outside ownership is known as the *minority interest*. The minority interest in the net assets of subsidiaries, if material, must be shown on the consolidated balance sheet as a separate item below the total for liabilities and above consolidated net worth. Similarly, the minority interest in the net income of subsidiaries, if material, must be separately shown on the income statement and deducted in arriving at consolidated net income.

Unconsolidated subsidiaries are accounted for as investments on the equity method, as discussed in Chapter 6.

[*165*]

REFERENCES

Official Pronouncements:

American Institute of Certified Public Accountants, Accounting Principles Board, Opinion No. 16, Business Combinations (1970); Opinion No. 17, Intangible Assets (1970).

American Institute of Certified Public Accountants, Accounting Research Bulletin No. 51, Consolidated Financial Statements (1959).

Secondary Sources:

Fiflis, Accounting for Mergers, Acquisitions and Investments, in a Nutshell: The Interrelationships of, and Criteria for, Purchase or Pooling, the Equity Method and Parent-Company-Only and Consolidated Statements, 37 Bus. Lawyer 89 (1981).

Wyatt, A Critical Study of Accounting for Business Combinations (AICPA Accounting Research Study No. 5) (1963).

Financial Accounting Standards Board, Discussion Memorandum on Analysis of Issues Related to Accounting for Business Combinations and Purchased Intangibles (1976).

Hong, Kaplan & Mandelker, Pooling vs. Purchase: The Effects of Accounting for Mergers on Stock Prices, 53 Acct.Rev. 31 (1978).

Bittker & Eustice, Federal Income Taxation of Corporations and Shareholders (4th ed. 1979), chapter 14.

Chapter Fourteen

ACCOUNTING FOR INFLATION

Fortune is like the market, where many times, if you can stay a little, the price will fall.

Francis Bacon, Of Delays

Introduction: The Effects of Inflation

Financial statements prepared in accordance with Generally Accepted Accounting Principles are based on historical costs. Assets are shown at the prices paid for them when they were acquired, less depreciation. Liabilities are reflected at the dollar amounts that will be required to discharge them. Income and expense are recorded in dollars realized or incurred at the time when the income was realized or the expense incurred. There is a reassuring sense of mathematical accuracy about the whole process: the dollar is the accepted unit of measurement, and all financial statement items are recorded on the basis of verifiable costs historically incurred.

There are major problems with this approach. First, the dollar is not a constant measuring unit. For many years, the purchasing power of the dollar has regularly declined. As a result, assets purchased with "older" dollars years ago were paid for with dollars worth more than assets purchased with "newer" dollars more recently. However, the balance sheet assumes that all dollars are the same.

Moreover, assets also change in value. Land purchased ten years ago for $1 million may today be worth $5 million, but the reader of the balance sheet will be given no hint of the change in value. GAAP requires that assets be shown at historical cost. In the case of a building, the distortion may be even greater. A 20 year old building might be almost fully depreciated and carried on the balance sheet at a nominal value, despite the fact that its fair market value is very substantial. Of what use is the balance sheet if it shows numbers that bear no relationship to reality?

Defenders of GAAP's historical cost approach to accounting argue that readers are aware of the deficiencies of the balance sheet and take appropriate steps to apprise themselves of current values. The more important statement, it is urged, is the statement of income, which must be based on historical costs to reflect fairly the actual results of operations. Neither of these arguments stand up well under careful scrutiny. Indeed, an increasing sense of the deficiencies in historical cost accounting has led both the SEC and the Financial Accounting Standards Board to require supplementary financial disclosure reflecting the effects of changes in values and changes in the purchasing power of the dollar. In order to understand these new requirements, and the direction in which contemporary accounting may be moving, we must first examine the effects of changing prices and consider how historical cost information may be adjusted to take account of those effects.

Suppose that on January 1, 1980 an investor purchased a bond for $1,000, and at the end of the year the investor received $100 interest on the bond and sold the bond for its original purchase price of $1,000. GAAP tells the investor that he has realized income of $100, and the Internal Revenue Code tells him that a tax is payable on that income. But in 1980, the annual inflation rate in the United States was 13.5%. By the end of 1980, the investor's $1,100 had less purchasing power than his original $1,000 at the beginning of 1980. Whatever GAAP and the Internal Revenue Code may say, the investor incurred a real economic loss. Indeed, he would have had to earn $135 simply to break even.

The fact that inflation has been sharply curtailed recently does not blunt the point of the illustration. If income represents an increase in the economic value of assets, the calculation of income is erroneous when it is based on a changing dollar. If the illustration above had taken place in 1982, when the inflation rate was 4.5%, the investor would have earned real income. However, his real income would still be considerably less than $100. One way of calculating his real income would be to restate his original $1,000 investment in end-of-1982 dollars; since the inflation rate was 4.5%, his January investment was the equivalent of $1,045 December dollars ($1,000 + 4.5% of $1,000). Therefore, the investor's real income was $55, rather than $100.

The illustration above demonstrates an important point about inflation. Even a "nominal" or "minor" rate of inflation has a substantial impact on the calculation of income. In the illustration, the 4.5% inflation rate in 1982 reduced the economic income of the investor by 45%. We shall see that similar effects are observable in the reported income of major companies.

Our first illustration was concerned with change in the value of the measuring unit, the dollar. Our second involves changes in the value of assets themselves. Suppose a jeweler buys gold to manufacture into jewelry at a price of $400 per ounce, but by the time the jewelry is ready for sale, gold costs $450 per ounce. When he sets the prices for his jewelry, should the jeweler calculate the cost of his gold at $400, or at $450? If he uses the $400 figure, he may sell at a "profit" but be less well off than he was before the sale. Consider another illustration. A homeowner purchased her house in Massachusetts in 1956 for $18,000. In 1983, a career change requires her to move to Michigan. She sells her Massachusetts home for $150,000. If a comparable home in Michigan will cost her $150,000, has she made a profit on the sale of her Massachusetts house? The point of both illustrations is that when assets are sold, only to be replaced by comparable assets, a strong argument can be made for measuring cost based on *replacement cost*, rather than historical cost. Note also that changes in the purchasing power of the dollar are not the same as changes in replacement cost, although assets held for any length of time will be affected by both factors.

Constant Dollar Accounting

Accounting as we have studied it so far is based on *nominal dollars* and historical costs. Nominal dollars are dollars actually spent at the time when they were spent, without adjustment for changes in purchasing power. A relatively simple set of calculations, readily amenable to computerization, may be used to adjust nominal dollars to *constant dollars*. Constant dollar accounting involves adjustment of all items on the financial statements to a single measurement unit: the dollar as of a given date. In most instances, constant dollar accounting will use the dollar as of the date of the financial statements. As a result, all earlier inflows and outflows of dollars will have to be *indexed*, or adjusted to reflect the relative value of the dollar as of the time they occurred. The most widely used index of the relative purchasing power of the dollar is the Bureau of Labor Statistics Consumer Price Index for All Urban Consumers (the CPI). Other indices include the Bureau of Labor Statistics Producer Price Index and the Implicit Price Deflator for the Gross National Product. Although these indices are not identical, over a period of years they yield strikingly similar results.

The index is applied to each of the items on the financial statements. Let us assume that financial statements are being prepared as of December 31, 1979, when the CPI was 229.9. If the balance sheet shows a building purchased on January 1, 1978 for $200,000, the historical purchase price must be adjusted to

December 31, 1979 dollars. Since the CPI was 187.2 in January 1978, the purchase price is adjusted as follows:

$$\$200,000 \times \frac{229.9}{187.2} = \$245,619$$

The figure of $245,619 does not represent what the building would cost as of December 31, 1979. Rather, it represents the building's *actual* 1978 purchase price, restated in 1979's less valuable dollars.

Gains and Losses on Monetary Items

Although the items on the financial statements are all restated in dollars as of the financial statement date, the *monetary items* as of the date of the financial statement—such as cash, accounts receivable and accounts payable—are not restated, since they are already stated in dollars as of the financial statement date. For example, cash as of December 31, 1979 needs no restatement on a December 31, 1979 balance sheet. However, in periods of inflation, an interesting phenomenon is revealed by the process of indexing: the company realizes gains or losses on monetary items. Consider the case of a company that holds $1,000 of cash for a year, during which inflation amounts to 5%. Although the company still has $1,000 of cash at the end of the year, it has suffered a decline in the *value* of that cash. Based on year-end dollars, the cash at the beginning of the year was worth $1,050 ($1,000 + 5% of $1,000). Therefore, in year-end dollars, the company lost $50 by holding the cash.

Correspondingly, if the company had a liability of $5,000 at the beginning of the same year, which it did not pay until the end of the year, the company recognized a gain by discharging its liability with cheaper dollars. The amount of the liability as of the beginning of the year, in year-end dollars, was $5,250 ($5,000 + 5% of $5,000). Therefore, in year-end dollars, the company gained $250 by owing the liability.

To bring the illustration closer to home, consider the buyer of a house on a thirty-year mortgage loan. Although the buyer pays interest on the debt, payment in later years is with cheaper dollars. In effect, inflation reduces the true interest rate of the loan. In general, during periods of inflation it is desirable to owe money and own goods. Correspondingly, in periods of declining prices, it is desirable to own money and be owed money.

Constant Dollar Financial Statements

The results of restating the financial statements in constant dollars can be startling. The illustration on the following page shows the comparative financial statements of ABC Corporation. The first two columns show financial position and results of operation for 1978 and 1979 in dollars actually spent (nominal dollars) in accordance with GAAP. The third and fourth columns present the same financial information restated to constant dollars as of the end of 1979.[1]

---

1. The ABC Corporation financial statements were prepared on the assumption that the corporation was formed on January 1, 1978, with the following opening Balance Sheet:

ABC Corporation
OPENING BALANCE SHEET
Jan. 1, 1978

Assets:

Cash	$100,000
Building (20-year useful life)	200,000
Land	50,000
Total Assets	$350,000

Liabilities & Equity:

Mortgage Note Payable	$150,000
Invested Capital	200,000
Total Liabilities & Equity	$350,000

Cost of Sales in the Statement of Income is based on the following historical cost data:

ABC Corporation
COST OF GOODS SOLD; HISTORICAL COST
Years Ended Dec. 31, 1978 and 1979

	1978	1979
Opening Inventory	$ –0–	$ 40,000
Purchases	140,000	160,000
Total Goods Available for Sale	$140,000	$200,000
Less: Ending Inventory	40,000	70,000
Cost of Goods Sold	$100,000	$130,000

The CPI, at the relevant dates used for indexing, was:

Jan. 1978	Dec. 1978	Dec. 1979	1978 Average	1979 Average
187.2	202.9	229.9	195.3	217.7

Further details on these financial statements and their theory and construction can be found in Siegel, Accounting and Inflation: An Analysis and a Proposal, cited in the references at the end of this chapter.

[*171*]

ABC Corporation
BALANCE SHEET
Dec. 31, 1978, 1979

	Historical Cost, Nominal Dollars		Adjusted to 12/31/79 Price Level	
	12/31/78	12/31/79	12/31/78	12/31/79
ASSETS:				
Cash	$ 85,000	$ 85,000	$ 96,311	$ 85,000
Accounts Receivable	60,000	80,000	67,984	80,000
Inventory	40,000	70,000	47,062	73,923
Building	200,000	200,000	245,619	245,619
Less: Accumulated Depreciation	(10,000)	(20,000)	(12,281)	(24,562)
Land	50,000	50,000	61,405	61,405
Total Assets	$425,000	$465,000	$506,100	$521,385
LIABILITIES & EQUITY:				
Liabilities:				
Accounts Payable	$ 50,000	$ 60,000	$ 56,654	$ 60,000
Mortgage Note Payable	150,000	150,000	169,961	150,000
Total Liabilities	$200,000	$210,000	$226,615	$210,000
Equity:				
Invested Capital	$200,000	$200,000	$245,620	$245,620
Retained Earnings	25,000	55,000	33,865	65,765
Total Equity	$225,000	$255,000	$279,485	$311,385
Total Liabilities & Equity	$425,000	$465,000	$506,100	$521,385

ABC Corporation
STATEMENT OF INCOME
Years Ended Dec. 31, 1978 and 1979

	Historical Cost, Nominal Dollars		Adjusted to 12/31/79 Price Level	
	1978	1979	1978	1979
SALES:	$170,000	$210,000	$200,015	$221,768
Less: Operating Expenses:				
Cost of Goods Sold	$100,000	$130,000	$117,657	$142,105
Depreciation	10,000	10,000	12,281	12,281
Other Operating Expenses	35,000	40,000	41,180	42,242
Total Operating Expenses	$145,000	$180,000	$171,118	$196,628
Operating Profit or Loss	$ 25,000	$ 30,000	$ 28,897	$ 25,140
Net Gain or Loss on Monetary Items	—	—	$ 4,968	$ 6,760
Net Earnings & Gain on Monetary Items	$ 25,000	$ 30,000	$ 33,865	$ 31,900

[*172*]

Note that on the balance sheet, the adjusted figure for cash as of December 31, 1978 is higher than the balance for cash as shown in nominal dollars for the same date. A moment's thought will reveal why this is so. We have chosen December 31, 1979 dollars as the constant measuring unit, and those dollars are worth less than the dollars as of the end of 1978. Accordingly $85,000 end of 1978 dollars are worth, by indexing, $96,311 of the "cheaper" dollars of December 31, 1979. Cash as of the end of 1979 is not restated since it is already presented in December 31, 1979 dollars. Similar restatements have been made for the other monetary items as of December 31, 1978: accounts receivable, and accounts and notes payable.

Also, on the balance sheet, building and land are shown in the last two columns at amounts greater than their historical costs, but the figures at the end of 1978 and 1979 are the same. This is explained by the fact that the actual assets are the same, and the values at the end of both years are written up to dollars of December 31, 1979. Note also that the invested capital (or common stock) of $200,000 becomes $245,620 in December 31, 1979 dollars; this increase is not a profit, since it reflects only the decline in the value of the dollar since the original investment was made.

It is the income statement that contains the surprise. The GAAP figures show an increase in net earnings, from $25,000 to $30,000. The restated figures, in constant dollars, show that net earnings have declined in real terms. Profits from operations dropped from $28,897 to $25,140. The company made substantial monetary gains during both years, since it owed much more than the total of its cash and accounts receivable. Even after these gains, however, the company's net income declined.

Lest you draw the conclusion that this illustration is atypical, refer to Note Q to the Times Mirror financial statements in Appendix A (pages 220–222). The *Five Year Summary of Selected Data Adjusted for Effects of Changing Prices* shows a steady decline in net income and net income per share from 1979 through 1981, a very different picture from the one shown by the GAAP financial statements. These differences are explained, and criticized, in the last section of *Management's Discussion* and *Analysis of Financial Condition and Results of Operation*, under the heading of *Inflation-Adjusted Data* (page 205).

Although financial statements adjusted for constant dollars provide important insights not otherwise offered by the GAAP financial statements, they do not reflect the actual *current* costs of the company's assets. They simply restate *historical* costs in current dollars. The restatement shows the effects of general inflation, but does not present the effects of specific changes in value in critical items like land, building and machinery. For this information, we must look to current cost accounting.

Current Cost Accounting

The objective of current cost accounting is to reflect assets and liabilities on the balance sheet, and income and expense on the income statement, at amounts that indicate their current costs. There are many definitions of current cost, but the most widely accepted is *replacement cost*, the cost of replacing existing assets or other items with comparable items. Financial statements prepared on the basis of current costs require adjustment of each item in a manner similar to the statements prepared on the basis of constant dollars. A major difference, however, is that the adjustment cannot be made on the basis of a readily-available index like the CPI. Instead, replacement costs must be separately determined for each item or group of items on the statements. As a result, the generation of current cost financial statements is likely to be more complex and expensive—and more subject to individual judgment—than development of constant dollar statements.

Current cost statements are also more difficult to read, though the unique information they present may be well worth the additional effort required to interpret them. The balance sheet prepared on the basis of current cost is the most realistic balance sheet available. The reader need not inquire about the current values of assets, since realistic judgments of those values (replacement costs) appear on the balance sheet itself.

The income statement is also based on current costs, and in an inflationary period the usual result will be that the major expenses of the business will be higher than those reflected on GAAP statements prepared on the basis of historical cost. A prominent example of this is depreciation, which will be based on the replacement cost of the asset being depreciated. In most cases, replacement costs of fixed assets have increased, with the result that depreciation under replacement cost accounting will also increase. Similar effects, though often not as dramatic, will be experienced with cost of sales and certain expense items. The figure for net income from operations is therefore likely to be lower than net income calculated on the basis of historical costs.

However, the income statement will contain an additional category, *holding gains and losses*, reflecting the gains and losses to the company of holding assets that have changed in value. For example, if in a given year the company's building increased in replacement cost from $200,000 to $240,000, the income statement would show an unrealized holding gain of $40,000. The holding gain would be *unrealized*, since the building was not sold. Holding gains on items sold or consumed as expenses would be shown on the income statement as *realized holding gains*. The important distinction between holding gains and income from operations may be illustrated with an example.

Suppose that during 1982 a jeweler purchased gold for $6,000 which he fashioned into jewelry and sold for $10,000. In 1983, he must pay $8,000 for the same amount of gold, which he will again fashion into jewelry for sale. If the jeweler had selling expenses of $2,000, his income statement prepared in accordance with GAAP would be as follows:

Sales	$10,000
Cost of Goods Sold	6,000
Gross Profit	$ 4,000
Less: Selling Expenses	2,000
Net Income	$ 2,000

If the jeweler's income statement is prepared in accordance with current cost accounting, however, it will look quite different:

Sales	$10,000
Cost of Goods Sold	8,000
Gross Profit	$ 2,000
Less: Selling Expenses	2,000
Net Income from Operations	$ 0
Realized Holding Gains on Sale of Gold	2,000
Net Income Plus Holding Gains	$ 2,000

The second income statement reveals that while the jeweler recognized income for the year, it was attributable solely to an increase in the price of gold. If the jeweler continues to operate on this financial basis, a levelling off or a decline in gold prices will lead to a business failure. The continuing vitality of most enterprises is based on operating income, not gains from inflationary forces. Current cost accounting provides an analytical tool for separating these items.

No business is as simple as the illustration, and the accumulation of current cost information does not generally yield results as obvious as those above. However, the results are often almost as dramatic. The managements of many corporations have been surprised and disappointed when they have applied current cost accounting to their financial statements.

You will find further analysis of current cost statements, and examples of those statements, in several of the references noted at the end of this chapter.

Current Cost, Constant Dollar Accounting

The illustrations above demonstrate that current cost accounting and constant dollar accounting do not achieve the same results. While constant dollar accounting recasts the financial statements to adjust for variations in the value of the dollar, it does not show the current costs of items on either the balance sheet or the income statement. Conversely, while current cost accounting reflects current costs on the financial statements, it does not measure the effects of changes in the value of the dollar. Both systems must be combined to reflect both elements of change in value. Accountants have shown great reluctance to accept any system that departs from historical cost, particularly when it is suggested that two sets of adjustment should be made. However, such statements have been prepared and are presented in several of the references cited at the end of this chapter. Financial statements based on current costs and constant dollars (referred to by some commentators as *real current costs*) provide a wealth of analytical material at the cost of considerable complexity.

FASB Statement No. 33

Although Generally Accepted Accounting Principles remain firmly rooted in historical costs, recent action by the Financial Accounting Standards Board has brought both constant dollar and current cost information to certain financial statements. The accounting profession has wrestled with the problems of inflation and deflation for some 60 years, but no definitive support for inflation adjustment of financial statements occurred until 1976. In that year, the SEC issued an Accounting Series Release requiring that the very largest of corporations (those with inventory, property, plant and equipment exceeding $100 million and comprising more than 10% of their assets) provide supplementary unaudited data on replacement costs of inventories and productive capacity, as well as cost of sales and depreciation based on replacement costs.

In so acting, the SEC had assumed its occasional role as gad-fly to the accounting profession. The action had the desired effect, for in 1979 the Financial Accounting Standards Board issued Statement No. 33, *Financial Reporting and Changing Prices*, and the SEC promptly withdrew its release. Statement No. 33 similarly requires disclosure of supplementary unaudited information by the largest of companies, those whose inventory, property, plant and equipment (before depreciation) exceed $125 million or whose total assets (after depreciation) exceed $1 billion. Two categories of supplementary information must be disclosed:

(1) *Constant dollar* information on income from continuing operations, and on the net gain or loss on monetary items for the current fiscal year.

(2) *Current cost* information on income from continuing operations, and the current cost amounts of inventory, property, plant and equipment.

In addition, Statement No. 33 requires the presentation of five-year summary data on sales and income per share from continuing operations, and on net assets, based on constant dollars and on current costs. There is no requirement, however, that full financial statements be prepared on either basis. Statement No. 33 represents an experiment with inflation adjusted accounting, and the FASB has indicated its intention to study the subject further.

The Times Mirror financial statements contain the required disclosure in Note Q (pages 220–222), which includes only constant dollar information. The Note indicates that current cost data did not differ materially from constant dollar data, and therefore was not disclosed.

REFERENCES

Official Pronouncements:

Financial Accounting Standards Board, Statement of Financial Accounting Standards No. 33, Financial Reporting and Changing Prices (1979).

Financial Accounting Standards Board, Illustrations of Financial Reporting and Changing Prices (1979).

Secondary Sources:

Financial Accounting Standards Board, Conceptual Framework for Financial Accounting and Reporting: Elements of Financial Statements and Their Measurement (Discussion Memorandum, 1976).

Revsine, Replacement Cost Accounting (1973).

Largay & Livingstone, Accounting for Changing Prices (1976).

Siegel, Accounting and Inflation: An Analysis and a Proposal, 29 U.C. L.A.L.Rev. 271 (1981).

Chapter Fifteen

FEDERAL INCOME TAX ACCOUNTING

Taxes are what we pay for civilized society.
O.W. Holmes, Jr. in Compania de Tobacos v. Collector,
275 U.S. 87 (1904)

Why Tax Accounting Differs From Financial Accounting

There are more similarities than differences between tax and financial accounting. This chapter explores some of the more important differences. The fundamental objective of financial accounting is to provide meaningful disclosure to creditors, shareholders and others of the financial condition and results of operation of the enterprise. The basic function of the Internal Revenue Code and Regulations is to raise revenue in accordance with the statutory policies. The United States Supreme Court, though perhaps exaggerating the flexibility of financial accounting and overstating the certainty of tax rules, noted in a recent decision that the differing goals of each sometimes require different principles:

> The primary goal of financial accounting is to provide useful information to management, shareholders, creditors, and others properly interested; the major responsibility of the accountant is to protect these parties from being misled. The primary goal of the income tax system, in contrast, is the equitable collection of revenue; the major responsibility of the Internal Revenue Service is to protect the public fisc. Consistently with its goals and responsibilities, financial accounting has as its foundation the principle of conservatism, with its corollary that "possible errors in measurement [should] be in the direction of understatement rather than overstatement of net income and net assets." In view of the Treasury's markedly different goals and responsibilities, understatement of income is not destined to be its guiding light.

> . . .

> [A] presumptive equivalency between tax and financial accounting would create insurmountable difficulties of tax administration. Accountants long have recognized that "generally accepted accounting principles" are far from being a

canonical set of rules that will ensure identical accounting treatment of identical transactions. "Generally accepted accounting principles," rather, tolerate a range of "reasonable" treatments, leaving the choice among alternatives to management. . . . Variances of this sort may be tolerable in financial reporting, but they are questionable in a tax system designed to ensure as far as possible that similarly situated taxpayers pay the same tax.

Thor Power Tool Co. v. Commissioner, 439 U.S. 522, 542–44 (1979).

Maintenance of Books and Records

Internal Revenue Code (Code) Section 6001 requires that taxpayers keep records, render statements, make returns and comply with the Treasury Regulations. The regulations, while not prescribing any particular form for keeping records, require that taxpayers maintain permanent records sufficient to establish the amount of gross income, deductions, credits or other matters required to be shown on the tax or information returns of the taxpayer. Most businesses will maintain a complete set of double entry books in manual or computer form. The entries in these books should be fully supported by originals or copies of orders, invoices, correspondence, cancelled checks, bank statements, diaries and similar documentation. In the event of a tax audit, this documentation will provide the basis for demonstrating the amounts entered on the tax return. Individual and business taxpayers who do not maintain full books of account must nevertheless retain adequate documentation to support their reported gross income, deductions and credits.

Taxable Year

Tax returns are filed, and taxable income is calculated, for the *taxable year* of the taxpayer. This may be a calendar year. Alternatively, if the taxpayer maintains books on an annual basis other than the calendar year, the taxable year may, subject to some limitations, be the *fiscal year* on which the books are maintained. The fiscal year is a twelve-month period ending on the last day of any month other than December. A permitted variation of the fiscal year is the *52–53 week year*, representing an annual period that always ends on the same day of the week closest to the end of the month. Examples of these taxable years are:

Calendar year: January 1 – December 31
Fiscal year: April 1 – March 31
52–53 week fiscal year: The year ending on the last Sunday
                                     in March

A taxpayer's first taxable year may be a *short period*, less than a full year, and so may its last. Moreover, when a taxpayer changes its taxable year, it must file a short period tax return. The Code contains detailed rules concerning tax returns for short periods.

A newly established business may choose its taxable year, which must be the same as the period used in keeping its financial books. The taxpayer may not change its taxable year without the prior approval of the Internal Revenue Service (the IRS).

Alternative Methods of Accounting; Clear Reflection of Income

The Code provides that taxable income shall be computed under the method of accounting used by the taxpayer in keeping its books. The two principal permissible methods are the *cash receipts and disbursements method* and the *accrual method.* Other permitted methods, applicable to certain businesses, are discussed in the references at the end of this chapter. These include the installment, percentage-of-completion and completed-contract methods. Taxpayers that manufacture or sell goods are required by the Code to maintain inventories and will therefore be required to apply the accrual method, at least with respect to their manufacturing or selling operations. As with the adoption of a taxable year, once a method of accounting has been adopted, it may not be changed without prior consent from the IRS.

Taxpayers in more than one business may use different methods for the different businesses. Moreover, the Code leaves open the possibility of using a combination of methods. Some taxpayers have, for example, successfully applied the accrual method to the inventory operations of a business and the cash receipts and disbursements method to other operations.

The Code provides that if the taxpayer's method of accounting "does not clearly reflect income," the computation of taxable income shall be made under a method that in the opinion of the Treasury does clearly reflect income. The Treasury Regulations provide little guidance as to the meaning of this vague standard, other than to indicate that consistency in the application of accounting methods is required in order to assure clear reflection of income. The United States Supreme Court has on several occasions broadly construed the authority of the IRS to reject accounting methods under this standard, unless specifically authorized by the Code.

Cash Receipts and Disbursements Method

The cash receipts and disbursements method, frequently called the *cash basis*, is not quite a purely cash method of accounting. The Treasury Regulations indicate that all items of gross income are included in the year when they are received, and expenditures are deductible in the year when they are paid. However, items of gross income include not only cash, but property and services as well. Moreover, the tests of receipt and payment are subject to important qualifications.

The cash receipts and disbursements method is very widely used by taxpayers who earn salaries and wages and who render services. Income is recognized under this method when payment is received, rather than when the services are rendered or a bill is submitted. There is obviously room for income shifting and tax abuse under this method. Several doctrines have developed to address this problem. The concept of *cash equivalence* is applied to require the inclusion in gross income of noncash items like property and services received. In general, debts owing to the taxpayer are not deemed the equivalent of cash unless they are in the form of notes or other obligations having characteristics (such as salability and negotiability) suggestive of immediate convertibility into cash.

Suppose the taxpayer receives checks from his clients or his employer in December, 1983 but does not cash or deposit the checks until January, 1984. Can he effectively defer taxes by claiming no cash receipt in 1983? If this ploy were effective, the cash receipts and disbursements method would be an open invitation to shifting taxes from year to year. The doctrine of *constructive receipt* addresses this issue. The Treasury Regulations provide that income not actually received during the year is constructively received by the taxpayer when it is "credited to his account, set apart for him, or otherwise made available so that he may draw upon it at any time." The constructive receipt doctrine applies to such items as savings bank interest that has been credited but not withdrawn, or funds set aside for the use of the taxpayer which the taxpayer chooses not to draw upon during the year. In situations where the taxpayer does not have free access to the funds, the doctrine is generally inapplicable.

Although deductions under the cash basis are generally taken in the year when payment is made, there are some exceptions to the rule. Assets with a useful life substantially longer than one year are subject to the usual rules of depreciation, depletion and amortization. A cash basis taxpayer who buys a machine for $35,000 may not deduct the full price as an expense in the year of purchase. Instead, the usual depreciation rules apply. If the machine is five-year property with no scrap value and the taxpayer elects straight-line depreciation, $7,000 per year may be deducted irrespective of cash payments. The weight of authority applies the same rule to prepayments of expenses applicable to substantially more than one year: the expenses should be allocated over the years to which they apply.

Despite these modifications to the "purity" of the cash receipts and disbursements method, it retains its attractiveness to many taxpayers principally because of its relative simplicity and because it allows taxpayers to forestall payment of taxes on income until the income is actually received. Moreover, it does leave room for some shifting of income and expense through timing of billings and payments. Remember, however, that this method does not comply with GAAP and will therefore not be acceptable for financial reporting purposes by companies that must distribute or file audited financial statements.

Accrual Method

The accrual method, frequently called *accrual basis*, is based on accrual accounting under GAAP, but departs from GAAP in several important areas. For tax purposes, accrual of income and expense occurs when all the events have occurred which fix the right to receive the income, or determine the fact of the liability, and the amount can be determined with reasonable accuracy. Historically, this test and the accrual method have been interpreted by the courts to produce results quite different from those of GAAP accrual accounting.

For example, a series of decisions by the United States Supreme Court established the general rule that advance receipts of income (such as subscriptions and dues) must be reflected by an accrual method taxpayer in the year of receipt, despite the fact that the taxpayer remains under an obligation to render services in later years. The harsh results of these holdings were ultimately mitigated by the IRS in the form of a Revenue Procedure and Regulations changes, and by Congress in amendments to the Code. Today, prepaid subscription income, prepaid dues of membership organizations and prepaid income for services to be performed by the end of the succeeding taxable year may, with certain limitations, be included in gross income by an accrual basis taxpayer when earned, rather than on receipt. Similarly, advance payments for goods, within certain limitations, may be reported as income in the year of delivery. Apart from these carefully drawn exceptions, however, the general rule remains intact: even for the accrual basis taxpayer, prepayments of income are included in taxable income in the year of receipt.

Tax and accounting approaches to accrual also part company on the subject of estimated and contingent liabilities. The Code specifically allows deduction of reasonable additions to a "reserve for bad debts," representing the estimated expense of uncollectible accounts receivable. With this exception, however, the courts have generally held that estimated expenses—such as estimated warranty claims, repair obligations and self-insurance provisions—are not deductible by an accrual basis taxpayer. The deduction is permitted in accordance with the general rule, when the fact of the liability is fixed and its amount can be determined with reasonable accuracy. In most such instances, the deduction therefore occurs on actual payment.

The tax requirements with respect to disputed items of income and expense are in partial accord with GAAP. In general, tax and accounting rules agree that unpaid income is not recognized when the party obligated to pay disputes his liability. The situation is less clear when the obligor concedes liability but disputes the amount. One very troublesome decision of the United States Supreme Court holds that the amount due must be estimated and immediately accrued as income. However, some subsequent lower court decisions indicate that a dispute as to amount renders the amount of income not determinable with reasonable accuracy, and therefore income should not be accrued until resolution of the dispute.

No accrual of a current deduction is permissible for tax purposes when the payment is the subject of dispute. In many instances this rule will be at odds with GAAP, which requires accrual of an estimated liability and the related expense when ultimate payment of some amount is reasonably probable. Occasionally a taxpayer will pay a disputed liability under protest and contest the liability subsequent to payment. The Code allows current deduction of the liability in that situation, and if a refund is ultimately received it is generally included in gross income in the year of receipt.

Inventories

The Code provides that inventories must be maintained whenever in the opinion of the IRS their use "is necessary in order clearly to determine the income of any taxpayer." In practice, all merchandising and manufacturing businesses will therefore be required to maintain inventories for tax purposes. In general the inventory methods permissible under GAAP may be used for tax purposes. The use of LIFO (last-in, first-out) is, however, subject to very detailed rules in both the Code and the Treasury Regulations. The Regulations provide that LIFO may be used only if it is also used in financial reports to creditors and investors. The Regulations detail the requirements for electing into and out of the LIFO inventory method.

The principle of *lower of cost or market* is generally available in valuation of inventories for tax purposes, with several important limitations. First, it may not be used in valuing inventories under LIFO. Second, lower of cost or market generally must be elected with respect to all inventories of the taxpayer. Third, the principle must in general be applied to each article of inventory. Finally, a recent decision of the United States Supreme Court held that inventory write-downs below replacement cost are forbidden unless the taxpayer actually sells inventory items below replacement cost in the normal course of business. This last rule contrasts sharply with the calculation of "market" required under GAAP, as discussed earlier in Chapter 4.

Depreciation

As a result of the Economic Recovery Tax Act of 1981 (ERTA), depreciation for tax purposes bears little or no relation to depreciation under GAAP. The depreciation system enacted in ERTA, known as the *Accelerated Cost Recovery System (ACRS)*, is a dramatic extension of the principle of accelerated depreciation, as earlier discussed in Chapter 5. ACRS divides all depreciable property into four categories, as follows:

Three-year property, including automobiles, some trucks and personal property used in research and development.

Five-year property, which includes most other personal property.

Ten-year property, including certain public utility property and a limited class of real property.

Fifteen-year property, which includes most real property.

Depreciation is calculated on the basis of these lives, applying declining balance depreciation at different rates, depending upon the year when the assets are acquired. The rates increase from 150% for assets acquired in 1981 through 1984, to 175% for assets acquired in 1985, to 200% for assets acquired thereafter. The complex calculations required by ACRS (which include switching to straight-line depreciation or sum-of-the-years'-digits depreciation at the most advantageous time) are summarized in tables showing the applicable depreciation percentage for each year and each class of assets. The tables treat all property acquired during a year as though it were put in service in the middle of the year.

Although ACRS is mandatory, taxpayers may elect alternatively to apply straight line depreciation for all property of a particular class placed in service in any year. Straight line depreciation may be applied for the same period as called for under ACRS, or for longer periods, as follows:

Three-year property:	3, 5 or 12 years
Five-year property:	5, 12 or 25 years
Ten-year property:	10, 25 or 35 years
Fifteen-year property:	15, 35 or 45 years

Another provision in ERTA permits taxpayers to charge directly to expense certain depreciable assets purchased during the year. The amount directly chargeable to expense increases from $5,000 for purchases made in 1982 and 1983, to $7,500 for purchases made in 1984 and 1985, to $10,000 for purchases made thereafter.

All of these provisions were apparently motivated by the desire to create incentives for the purchase of depreciable property. The availability of more rapid, and within limits immediate, depreciation for tax purposes affords substantial tax benefits. But the corollary of early depreciation under ACRS is that no depreciation is available for tax purposes in later years, when the assets will still be in use. Furthermore, if the assets are sold at a profit after being depreciated under ACRS, the applicable provisions of the Code requiring "recapture" will call for recognition of ordinary income to the extent of all or a portion of the gain on sale.

Amortization of Intangible Assets

The cost of certain intangible assets, like copyrights and patents, may be amortized over their useful lives in a manner consistent with GAAP. Goodwill does not follow this rule. Though GAAP requires that it be amortized over a period not in excess of 40 years, no amortization of goodwill is permissible for tax purposes.

Organizational expenses, including expenditures incident to the creation of a corporation, may at the election of the corporation be deducted ratably over a period not less than 60 months, beginning with the organization of the corporation. However, reorganization expenses incurred in connection with corporate acquisitions and restructuring have been held by the United States Supreme Court to be capital in nature. They are not deductible when incurred, and may not be amortized.

Net Operating Losses

The federal income tax structure is based on taxation of income for the taxable year. However, a company may have substantial taxable income in some years and losses in others. Unless the losses were taken into account in determining the company's tax liability, the annual calculation of taxable income would create an unfair tax burden on the company. The Code provides for determination of a company's *net operating loss*, which may then, subject to certain rules and limitations, be applied against the taxable income of earlier or later years to reduce the tax payable. Under present law, corporations may *carry back* net operating losses to the three preceding taxable years and may *carry forward* net operating losses for years ending after 1975 to the succeeding 15 taxable years.

A moment's thought will reveal that net operating loss carryovers are of considerable value to a corporation, since they afford insulation against taxation of subsequent income. For this reason, companies with substantial carryforward losses frequently are viewed as attractive candidates for acquisition by other companies. Several sections of the Code deal with the subject known as "trafficking in loss carryovers," and impose limitations, and in some instances reductions, with respect to the use of carryover losses after an acquisition. This subject can be examined in detail in one of the references cited at the end of this chapter.

[*187*]

A Word on Taxation of Individuals, Partnerships and Corporations

Although this is not a text on taxation, it is important that for accounting purposes we note certain fundamental differences in tax accounting for individuals, partnerships and corporations. The calculations of taxable income for a business owned by an individual (a proprietorship) and for a corporation are fundamentally similar, although there are numerous detail differences with respect to certain items of gross income, deductions and credits. The proprietorship net income for tax purposes will be calculated on a separate schedule (Schedule C) of the owner's individual tax return on Form 1040, and will enter into the calculation of the owner's personal income tax.

A corporation is a separate entity for tax as well as legal purposes. The corporation's taxable income is calculated and for most corporations reported on Form 1120, and a tax is paid at graduated rates, with all taxable income in excess of $100,000 taxed at the rate of 46%. When a corporation makes distributions of current or accumulated income to its shareholders, in the form of dividends, the shareholders in turn must include the dividends in their personal taxable income. The corporation takes no deduction for dividend distributions. Therefore, the basic structure of corporate taxable income and distributions contemplates taxation at two levels: the corporation is taxed on its income, and the shareholders are taxed on distributions of the corporation's income. Corporate and shareholder conduct have taken account of this structure in various ways. Corporations tend to retain the bulk of their income and grow internally, rather than make substantial distributions of taxable dividends. Often, corporate capital structures are arranged to provide for distributions that—unlike dividends—avoid double taxation by providing the corporation with a deduction. For example, it is not uncommon for the shareholders of a closely-held corporation to make a portion of their investment in long-term debt, so that the corporation has an interest deduction on some portion of the income distributed to them. Like many business and tax arrangements, this structure is subject to possible abuse, and it has been addressed by the Code, the Treasury Regulations and the courts. The details of these structures, and the provisions of the Code and Regulations adopted to deal with them, are the subject of a text on corporate taxation. Awareness of them often explains what might otherwise be a puzzling aspect of the corporate financial statements.

A partnership does not have entity status for federal income tax purposes. It files an information return on Form 1065, but its items of gross income, deductions and credits are allocated to the individual partners directly. The partnership provides this allocation, consistent with the partnership agreement, by supplying each partner with a Schedule K–1 showing the items of gross income, deductions and credits allocable to that partner for the taxable year. The fact that a partnership is not treated as a separate taxable entity affords potential advantages and disadvantages to the use of that form of organization. An entire practice in the area of "tax shelters" now occupies the efforts of many talented accountants, attorneys and business people. Most of these shelters are organized in partnership form in order to pass through to the investor-partners the income and expenses of the partnership. You may pursue this subject further in a text on partnership taxation.

Our purpose in examining these forms of organization in this chapter on tax accounting was to suggest that organization form and structure, as well as financial reporting, may be heavily affected by income tax motivations.

REFERENCES

Official Pronouncements:

Internal Revenue Code of 1954, as amended. See particularly sections 441–443 (accounting period); 446, 447 (method of accounting); 471–473 (inventories); 168 (depreciation).

Secondary Sources:

Bittker, Federal Taxation of Income, Estates and Gifts (1981), chapters 105–107.

Bittker & Eustice, Federal Income Taxation of Corporations and Shareholders (4th ed. 1979).

McKee, Nelson & Whitmire, Federal Taxation of Partnerships and Partners (1978).

*

Appendix A

ILLUSTRATIVE FINANCIAL STATEMENTS *

Responsibility for Financial Statements

The integrity of the financial information appearing in this Annual Report is the responsibility of Times Mirror management. The information has been prepared by the Company in accordance with generally accepted accounting principles appropriate in the circumstances and necessarily includes amounts based on management's best estimates and judgments. The Company's independent auditors, Ernst & Whinney, have examined the accompanying financial statements and tested the accounting records as described in their report on page 55.

The Company maintains a system of internal accounting control which it believes is sufficient to provide reasonable assurance that in all material respects transactions are properly authorized and recorded, financial reporting responsibilities are met and accountability for assets is maintained.

In establishing and maintaining any system of internal control, judgments are required to assess and balance the relative costs and expected benefits.

The internal control system is augmented by the selection and training of qualified personnel, clearly established and communicated accounting and business policies, and an organizational structure designed to appropriately divide duties and delegate authority. The system is monitored by the Company's staff of internal auditors who evaluate and report on the effectiveness of the system to management.

An Audit Committee of the Board of Directors, composed solely of outside directors, has existed since 1971. This Committee meets at least semi-annually with the Company's management, internal auditors and independent auditors to consider the discharge of responsibility by each.

---

* This Appendix contains the consolidated financial statements of Times Mirror Company, together with the notes and comments thereto, as published in the Times Mirror Annual Report for the year 1981.

Summary of Selected Consolidated Financial Data and Other Information

(In thousands of dollars except per share amounts)	1981	1980	1979	1978	1977
Operating Results					
Operating revenues	$2,130,756	$1,857,349	$1,638,535	$1,411,356	$1,129,630
Operating profit	305,393	253,826	268,577	243,405	181,446
Interest expense	48,582	24,097	14,528	2,996	2,417
Income before income taxes	256,811	229,729	254,049	266,250[1]	179,029
Net income	150,331	139,217	146,493	142,399[1]	96,110
Per Share Information					
Earnings per share	$4.40	$4.08	$4.31	$4.13[1]	$2.77
Dividends declared[2]	1.79	1.51	1.26	1.05	.85
Dividends paid	1.72	1.44	1.20	1.00	.75
Financial Information					
Current assets	$ 555,551	$ 514,010	$ 443,555	$ 486,751	$ 427,280
Timberlands less depletion	115,998	103,583	105,990	99,847	101,184
Property, plant and equipment—net	796,498	676,660	499,386	294,901	241,314
Total assets	1,917,212	1,734,788	1,349,708	1,002,253	843,288
Long-term debt	478,273	447,029	214,514	33,658	28,288
Shareholders' equity	915,203	822,735	731,829	625,645	547,458
Working capital	226,845	210,451	167,863	247,804	247,706
Total funds from operations	265,999	233,334	210,019	166,569	139,207
Purchase of property, plant and equipment[3]	188,696	195,815	177,158	73,037	50,341
Additions to timberlands	27,182	15,531	20,482	18,443	22,488
Other					
Price range of Common Stock	$58½ to 39¾	$45⅝ to 28¾	$37½ to 28	$35¼ to 22⅜	$ 26 to 20
Book value of Common Stock[4]	$26.81	$24.13	$21.56	$18.46	$15.77
Number of shareholders	5,450	5,626	5,713	5,767	5,954
Number of employees	27,049	26,856	24,256	21,937	19,396

Summary of Selected Consolidated Financial Data and Other Information

(In thousands of dollars except per share amounts)	1976	1975	1974	1973	1972
Operating Results					
Operating revenues	$972,460	$806,475	$741,772	$701,880	$610,743
Operating profit	133,329	92,713	107,951	108,663	86,505
Interest expense	2,311	2,405	2,424	2,612	2,711
Income before income taxes	131,018	90,308	105,527	106,051	83,794
Net income	70,667	48,212	59,407	55,651	42,790
Per Share Information					
Earnings per share	$2.03	$1.39	$1.72	$1.61	$1.24
Dividends declared[2]	.60	.50	.45	.31	.26
Dividends paid	.575	.50	.45	.31	.26
Financial Information					
Current assets	$365,607	$295,923	$235,826	$239,978	$210,489
Timberlands less depletion	94,804	75,980	73,074	50,397	35,610
Property, plant and equipment—net	216,908	213,836	214,938	192,184	179,220
Total assets	738,798	650,157	592,611	551,270	485,559
Long-term debt	32,556	33,843	35,983	43,326	43,878
Shareholders' equity	481,818	430,372	403,118	359,338	314,543
Working capital	209,136	169,244	137,020	133,583	120,310
Total funds from operations	111,109	83,043	91,912	87,607	69,449
Purchase of property, plant and equipment[3]	27,267	23,408	37,448	30,713	30,761
Additions to timberlands	34,171	13,011	33,392	14,562	10,703
Other					
Price range of Common Stock	$ 23¾ to 18¼	$ 19⅞ to 10¼	$ 17⅝ to 8¾	$ 25⅞ to 15¾	$ 30¾ to 21⅞
Book value of Common Stock[4]	$13.86	$12.41	$11.63	$10.40	$ 9.10
Number of shareholders	5,873	6,023	6,286	5,885	5,300
Number of employees	17,654	16,057	15,130	15,961	15,293

This summary should be read in conjunction with the consolidated financial statements and notes thereto.

[1]Included in income before income taxes and net income are $25,841 and $17,252 ($.50 per share), respectively, from the sale of forest products assets.
[2]Excludes cash dividends on Series A Convertible Preferred Stock of $.35 in 1977 and $.70 in prior years.
[3]Excludes capital assets acquired in business combinations accounted for as purchases.
[4]Calculations assume conversion of Series A Convertible Preferred Stock for 1976 and prior years.

Five-Year Summary of Business Segment Information

(In thousands of dollars)	1981	1980	1979	1978	1977
Total Revenues					
Newspaper Publishing	$1,065,479	$ 874,343	$ 724,300	$ 622,304	$ 510,688
Newsprint and Forest Products	324,391	296,319	323,141	311,022	301,206
Book Publishing	289,773	263,601	234,652	214,193	176,206
Information Services	246,066	227,266	203,665	162,994	97,048
Broadcast and Cable Television	190,591	139,935	86,209	36,537	29,813
Other Operations	185,415	179,202	169,875	154,766	112,048
Corporate and Investments	7,490	3,624	7,255	13,038	11,374
Consolidated					
Total revenues	2,309,205	1,984,290	1,749,097	1,514,854	1,238,383
Intersegment sales*	(153,235)	(115,427)	(101,621)	(86,923)	(94,639)
Total sales to unaffiliated customers	$2,155,970	$1,868,863	$1,647,476	$1,427,931	$1,145,744
Operating Profit					
Newspaper Publishing	$ 169,918	$ 155,326	$ 134,257	$ 115,647	$ 81,316
Newsprint and Forest Products	(1,590)	(7,484)	43,730	40,709	39,381
Book Publishing	44,642	40,666	35,187	38,818	31,362
Information Services	31,352	23,974	23,204	20,403	12,289
Broadcast and Cable Television	64,150	47,223	32,245	18,183	14,030
Other Operations	16,519	13,342	12,963	16,029	9,230
Corporate and Investments	(19,598)	(19,221)	(13,009)	(6,384)	(6,162)
Consolidated	305,393	253,826	268,577	243,405	181,446
Sale of forest products assets				25,841	
Interest expense	(48,582)	(24,097)	(14,528)	(2,996)	(2,417)
Income before Income Taxes	$ 256,811	$ 229,729	$ 254,049	$ 266,250	$ 179,029

*Intersegment sales consist primarily of newsprint as follows (in thousands): $152,221 in 1981; $113,643 in 1980; $97,822 in 1979; $83,388 in 1978; and $91,466 in 1977.

Five-Year Summary of Business Segment Information

	1981	1980	1979	1978	1977
Identifiable Assets					
Newspaper Publishing	$ 603,639	$ 519,870	$ 359,218	$ 191,102	$154,501
Newsprint and Forest Products	433,208	412,868	342,165	294,928	259,052
Book Publishing	186,166	187,505	175,280	144,537	123,961
Information Services	161,787	165,988	158,541	141,245	48,967
Broadcast and Cable Television	421,895	338,723	195,223	37,637	32,305
Other Operations	95,947	95,271	91,725	87,638	78,496
Corporate and Investments	110,658	88,136	72,066	145,087	179,633
Eliminations	(96,088)	(73,573)	(44,510)	(39,921)	(33,627)
Consolidated	$1,917,212	$1,734,788	$1,349,708	$1,002,253	$843,288
Depreciation, Amortization and Depletion					
Newspaper Publishing	$ 20,223	$ 14,636	$ 9,784	$ 7,699	$ 7,407
Newsprint and Forest Products	39,048	32,500	25,916	23,098	26,807
Book Publishing	2,114	1,722	1,587	1,214	990
Information Services	6,410	5,654	4,845	3,955	1,444
Broadcast and Cable Television	19,560	17,361	11,049	3,505	3,193
Other Operations	1,778	1,921	1,458	659	489
Corporate and Investments	1,173	957	885	901	842
Consolidated	$ 90,306	$ 74,751	$ 55,524	$ 41,031	$ 41,172
Capital Expenditures					
Newspaper Publishing	$ 75,219	$ 61,676	$ 54,041	$ 24,317	$ 25,889
Newsprint and Forest Products**	59,934	94,964	98,954	47,621	35,413
Book Publishing	5,293	3,214	2,690	2,596	2,521
Information Services	8,166	8,313	12,296	7,822	3,909
Broadcast and Cable Television	64,077	40,277	27,603	4,322	2,997
Other Operations	1,720	2,029	1,612	2,895	507
Corporate and Investments	1,469	873	444	1,907	1,593
Consolidated	$ 215,878	$ 211,346	$ 197,640	$ 91,480	$ 72,829

**Includes additions to owned timberlands and capitalized timber harvesting rights as follows (in thousands): $27,182 in 1981; $15,531 in 1980; $20,482 in 1979; $18,443 in 1978; and $22,488 in 1977.

Management's Discussion and Analysis of
Financial Condition and Results of Operations

Results of Operations

During 1981, Times Mirror achieved new highs in revenues and income despite a national recession and interest rates that remained at record levels for much of the year. Consolidated revenues reached $2.16 billion, a 15% improvement over 1980. Operating profit, or income before interest and taxes, was $305.4 million, a 20% increase over the prior year. Pretax income rose 12% to $256.8 million from $229.7 million in 1980. Consolidated net income was $150.3 million, or $4.40 per share, up 8% over the previous year's $139.2 million and $4.08 per share.

Each of the Company's operating groups, led by Newspaper Publishing and Broadcast and Cable Television, reported improved operating results for the year. In Newspaper Publishing, all of the Company's metropolitan newspapers attained record-high sales and profits despite recessionary pressures on advertising volume in the second half of the year. Broadcast and Cable Television profits advanced 36% due to the strong performance of KDFW-TV in Dallas and the inclusion of a full year's results of five television stations acquired in March 1980.

Consolidated pretax income increased less than operating profit because of the Company's additional borrowing costs. Interest expense for the year reached $48.6 million, more than double 1980's $24.1 million, due to increased borrowings and higher interest rates. Capitalization of interest benefited pretax income by $6.7 million (or 10 cents per share) in 1981 compared with $11.4 million (17 cents per share) in 1980. The amount of interest capitalized in 1982 should be higher than in 1981 due to major expansions in the Company's cable television operations.

Consolidated net income increased 8% over 1980, which was lower than the 12% pretax gain. In 1980, the Company enjoyed a lower effective tax rate due to the investment tax credits associated with the new newsprint machine in Newberg, Oregon, and more capital gains benefits from the cutting of timber.

In 1981, the Company sold two operating units — the Denoyer-Geppert Company at a $2 million gain and New English Library at a $2 million loss. The absence of these subsidiaries will not significantly affect Times Mirror's future results.

Consolidated 1980 Results

Consolidated 1980 revenues totaled $1.87 billion, an increase of $221.4 million or 13% over the prior year. The acquisition of The Hartford Courant in August 1979 and five television stations in March 1980 contributed to the growth in revenues.

Consolidated operating profit for 1980 was $253.8 million, a decline of $14.8 million or 5% from 1979. A substantial decline in Newsprint and Forest Products results caused by a depressed housing market was largely offset by strong 1980 performances by Newspaper Publishing, Book Publishing and Broadcast and Cable Television. In the Newspaper Publishing segment, retail and national advertising linage at each metropolitan newspaper exceeded records established in 1979. A 16% profit gain by Book Publishing reflected the strength of the Company's professional publishing subsidiaries and significantly improved results at New American Library. Broadcast and Cable Television profits advanced 46% due to the strong performance of KDFW-TV in Dallas, the inclusion of the additional television stations and substantial growth in cable television subscribers.

1980 consolidated pretax income declined more than operating profit because of the Company's higher interest costs. Pretax income of $229.7 million represented a $24.3 million decrease from 1979 as interest expense rose $9.6 million between years. Interest expense was reduced by $11.4 million (or 17 cents a share) due to capitalization, which was first required for 1980 results.

While pretax income declined 10%, 1980 consolidated net income was off only 5% from 1979 as a result of increased investment tax credits and capital gains benefits from the cutting of timber.

The following paragraphs discuss the revenues and operating profit of the Company's principal lines of business.

Newspaper Publishing

Revenues for 1981 reached $1.07 billion, exceeding 1980 by $191.2 million or 22%. A significant portion of the revenue increase resulted from the inclusion of The Denver Post, which was acquired in December 1980. Rate increases accounted for most of the remaining revenue growth. Advertising revenues rose 24% to $855.2 million and circulation revenues and other income climbed 15% to $210.3 million. Excluding The Denver Post, advertising revenues declined slightly on a volume basis despite a 2% gain in total linage. Linage in the suburban part-run and preprinted sections categories increased more than total full-run advertising, resulting in a moderately less profitable overall linage mix in 1981.

Operating profit was $169.9 million, an increase of $14.6 million or 9% above 1980. The profit gain was primarily attributable to rate increases. 1981 results also benefited from the addition of the operating profit of The Denver Post.

The group's 1981 operating profit margin was 15.9% compared with last year's 17.8%. A major reason for this reduction was the lower profit contribution of The Denver Post. A number of major steps implemented by The Post to cut costs, improve productivity, and increase market share should result in steadily improving profitability in the years ahead. Reduced classified advertising volume also affected the profit margins of several newspapers this year.

Partially offsetting these factors were effective cost control programs at several of the Company's newspapers. Also, the group benefited in 1981 from the return of a stable market for newsprint from 1980's shortages. The substantial premiums paid for newsprint obtained from distant sources last year were almost completely eliminated in 1981. This market stability is expected to continue during 1982.

Over the near term, the Company anticipates continued pressures on classified and other advertising categories as long as the overall economy remains weak. The Company's newspapers will diligently continue to monitor and control operating expenses to minimize the adverse effects on profits of the business downturn.

1980 revenues exceeded 1979 by 21%, and operating profit increased 16%. Rate increases and the inclusion of the results of The Hartford Courant for a full year versus only four months in 1979 primarily accounted for the year-to-year improvement.

The following table shows Newspaper Publishing revenues by category:

(In millions of dollars)	1981	1980	1979
Advertising	$ 855.2	$691.4	$579.1
Circulation and Other	210.3	182.9	145.2
	$1,065.5	$874.3	$724.3

Newsprint and Forest Products

Revenues for 1981 totaled $324.4 million, up 9% from 1980's $296.3 million.

Pulp and paper revenues advanced 34% due primarily to price increases and the additional production of a new paper machine in Newberg, Oregon, which began limited production in mid-November 1980.

Wood products revenues declined $27.9 million, or 21% from 1980's results. The protracted downturn in U.S. housing construction that depressed 1980's results was even more severe in 1981. New housing starts, a leading industry indicator, sank to a 35-year low of 1,085,000 for the year as mortgage interest rates rose to record levels. As a result, most of the Company's sawmill and plywood operations had been closed down by the fall of 1981. In January 1982, one of the lumber mills resumed limited operations, but it is not known how long it will continue operating or when the Company's other mills will resume operations.

Newsprint and Forest Products posted a $1.6 million operating loss in 1981, compared with a $7.5 million loss in 1980. The improvement was entirely attributable to pulp and paper operations. In addition to substantially increased sales, the profit margins of the Company's paper mills improved. The cost of wood chips used in newsprint manufacture fell substantially as a percentage of sales. In 1980, wood chip prices doubled during a period of sawmill curtailments. Also, the increases in energy costs in 1981 were not as great as the prior year, when average electrical rates rose 34%.

Profitability in the wood products sector, however, was materially impacted by the depressed market conditions. Substantial sales volume declines resulted in a significantly larger operating deficit this year.

The Company will enter labor negotiations with its paperworkers during the first half of 1982 upon the expiration of the current collective bargaining agreements. The current contracts with the Company's woodworkers expire in 1983.

In 1980, revenues of $296.3 million were 8% below 1979. Operating profit dipped from $43.7 million in 1979 to a deficit of $7.5 million in 1980. Wood products operations primarily contributed to the group's downturn due to the severe housing slump. Also, pulp and paper results suffered from substantial increases in the costs of wood chips and energy.

The following table summarizes Newsprint and Forest Products revenues by major category for the last three years:

(In millions of dollars)	1981	1980	1979
Pulp and Paper	$221.3	$165.3	$141.5
Wood Products	103.1	131.0	181.6
	$324.4	$296.3	$323.1

Book Publishing

The group's 1981 revenues were $289.8 million, a $26.2 million (10%) increase over 1980. Higher average prices in both the professional book and general book sectors primarily accounted for the group's revenue growth. On a volume basis, the group enjoyed substantial gains from new legal products introduced in the year and from increased subscriptions to legal reference services. Largely offsetting these volume gains was the absence of a full year's sales from New English Library, which was sold in May 1981.

Group operating profit increased $4.0 million to $44.6 million primarily due to increased professional publishing sales. The group's operating profit margin of 15.4% was unchanged from 1980 despite a substantial increase in inventory writeoffs due to the discontinuation of several medical book lines this year. 1981's profit margin did, however, benefit from the sale of New English Library, which provided a significantly lower profit carrythrough than the Company's other book publishers in 1980.

1980 Book Publishing revenues advanced 12% over 1979 and operating profit increased 16%. The group's improved performance was attributable to substantial revenue gains in legal publishing and the absence of 1979's large inventory adjustments. A major contribution was also made by the Company's paperback operations, which benefited from improved sales and cost cutting.

The following table summarizes Book Publishing revenues for the past three years:

(In millions of dollars)	1981	1980	1979
Professional Books	$166.3	$141.7	$123.8
General Books	123.5	121.9	110.9
	$289.8	$263.6	$234.7

Information Services

Group revenues for 1981 were $246.1 million, an $18.8 million (8%) gain over 1980. Price increases accounted for the predominate portion of the revenue growth. However, volume increases were recorded in several of the group's major product lines, including charts for recording medical and scientific information. Offsetting these volume gains was the loss of revenues from the Denoyer-Geppert Company, which was sold in February 1981.

Group operating profit was $31.4 million, up $7.4 million from 1980. The group's profit margin also improved from 10.5% in 1980 to 12.7% in 1981. The Company's directory printing subsidiary,

Times Mirror Press, was the major contributor to the group's improved profit performance. Directory printing operations were significantly more efficient this year following 1980's production problems related to paper quality and other factors. In addition, the settlement of claims against the Company's directory paper supplier added approximately $1 million in operating profit this year. Another major factor in the group's profit improvement was the absence of 1980's loss at the Denoyer-Geppert Company.

During the year, Times Mirror Press was unsuccessful in its attempt to renew production contracts which account for most of the firm's present volume. These contractual commitments expire at the end of 1983 and in 1984. The loss of this business will not materially affect Times Mirror's future earnings.

In 1980, group revenues totaling $227.3 million were 12% ahead of 1979, and operating profit of $24.0 million rose 3%. Profit gains from price increases were partially offset by production difficulties in directory printing, recession-related profit pressures in the recording charts and marking systems lines, and adverse foreign exchange translation adjustments.

The following table shows Information Services revenues for the past three years:

(In millions of dollars)	1981	1980	1979
Information Services	$246.1	$227.3	$203.7

Broadcast and Cable Television

1981 group revenues of $190.6 million advanced 36% over 1980. Broadcast television revenues rose 40% due to the substantial growth in the Company's major markets and a full year's results of the five stations acquired in March 1980. Cable television revenues climbed 34% on the strength of substantial gains in subscribers to basic and premium cable services. In those franchises in which the Company held at least 50% of the ownership interest, subscribers to the basic cable service grew to 641,000 at year end, while subscriptions to premium or pay-TV services rose to 343,000.

Group operating profit of $64.2 million was a 36% increase over 1980. Sales gains and cost control at the Company's television stations, primarily KDFW-TV in Dallas, Texas, accounted for the major share of the group's profit improvement.

Cable television operating profit also increased between years largely due to a capital gain on the exchange of the Company's interest in one franchise for another. The operating profit margin in cable television declined, however, primarily as a result of higher franchising costs and the Company's increasing participation in premium services, including the start-up of the Company's pay-TV service, Spotlight. In 1982, the Company anticipates a continuation of the dramatic subscriber and revenue gains of recent years. Additional premium services costs and cable system development expenses should, however, cause further short-term profit margin deterioration.

In 1980, group revenues exceeded 1979 by 62% and operating profit advanced 46%. The inclusion of five newly-acquired broadcasting properties and substantial growth at KDFW-TV were primarily responsible for this major improvement in operating results. Profit growth lagged revenue gains due to the ongoing cable television expansion and the lower margins of the new television stations.

The table below summarizes Broadcast and Cable Television revenues:

(In millions of dollars)	1981	1980	1979
Broadcast Television	$ 87.0	$ 62.3	$27.1
Cable Television	103.6	77.6	59.1
	$190.6	$139.9	$86.2

Other Operations

Revenues for the Company's Art and Graphic Products and Magazine Publishing companies increased $6.2 million, or 3% during 1981. Price increases accounted for most of the revenue gain. Adverse economic conditions resulted in reduced volume in the group's magazine advertising and art materials product lines. In addition, book club unit sales were substantially lower principally due to the loss of sales from two discontinued book clubs.

Operating profit advanced 24% to $16.5 million. The major contributor to the group's strong profit gain was Times Mirror Magazines, which substantially improved its profitability due to increased subscription revenues and reduced production and distribution expenses.

In 1980, revenues advanced 5% and operating profit 3% over 1979. The Company's art materials subsidiary turned in a major improvement over 1979, which offset decreased magazine publishing profits and the costs of trimming certain product lines in Art and Graphic Products.

Revenues of the Company's Other Operations were as follows:

(In millions of dollars)	1981	1980	1979
Art and Graphic Products	$ 73.1	$ 65.1	$ 61.0
Magazine Publishing	112.3	114.1	108.9
	$185.4	$179.2	$169.9

Corporate and Investments

Corporate revenues of $7.5 million more than doubled 1980's $3.6 million. The major factor underlying this variance was a $3.8 million gain before taxes on the repurchase of $12.6 million of the Company's 5% debentures during the year. The $2.0 million gain on the sale of the Denoyer-Geppert Company and an offsetting loss on the sale of New English Library were included in Corporate's 1981 results.

The Corporate deficit of $19.6 million was slightly higher than 1980's $19.2 million loss. Higher administrative expenses and the costs associated with the Company's videotex experiment essentially offset the gain on the sale of debentures. As a percentage of consolidated revenues, corporate operating costs were 1.3%, which was little changed from the past several years.

Capital Investment

Times Mirror's substantial program of capital investment in recent years has been undertaken in conjunction with the Company's strategic plan to expand its media presence and to enhance the potential for future earnings. Over the past few years, the pace of investment has quickened as a number of major opportunities have arisen for growth by acquisition and internal capital expansion. In Newspaper Publishing, The Hartford Courant and The Denver Post were acquired to strengthen the Company's base of metropolitan newspapers. The purchase of Communications Properties, Inc. has placed Times Mirror as the country's seventh largest cable television operation, and the acquisition of five television stations in March 1980 has established the Company as a significant operator of broadcasting properties.

In 1978 and 1979, Times Mirror began three major programs of internal capital spending. The largest of these is the three-phase expansion and modernization of the Los Angeles Times' production facilities at a total estimated cost of $215 million, excluding capitalized interest. The first phase, the expansion of The Times' Orange County plant, was completed in 1981 at the budgeted cost of $56.8 million. The second phase involves the construction of a second satellite plant in the San Fernando Valley. As of year-end 1981, land had been purchased, certain equipment, including several new offset presses, had been ordered, and site construction had begun. The completion of this satellite plant is expected in 1984. The third phase, the modernization of the downtown Los Angeles pressroom, is well underway, and is planned for completion in 1983. Through December 31, 1981, $81.8 million, exclusive of capitalized interest, had been expended on all phases of The Times' press expansion and improvement program.

The second major capital program relates to the expansion and modernization of the Company's newsprint and wood products production facilities. The expansion of the Newberg, Oregon, newsprint plant was completed in 1980 within its $127 million budget.

The Company's third major area of expansion during the last three years has been in cable television. Following the January 1979 purchase of Communications Properties, Inc., the Company's basic cable operations have been substantially expanded through plant extension in currently held franchises and the acquisition of interests in other cable operations. In addition, the Company has become active in premium cable services, and has begun to investigate new services and technologies.

Over the past three years, the Company's cable television capital expenditures have totaled $124.5 million. In addition, the Company has invested $24.7 million in partially owned franchises. In 1982, cable television capital spending should reach a new high, and the Company's investments in cable affiliates should also increase. Actual purchase commitments at December 31, 1981, amounted to $27 million.

On a consolidated basis, Times Mirror plans to spend more than $250 million on capital projects during 1982. Expenditures for cable television and The Times' expansion project are the major components of the Company's 1982 projection. Actual capital commitments as of December 31, 1981 amounted to approximately $120 million. The Company has the flexibility to delay or cancel much of the planned capital spending should business or economic conditions warrant.

Liquidity and Capital Resources

In undertaking a considerably expanded program of internal capital expansion and acquisitions during the three years 1979 – 1981, Times Mirror has utilized its substantial funds flow from operations and has also judiciously utilized leverage to meet its growing requirements for capital.

The cornerstone of Times Mirror's cash generation capability is the strength of its operations. The dependability of the Company's cash flow has been demonstrated by historical performance. Over the past five years, the Company has generated more than $1 billion in funds from operations. Funds provided in 1981 alone were $266 million. The Company has been able to maintain cash flow growth even in periods of economic downturn. In 1981, the Company generated 14% more funds from operations than in 1980, almost double the amount recorded four years earlier, despite the recession and record high interest rates. Furthermore, one of the objectives of the Company's acquisition strategy is to further enhance the stability of the Company's earnings.

The Company's cash flow is augmented by tax benefits arising from certain inherent characteristics of its business. The cutting of timber is accorded capital gains tax treatment. Accelerated depreciation for tax purposes provides further near-term cash benefits from the Company's current internal capital expansion programs. This factor will become substantially more favorable to the Company in 1982 and beyond due to the new depreciation provisions of the Economic Recovery Tax Act of 1981. In addition, the use of the LIFO (last-in, first-out) method of costing major categories of the Company's inventory matches the current costs of labor and materials against current sales, thus reducing income taxes during periods of inflation and stable or expanding inventories.

In the past few years, the Company's capital needs have exceeded its cash flow from operations. As a result, Times Mirror has drawn upon its considerable borrowing capacity through a number of financing moves designed to maintain a balanced capital structure. Beginning in 1979, the Company initiated a commercial paper issuance program to complement its internal funds flow. By year-end 1979, total debt increased to $230.6 million, including $100 million funded at a fixed rate of 9⅝% for seven years and $47.0 million assumed in the acquisition of Communications Properties, Inc. During 1980, total debt increased $231.7 million, including $100 million of five-year notes at 10¼%, and at year end amounted to $462.3 million, or 36.0% of adjusted capitalization. At December 31, 1981, total debt was $502.8 million, or 35.5% of adjusted capitalization. Commercial paper and short-term bank debt amounted to $168.2 million.

The Company's strategic plans for the next few years indicate that capital requirements could continue to outpace internal cash flow. To meet any temporary cash deficiencies in the future, the Company will continue to exercise its substantial liquidity while maintaining a high degree of financial flexibility. The Company's commercial paper borrowings, which are given the highest credit ratings available by Moody's Investors Service and Standard & Poor's Corporation, two of the leading rating agencies, are backed by revolving credit agreements with commercial banks. These borrowing arrangements could be expanded significantly at Times Mirror's option. The Company's bonds are also highly rated (AA by Moody's and AA- by Standard & Poor's).

The Company also has utilized other means of leverage to help finance growth. For instance, in the acquisition of The Denver Post, seller financing was a major component of the total financing package. Also, by acquiring less than majority interests in cable television franchises, the Company can expand into large growing markets while limiting its cash commitments to just its invested capital. At December 31, 1981, the Company's 50% or less owned cable television franchises reported total indebtedness to non-related parties of $32.1 million. The Company anticipates that these operations, which are not consolidated with Times Mirror's majority-owned subsidiaries, will require substantially more financing to fund future growth. It is expected, however, that most of this financing will be provided by outside lenders.

The Company continuously monitors investment plans to anticipate their impact on corporate liquidity. Times Mirror's capital base is structured to assure adequate funding to meet near and medium-term spending needs, and the Company's capital structure can easily accommodate additional longer-term debt if necessary. The Company expects that any increased level of indebtedness will be in keeping with a stable and secure capital structure. Furthermore, the Company intends to maintain as much flexibility as practical and prudent in timing its future capital outlays.

Inflation's Impact

To lessen the impact of rising costs, Times Mirror has pursued a strategy of improving productivity, controlling costs, and increasing selling prices where competitive conditions permit. The Company's intensive capital expansion program will provide the benefits of innovative and cost efficient new technologies in replacing obsolete plant and equipment. Management has also pursued acquisitions in specific industries which it feels are least affected by inflationary costs, such as television broadcasting and cable television. In addition, it has approved acquisitions of newspaper properties, which, when combined with the Company's inherent management skills in that industry and new cost saving technologies, will serve as a buffer against inflation.

Over the past five years, Times Mirror's earnings per share have increased an average 17% per year and dividends to shareholders have increased 24% per year, while inflation has averaged about 10% per annum over the same period. Market prices of the Company's stock have also increased at a faster pace than general inflation.

Inflation-Adjusted Data

Note Q of this year's consolidated financial statements restates certain historical data into 1981 constant dollars through the use of the Consumer Price Index for all Urban Consumers (CPI-U). Whereas the primary financial statements of the Company combine dollars spent at various times in the past, the constant dollar approach attempts to make all dollars comparable. This essentially equates the purchasing power of a dollar spent in prior years to what the dollar would purchase in 1981.

This disclosure is designed to quantify the effects of inflation on the Company's financial results using methods prescribed by the Financial Accounting Standards Board. This information as set forth is experimental in nature and uses subjective assumptions in the measurement of the effects of inflation. The reader is therefore cautioned to use these data only as a broad indicator and not as a specific statement of the impact of inflation on the Company.

The first table in Note Q compares Times Mirror's operating results in historical dollars with results restated in constant dollars. The restated net income is $41 million (27%) below the net income reported in the Company's primary financial statements.

This decline results principally from the restatement of depreciable assets and their corresponding depreciation to current year dollars. Applying constant dollar indexing, restated depreciation, amortization and depletion expense is $32 million higher than reported on an historical cost basis. This approach logically assumes that the Company could not replace all existing plant and equipment at the cost values at which they are carried in the historical financial statements. It also, however, unrealistically assumes that all plant and equipment will be replaced simultaneously. In addition, constant dollar indexation ignores the self-replenishing nature of timberlands and assumes that the Company's timberlands will be replaced primarily by outside purchases. In reality, the Company acquires timberland acreage to augment rather than replace the existing timberlands base.

Another factor underlying the decline in 1981 earnings on a constant dollar basis is the restatement of inventories and the corresponding cost of sales. In 1981, the Company's cost of sales is estimated to be $9 million greater after adjusting for inflation. The Company reduces the effects of this adjustment by using the LIFO (last-in, first-out) method of costing major inventory categories.

The second table in Note Q shows that in constant dollars, 1981 net income dropped 3% from 1980. This analysis is designed to portray the year-to-year disparity between inflation, as measured by the CPI-U, and the change in a company's earnings. In Times Mirror's case, 1981's earnings fell below the prior year's on a constant dollar basis primarily because the Company's gain in reported net income trailed the increase in the CPI-U. This decline, however, primarily was the result of adverse economic conditions, principally the severe housing slump, rather than an inability to keep pace with inflationary cost increases.

It should be noted that inflation also affects the Company's assets and liabilities. Since the Company maintained more monetary liabilities, principally long-term debt, than monetary assets, a purchasing power gain resulted in 1981. That purchasing power gain is excluded from the restatement of net income on a constant dollar basis because it will be realized only over time as the liabilities are paid with dollars of decreased purchasing power.

Consolidated Balance Sheets

(In thousands of dollars)

Assets

December 31	1981	1980
Current Assets		
Cash	$ 25,165	$ 25,733
Marketable securities	8,519	3,944
Accounts receivable, less allowances for doubtful accounts and returns (1981—$40,178, 1980—$36,426)	309,684	285,240
Inventories	164,628	153,099
Prepaid expenses	47,555	45,994
Total Current Assets	555,551	514,010
Timberlands, less depletion	115,998	103,583
Property, Plant and Equipment		
Buildings	204,068	194,165
Machinery and equipment	865,005	699,281
	1,069,073	893,446
Less allowances for depreciation and amortization	324,204	267,790
	744,869	625,656
Land	51,629	51,004
	796,498	676,660
Other Assets		
Goodwill	353,682	356,835
Deferred charges	35,191	38,173
Other assets	60,292	45,527
	449,165	440,535
	$1,917,212	$1,734,788

See notes to consolidated financial statements

Consolidated Balance Sheets

Liabilities and Shareholders' Equity		The Times Mirror Company and Subsidiaries	
December 31		1981	1980
Current Liabilities			
Accounts payable		$ 199,343	$ 189,208
Employees' compensation		55,388	51,092
Income taxes		20,518	22,060
Other taxes		11,869	11,240
Dividends payable		17,071	14,663
Current portion of long-term debt and notes payable		24,517	15,296
Total Current Liabilities		328,706	303,559
Long-Term Debt		478,273	447,029
Other Liabilities and Deferrals			
Unearned income		52,038	50,303
Deferred income taxes		85,316	59,954
Other liabilities		57,676	51,208
		195,030	161,465
Shareholders' Equity			
Common stock		32,908	32,868
Additional paid-in capital		43,672	40,465
Retained earnings		838,623	749,402
		915,203	822,735
Contingent Liabilities and Commitments			
		$1,917,212	$1,734,788

Statements of Consolidated Income

(In thousands of dollars except per share amounts)

The Times Mirror Company and Subsidiaries

Year Ended December 31	1981	1980	1979
Revenues			
Operating revenues	$2,130,756	$1,857,349	$1,638,535
Other income	25,214	11,514	8,941
	2,155,970	1,868,863	1,647,476
Costs and expenses			
Cost of sales	1,296,536	1,158,972	1,005,096
Selling, administrative and general expenses	554,041	456,065	373,803
Interest expense	48,582	24,097	14,528
	1,899,159	1,639,134	1,393,427
Income before income taxes	256,811	229,729	254,049
Income taxes	106,480	90,512	107,556
Net income	$ 150,331	$ 139,217	$ 146,493
Earnings per share	$4.40	$4.08	$4.31

See notes to consolidated financial statements

[*208*]

Statements of Shareholders' Equity

(In thousands of dollars except for number of shares)

The Times Mirror Company and Subsidiaries

Three Years Ended December 31, 1981	Common Stock		Additional Paid-In Capital	Retained Earnings
	Shares	Amount		
Balance at January 1, 1979	33,885,241	$32,661	$34,848	$558,136
Transactions related to executive stock option and restricted stock plans	56,775	55	2,558	
Dividends on Common Stock				(42,922)
Net income				146,493
Balance at December 31, 1979	33,942,016	32,716	37,406	661,707
Transactions related to executive stock option and restricted stock plans	158,900	152	3,059	
Dividends on Common Stock				(51,522)
Net income				139,217
Balance at December 31, 1980	34,100,916	32,868	40,465	749,402
Transactions related to executive stock option and restricted stock plans	41,385	40	3,207	
Dividends on Common Stock				(61,110)
Net income				150,331
Balance at December 31, 1981	34,142,301	$32,908	$43,672	$838,623

See notes to consolidated financial statements

Statements of Consolidated Changes in Financial Position

(In thousands of dollars)

The Times Mirror Company and Subsidiaries

Year Ended December 31	1981	1980	1979
Source of Funds			
From Operations:			
Net income	$150,331	$139,217	$146,493
Add items not requiring outlay of funds:			
Depreciation, amortization and depletion	90,306	74,751	55,524
Noncurrent deferred income taxes	25,362	19,366	8,002
Total from operations	265,999	233,334	210,019
Increase in long-term debt	51,860	242,034	143,840
Increase in other liabilities and deferrals	8,203	11,521	15,230
Net book value of property, plant and equipment sold	3,749	2,683	6,773
Total source of funds	329,811	489,572	375,862
Application of Funds			
Net noncurrent assets of businesses purchased:			
Property, plant and equipment		30,653	70,573
Goodwill		129,876	164,202
Other—net		1,859	6,134
Long-term debt			(44,110)
		162,388	196,799
Purchases of property, plant and equipment	188,696	195,815	177,158
Additions to timberlands	27,182	15,531	20,482
Decrease in long-term debt	21,940	9,519	7,094
Dividends	61,110	51,522	42,922
Other—net	14,489	12,209	11,348
Total application of funds	313,417	446,984	455,803
Increase (Decrease) in Working Capital	$ 16,394	$ 42,588	$ (79,941)

Statements of Consolidated Changes in Financial Position

(In thousands of dollars)

The Times Mirror Company and Subsidiaries

Year Ended December 31	1981	1980	1979
Change in Working Capital			
Increase (decrease) in current assets:			
Cash and marketable securities	$ 4,007	$ 2,522	$ (76,164)
Accounts receivable	24,444	39,455	20,621
Inventories	11,529	19,814	2,321
Prepaid expenses	1,561	8,664	10,026
	41,541	70,455	(43,196)
(Increase) decrease in current liabilities:			
Accounts payable	(10,135)	(18,327)	(29,944)
Employees' compensation	(4,296)	(7,867)	(6,487)
Income taxes	1,542	1,284	16,968
Other taxes	(629)	(1,291)	(2,226)
Dividends payable	(2,408)	(2,444)	(2,053)
Current portion of long-term debt and notes payable	(9,221)	778	(13,003)
	(25,147)	(27,867)	(36,745)
Increase (Decrease) in Working Capital	$ 16,394	$ 42,588	$ (79,941)

See notes to consolidated financial statements

Notes to Consolidated Financial Statements

Note A

Summary of Significant Accounting Policies

Principles of Consolidation

The consolidated financial statements include the accounts of the Company and its subsidiaries.

Marketable Securities

Marketable securities are carried at cost which approximates market at the respective balance sheet dates.

Inventories

Inventories are carried at the lower of cost or market and are determined under the first-in, first-out method for books and certain finished products, and under the last-in, first-out method for newsprint, paper, lumber, logs and certain other inventories (see Note D).

Timberlands

Contracts for timber harvesting rights are recorded when the gross prices to be paid are fixed (see Note E). Depletion of timberlands is provided on the unit-of-production method based upon estimated recoverable timber.

Property, Plant and Equipment

Property, plant and equipment are carried on the basis of cost. Generally, depreciation is provided on the straight-line method for buildings, machinery and equipment.

Goodwill

Goodwill recognized in business combinations accounted for as purchases subsequent to October 31, 1970 ($334,356,000 at December 31, 1981 and $337,182,000 at December 31, 1980 — net of amortization of $23,148,000 and $14,236,000, respectively) is being amortized over a period of 40 years. Goodwill arising from business combinations consummated prior to November 1, 1970 is not being amortized because, in the opinion of management, it has not diminished in value.

Investment Tax Credit

The investment tax credit is recognized on the flow-through method as a reduction of the provision for Federal income taxes.

Book and Magazine Revenue

Book sales, less provisions for estimated returns, are recorded at the time of shipment. Magazine subscription sales are deferred as unearned income at the time of sale. As magazines are delivered to subscribers, the proportionate share of the subscription price is taken into revenue. Subscription selling expenses are deferred and charged to expense over the same period as the related subscription income is earned.

Employee Retirement Plans

The Company has various contributory and non-contributory retirement plans covering substantially all employees. The costs charged to earnings relative to such plans include current service costs and the amortization of past service costs over periods ranging from ten to thirty-five years. It is the Company's policy to fund all pension costs accrued (see Note K).

Note B
Business Combinations

On December 31, 1980, the Company purchased the assets of The Denver Post, Inc., a newspaper publishing company located in Denver, Colorado, for approximately $95,000,000. The transaction involved an initial cash payment of $25,000,000, and the issuance of notes in the amount of $70,000,000 (see Note G). Also in 1980, the Company completed the acquisition of five television stations from the Newhouse Broadcasting Corporation, for approximately $83,000,000 in cash. Operations of the purchased companies have been included since the dates of acquisition.

Note C
Interest Expense

For the years ended December 31, 1981 and December 31, 1980, interest cost of $55,302,000 and $35,538,000 was incurred; $6,720,000 and $11,441,000 of which was capitalized.

Note D
Inventories

Inventories consist of the following:

(In thousands of dollars)	1981	1980	1979
Newsprint and paper	$ 46,342	$ 29,521	$ 20,574
Books and other finished products	53,754	60,965	53,250
Lumber, veneer and plywood	2,489	4,215	5,290
Work-in-process	19,469	15,563	15,554
Raw materials and logs	42,574	42,835	38,617
	$164,628	$153,099	$133,285

The total inventories would have been higher by $28,309,000 in 1981, $17,412,000 in 1980 and $12,674,000 in 1979 had the first-in, first-out method (which approximates current cost) been used exclusively.

Note E
Timberlands

Timberlands, less depletion, consist of the following:

(In thousands of dollars)	1981	1980
Owned	$ 82,097	$ 76,497
Capitalized timber harvesting rights	33,901	27,086
	$115,998	$103,583

Note F

Income Taxes

The Company reports certain income and expense items in different years for financial and tax reporting purposes. Deferred income taxes have been provided with respect to such items which relate principally to accelerated depreciation, magazine subscription expenses, deferred compensation and book returns.

Income tax expense consists of the following:

(In thousands of dollars)	1981	1980	1979
Current			
Federal	$ 60,386	$48,639	$ 83,566
State	14,048	15,833	18,146
Foreign	5,596	5,183	4,863
Deferred			
Federal	22,793	17,978	2,821
State	3,657	2,879	(1,840)
	$106,480	$90,512	$107,556

Income tax expense is different from the amount computed by applying the Federal statutory rate to income before income taxes. Such difference is reconciled as follows:

(In thousands of dollars)	1981	1980	1979
46% of pretax income	$118,133	$105,675	$116,863
State and local income taxes, net of Federal effect	9,561	10,104	8,805
Effect from income taxed at capital gains rates principally related to the cutting of timber	(8,938)	(11,364)	(7,449)
Investment tax credit	(16,400)	(17,196)	(12,714)
Other	4,124	3,293	2,051
	$106,480	$90,512	$107,556

Deferred income tax expense resulted from the following:

(In thousands of dollars)	1981	1980	1979
Accelerated depreciation	$16,945	$14,543	$6,869
Other	9,505	6,314	(5,888)
	$26,450	$20,857	$ 981

Note G
Long-Term Debt

Long-term debt consists of the following:

(In thousands of dollars)	1981	1980
Commercial paper effectively due in 1983 with average interest rates at December 31, 1981 and 1980 of 12.36% and 19.34%	$153,229	$107,225
10¼% Notes due May 15, 1985	100,000	100,000
9⅜% Notes due September 15, 1986, net of unamortized discount	99,832	99,796
10% Notes due December 30, 1990	55,000	55,000
5% Sinking Fund Debentures due January 1, 1990	6,091	18,668
Other, maturing through 2028 with interest from 5¼% to 21⅛%	64,121	66,340
	$478,273	$447,029

The Company maintains revolving credit agreements with several domestic banks to serve as backup for commercial paper the Company has issued. The agreements, which expire March 31, 1983, allow the Company to borrow up to $155,000,000. Interest on borrowings would be computed at 110% of the prime rate. A commitment fee of ⅜ of 1 per cent per annum is payable on the average unused portion of the commitment. As of December 31, 1981, the Company had not borrowed under the agreements.

Notes with an aggregate principal amount of $100,000,000 bear interest at 10¼% per annum payable each May 15 and November 15. On or after May 15, 1983, the Notes will be subject to redemption at the option of the Company at a price equal to 100% of the principal amount together with accrued and unpaid interest to the date fixed for redemption.

The 9⅜% Notes issued in September 1979 for an aggregate amount of $100,000,000 (less discount) require interest payments each March 15 and September 15. On or after September 15, 1983, the Notes will be subject to redemption at the option of the Company for a redemption price equal to 100% of the principal amount together with accrued and unpaid interest to the date fixed for redemption.

In connection with the purchase of the assets of the Denver Post, Inc., the Company issued notes with an aggregate principal of $70,000,000. Of this amount, $55,000,000 is due in December 1990 and bears interest at the rate of 10% per annum payable each January 15 and July 15. The remaining $15,000,000 is represented by noninterest bearing installment notes with principal payments due each December from 1991 through 2000. The installment notes have been discounted at an effective interest rate of 10% per annum.

The 5% Sinking Fund Debentures, which are redeemable at the option of the Company, require payments of $2,100,000 each year through 1989. As of December 31, 1981, the Company held $16,734,000 of debentures purchased on the open market, an amount sufficient to meet sinking fund requirements through 1988. In 1981, the Company purchased $12,577,000 of the debentures, resulting in a gain of approximately $3,800,000 which is included in other income.

The aggregate maturities of the Company's long-term debt for the five years subsequent to December 31, 1981 are as follows:

(In thousands of dollars)

1982	$ 9,517
1983	161,775
1984	13,658
1985	106,738
1986	105,839

Note H
Capital Stock

The Company's authorized capital stock consists of 40,000,000 shares of Common Stock without par value and 4,500,000 shares of Convertible Preferred Stock without par value. The Convertible Preferred Stock is issuable in series under such terms and conditions as the Board of Directors may determine.

Note I
Stock Options

The Executive Stock Option Plans provide that options may be granted to key executive employees to purchase shares of the Company's Common Stock at a price at least equal to 75% of the fair market value at the date of grant. According to the plans, the options have a five-year term of existence and are exercisable either one or two years from the date of grant. At such time the options are exercisable in whole or in increments during the remaining term.

The following tabulation sets forth information relative to the plans:

	Number of Shares	Option Price Per Share
Options Outstanding		
January 1, 1979	142,725	$10.87 to $25.79
Changes during 1979:		
Exercised	53,025	10.87 to 17.58
Cancelled	1,700	
Options Outstanding		
December 31, 1979	88,000	13.87 to 25.79
Changes during 1980:		
Granted	96,650	27.29
Exercised	41,775	13.87 to 25.79
Cancelled	5,200	
Options Outstanding		
December 31, 1980	137,675	17.58 to 27.29
Changes during 1981:		
Granted	2,000	30.80 to 38.66
Exercised	36,235	17.58 to 27.29
Cancelled	6,050	
Options Outstanding		
December 31, 1981*	97,390	17.58 to 38.66

*Includes 80,190 options exercisable at December 31, 1981.

At December 31, 1981 there were 166,000 shares reserved for future grants under executive stock option plans.

For options granted, any difference between the market price and the option price is charged to operations over the period from the date of grant to the date the option becomes exercisable. At the time options are exercised, the stated value per share is credited to Common Stock and the excess of the proceeds over the stated value is credited to Additional Paid-In Capital. Under the plans, operations were charged $201,000 in 1981, $578,000 in 1980 and $40,000 in 1979.

Note J
Restricted Stock Plans

The 1971 and 1976 Restricted Stock Plans provide for the sale of a maximum of 530,000 shares of the Company's Common Stock to key employees, including officers. Under the plans, the restrictions are for a period of five years and are removed annually in cumulative 25% increments commencing after the second anniversary of the sale. The stock sold to the employee may not be sold or encumbered until the restrictions are terminated.

Under the plans, the Company sold (net of repurchases) 5,150 shares in 1981, 117,125 shares in 1980 and 3,750 shares in 1979 for an aggregate amount of $5,269, $117,315, and $3,750, respectively. At December 31, 1981, there were 48,400 shares reserved for future sales.

The difference between the sales price and the fair market value of the stock is charged to operations over the period during which the restrictions are in effect. The charge to operations was $1,449,000 in 1981, $1,355,000 in 1980 and $874,000 in 1979.

Note K
Employee Retirement Plans

Employee retirement plan expenses amounted to $31,630,000 for 1981, $31,652,000 for 1980 and $24,769,000 for 1979. The actuarially computed value of plan assets at the most recent valuation date (January 1, 1981) was $333,057,000. At the same date the actuarial value of the vested benefits was $196,834,000 and for nonvested benefits was $10,794,000. The assumed rate of return used in determining the actuarial value of plan benefits was 7%.

Note L
Leases

The rental expense under operating leases amounted to $25,861,000, $20,941,000 and $17,675,000 for the years ended December 31, 1981, 1980 and 1979 respectively. Capital leases and contingent rentals are not significant. The future minimum lease payments as of December 31, 1981, for all noncancelable operating leases are as follows:

(In thousands of dollars)

1982	$ 19,954
1983	19,387
1984	18,558
1985	18,475
1986	9,407
Later years	16,205
Total	$101,986

Note M

Litigation

In August 1977 the Federal Trade Commission issued a complaint alleging that the retail display advertising rates of the *Los Angeles Times* discriminate in favor of high volume advertising in violation of Section 5 of the Federal Trade Commission Act (which prohibits unfair trade practices) and Section 2(a) of the Robinson-Patman Act (which prohibits price discrimination between the purchasers of commodities). Times Mirror answered by denying the allegations of the complaint and asserting several alternative defenses. In November 1980 tentative settlement of this proceeding was announced and the matter was withdrawn from adjudication. Thereafter, in view of changed circumstances, Times Mirror decided to press for dismissal of the complaint. In September 1981 the Commission announced tentative approval of the settlement, subject to a 60-day public comment period and further Commission consideration. The period for public comment closed on December 13, 1981. Times Mirror will continue to press for the dismissal of the complaint on the ground that this proceeding is not in the public interest. The Company believes that the ultimate disposition of this matter will not have a material effect on the financial position of the Company.

Note N

Earnings and Dividends per Share

Earnings per share computations are based upon the weighted average number of shares of Common Stock and Common Stock equivalents outstanding during the year. Fully diluted earnings per share are the same as the earnings per share indicated.

Cash dividends declared per share of Common Stock amounted to $1.79 in 1981, $1.51 in 1980 and $1.26 in 1979.

Note O

Business Segments

Financial data regarding the Company's business segments presented in the supplementary financial information section (page 36 of this report) are incorporated herein by reference.

The Company operates principally in five industries: Newspaper Publishing, Newsprint and Forest Products, Book Publishing, Information Services and Broadcast and Cable Television. Operations in Newspaper Publishing include the production and sale of five metropolitan newspapers. Operations in Newsprint and Forest Products include timber growing and the manufacture and sale of newsprint, pulp, logs, lumber, plywood, hardboard and particleboard. Operations in Book Publishing include the publishing and sale of various types of books, including law and medical books. Operations in Information Services include the publishing of aeronautical charts, flight information and road maps, the manufacturing of recording charts and marking systems, and the printing of directories and other publications. Operations in Broadcast and Cable Television include seven network affiliated broadcast television stations and basic and premium cable television services. Other Operations include magazine publishing and art and graphic products. Total revenue by industry includes sales to unaffiliated customers and intersegment sales which are accounted for at market price.

The Company's foreign operations are not significant.

Note P

Quarterly Results of Operations (Unaudited)

In 1981, the Company changed from thirteen to twelve reporting periods. As a result, operations for the first, third and fourth quarters of 1981 include five, seven and eight more days, respectively, than the corresponding quarters of 1980. Second quarter operations in 1981 include twenty-one fewer days than the second quarter of 1980.

A summary of the unaudited quarterly results of operations follows (in thousands of dollars except for per share amounts):

1981 Quarters Ended	March 29	June 28	Sept. 27	Dec. 31
Revenues				
Operating revenues	$494,816	$535,804	$535,122	$565,014
Other income	5,877	3,660	4,432	11,245
	500,693	539,464	539,554	576,259
Costs and expenses				
Cost of sales	306,932	323,928	326,701	338,975
Selling, administrative and general expenses	136,235	135,750	138,929	143,127
Interest expense	11,633	11,957	12,212	12,780
	454,800	471,635	477,842	494,882
Income before income taxes	45,893	67,829	61,712	81,377
Income taxes	19,908	29,334	25,861	31,377
Net income	$ 25,985	$ 38,495	$ 35,851	$ 50,000
Earnings per share	$ .76	$ 1.13	$ 1.05	$ 1.46

1980 Quarters Ended	March 23	July 13	Oct. 5	Dec. 31
Revenues				
Operating revenues	$401,490	$513,357	$450,646	$491,856
Other income	1,792	4,421	2,212	3,089
	403,282	517,778	452,858	494,945
Costs and expenses				
Cost of sales	256,421	324,972	276,419	301,160
Selling, administrative and general expenses	100,884	126,206	110,831	118,144
Interest expense	3,332	7,814	5,616	7,335
	360,637	458,992	392,866	426,639
Income before income taxes	42,645	58,786	59,992	68,306
Income taxes	18,295	22,987	23,287	25,943
Net income	$ 24,350	$ 35,799	$ 36,705	$ 42,363
Earnings per share	$ .71	$ 1.05	$ 1.08	$ 1.24

Note Q

Supplementary Data on Changing Prices (Unaudited)

The following financial data have been prepared in conformity with requirements prescribed by the Financial Accounting Standards Board's Statement No. 33 "Financial Reporting and Changing Prices." Management's comments relative to the impact of changing prices (inflation) on the Company are included in Management's Discussion and Analysis of the Company's Financial Condition and Results of Operations. Statement No. 33 calls for two supplementary computations: one dealing with the effects of general inflation (purchasing power) and the second dealing with changes in specific prices (current cost) on certain assets described in the succeeding paragraph. The computations inherently involve the use of assumptions, approximations, and estimates; therefore, the resulting measurements should be viewed in that context and not as precise indicators of the effects of inflation.

Inventories, cost of sales, net timberlands and property, plant and equipment, and depreciation, amortization and depletion have been adjusted for general inflation as measured by the Consumer Price Index for All Urban Consumers. Revenues and other expenses have not been restated as they are considered to have occurred proportionately throughout the year, and already reflect average 1981 dollars. Supplementary computations reflecting changes in specific prices (current cost) did not differ materially from those for general inflation. Therefore, the following summary reflects only one set of inflation adjusted amounts.

Statement of Consolidated Income
Adjusted for Changing Prices

For the Year Ended December 31, 1981

(In millions of dollars except per share amounts)	As Reported in the Primary Financial Statements	Adjusted for General Inflation
Net sales and other revenues	$2,156	$2,156
Cost of sales (exclusive of depreciation, amortization and depletion)	1,223	1,232
Depreciation, amortization and depletion	90	122
Other expenses	586	586
	1,899	1,940
Income before income taxes	257	216
Income taxes	107	107
Net income	$ 150	$ 109
Earnings per share	$ 4.40	$ 3.19

Depreciation, amortization and depletion were computed using the same methods as reflected in the historical cost financial statements. Although the adjustments for depreciation, amortization and depletion and cost of sales affect income before income taxes, no adjustments have been made to the provision for income taxes in accordance with requirements of Statement No. 33.

A gain or loss in purchasing power of net monetary items results from holding monetary items such as cash or claims to cash which are fixed in terms of numbers of dollars. In 1981 the Company increased its net monetary liabilities by $55 million. Thus, during this period of declining purchasing power of the dollar, the Company experienced a gain in purchasing power of $48 million.

Five-Year Summary of Selected Data
Adjusted for Effects of Changing Prices

(In millions of dollars except per share amounts)

Year Ended December 31	1981	1980	1979	1978	1977
Net sales and other revenues					
As reported	$2,156	$1,869	$1,647	$1,428	$1,144
In average 1981 dollars	$2,156	$2,063	$2,064	$1,991	$1,717
Historical cost information adjusted for general inflation and stated in average 1981 dollars*					
Net income	$ 109	$ 112	$ 148		
Net income per share	$3.19	$3.28	$4.36		
Net assets at year end	$1,223	$1,176	$1,141		
Purchasing Power Gain	$ 48	$ 48	$ 26		
Cash dividends declared per common share					
As reported	$1.79	$1.51	$1.26	$1.05	$ .85
In average 1981 dollars	$1.79	$1.67	$1.58	$1.46	$1.28
Market price per common share at year-end					
Unadjusted	$45.75	$41.50	$36.50	$29.75	$25.50
In average 1981 dollars	$44.13	$43.66	$43.25	$39.94	$37.33
Average Consumer Price Index**	272.4•••	246.8	217.4	195.4	181.5

*Current cost amounts are not shown for 1981, 1980, or 1979 as they do not differ materially from amounts adjusted for general inflation.

**(1967=100)

•••Estimated

Report of Independent Accountants

To the Shareholders and Board of Directors
The Times Mirror Company
Los Angeles, California

We have examined the consolidated balance sheets of The Times Mirror Company and subsidiaries as of December 31, 1981 and 1980, and the related statements of consolidated income, shareholders' equity, and changes in financial position for each of the three years in the period ended December 31, 1981. Our examinations were made in accordance with generally accepted auditing standards and, accordingly, included such tests of the accounting records and such other auditing procedures as we considered necessary in the circumstances.

In our opinion, the financial statements referred to above present fairly the consolidated financial position of The Times Mirror Company and subsidiaries at December 31, 1981 and 1980, and the consolidated results of their operations and changes in financial position for each of the three years in the period ended December 31, 1981, in conformity with generally accepted accounting principles applied on a consistent basis.

Ernst & Whinney

Los Angeles, California
February 8, 1982

Appendix B

DOUBLE–ENTRY BOOKKEEPING: THEORY AND OPERATION

The Books of Account

This Appendix explains and illustrates the processes of double-entry bookkeeping as applied to transactions discussed in various chapters of this book. We suggest that you read Chapters 1 and 2 before beginning your study of bookkeeping, and that you read the other chapters of the book as appropriate before attempting to master the bookkeeping processes in each area.

Bookkeeping involves the entry of financial and related information into business records generally known as *books of account*. Since most businesses carry out many transactions daily, books of account are generally divided by function and are often subdivided. Transactions are initially recorded as they take place, in chronological order, in a daily record called a *journal*. The word journal derives from the French word for day, *jour*. A large business might maintain several specialized journals that combine in one place all similar transactions. Ordinarily these would include separate journals for cash receipts, cash disbursements, sales and purchases. Transactions not entered in the specialized journals are recorded in the general journal.

The many transactions entered in the journals are not in a form usable by the business to report on its status and performance. The financial information must be summarized and collected as part of the process of generating financial statements. The first step in this process is to transfer each of the items in every journal entry to *accounts* in a *ledger*. Separate ledger accounts are maintained for each type of asset and liability, as well as for income, expense and net worth. For example, a ledger account (or accounts) will be maintained for the asset furniture, and every journal entry that increases or decreases this asset will be *posted*, or transferred, to that ledger account. The process of posting is usually carried out daily, with the result that the ledger contains summaries—by separate categories—of all of the transactions entered into the journals.

Ledgers are also subdivided in order to provide necessary detail on the status of certain accounts. Typically, a business will have *subsidiary ledgers* for such items as accounts receivable and accounts payable. For example, the accounts receivable ledger will contain a separate ledger account for each individual or company that owes money to the enterprise. The total of all of the separate accounts receivable will, of course, equal the total figure for accounts receivable shown in the main ledger, known as the *general ledger*.

When the management of the enterprise wishes to generate financial statements, the bookkeeping department will be instructed to prepare a *Trial Balance*, which is a listing of the balances in all of the accounts in the ledger. The trial balance will then be divided into balance sheet and income statement items for purposes of preparing the financial statements.

This Appendix explores each of these steps, from original entry of the transactions in the journals, through posting in the ledgers, to summarization in the trial balance and preparation of the financial statements. The discussion of journals and of other documents involved in the bookkeeping process may bring to mind archaic visions of clerks with green eyeshades recording the daily business transactions with quill pens, in the manner of Dickens' immortal character, Bob Cratchitt. Today the eyeshades and quill pens are gone. Even the most rudimentary bookkeeping systems generally use time-saving printed forms, and most systems involve mechanization to a substantial degree. In the most sophisticated systems, transactions are entered directly at computer terminals, and the financial data is recorded on magnetic tape or disks rather than with pen on paper. However, the principles of bookkeeping remain unchanged. The journal remains a journal, the ledger a ledger, whatever their form, and the processes of initial entry, posting and summarization that we describe in this Appendix do not change in any substantive aspect.

The Fundamental Equation

Double-entry bookkeeping is based on the Fundamental Equation:

$$Assets = Liabilities + Net\ Worth$$

As we noted in Chapter 2, *Assets* are the items of value owned by the enterprise, *Liabilities* are the debts and obligations owed by the enterprise, and *Net Worth* represents the interest of the owner or owners in the enterprise. The Fundamental Equation must, by definition, remain in balance. If the Fundamental Equation must remain in balance, it follows that the recording of any transaction will require two entries. Let us illustrate this point with a simple example. Suppose that E. Scrooge has two assets, cash of $5,000 and furniture of $3,000, and that he owes creditors a total of $1,000. We may summarize his business as follows in accordance with to the Fundamental Equation:

Assets ($8,000) = Liabilities ($1,000) + Net Worth ($7,000)

Although we were not given the figure for Scrooge's net worth, we know that it is $7,000 because the Fundamental Equation must be in balance. Moreover, we can readily deduce the accuracy of this simple calculation (and of the Fundamental Equation) by reasoning that if Scrooge owns items of value worth $8,000 and owes debts of $1,000, the remaining value of $7,000 is his net ownership interest, or net worth.

Every financial transaction that Scrooge undertakes will have two effects. For example, if he buys $200 of merchandise on credit, he will increase his assets (merchandise) by $200 but also increase his liabilities (accounts payable) by $200. The Fundamental Equation remains in balance:

Assets ($8,200) = Liabilities ($1,200) + Net Worth ($7,000)

Obviously, an accounting system that simply maintains a running balance in the Fundamental Equation will be unsatisfactory. The bookkeeping process records each transaction, however, in accordance with its *effect* on the Fundamental Equation. Scrooge's purchase of merchandise would be entered in the journal as follows:

Merchandise $200.00
    Accounts Payable $200.00
    (To record purchase of merchandise on credit.)

Journal entries are made in two columns, left and right, corresponding to the left and right sides of the Fundamental Equation. The entries will retain their character as left or right throughout the entire bookkeeping process and on the financial statements. Thus, increases in assets will be made by entries on the left side, while increases to liabilities and net worth will be reflected by entries on the right side. In the entry above, merchandise (an asset) was increased by a left side entry and accounts payable (a liability) was increased by a right side entry.

It is customary to provide an explanation beneath each journal entry to document the basis of the entry for purposes of subsequent review, or audit, of the financial records. Each entry will also be dated. In this Appendix, we will occasionally omit dates or explanations in the interests of brevity.

Suppose that Scrooge buys additional merchandise for $500 cash. The entry must now reflect an increase in one asset (mer-

chandise) and a decrease in another asset (cash). We might
show the entry as follows:

Merchandise	$500.00
Cash	−$500.00

(To record purchase of merchandise for cash.)

However, entries of this type would require that the bookkeeping system maintain positive and negative numbers in the journals and ledgers. To avoid the confusion and possible error that
such a procedure might create, a convention has been adopted.
The convention is simple, but fundamental enough to require
emphasis:

> *Increases in assets (the left side of the equation) are re-
> corded by left side entries. Decreases in assets are re-
> flected by right side entries.*

> *Correspondingly, increases in liabilities or net worth
> (the right side of the equation) are recorded by right side
> entries. Decreases in liabilities or net worth are shown by
> left side entries.*

Therefore, Scrooge will record the purchase of merchandise
for cash as follows:

Merchandise	$500.00
Cash	$500.00

(To record purchase of merchandise for cash.)

The value of this approach becomes more evident when we consider a business with thousands of cash receipts and disbursements. The company's ledger account for cash will contain
records of every cash transaction. Every left side entry will reflect a receipt of cash, and every right side entry will reflect a
disbursement of cash. The cash balance at any time is found by
totalling the entries on the left and right sides, and subtracting
the right (negative) from the left (positive).

Debit and Credit: A Very Short Explanation

At the risk of inserting confusion into this simple process, we
now introduce two terms that have—without reason—confused
generations of accounting students and given rise to many apoc-
ryphal stories. They are:

> *Debit*, meaning *left*, and

> *Credit*, meaning *right*.

When accountants speak of "debit", they mean "left", nothing
more and nothing less. "Credit", as an accounting term, means

only "right." The left-side columns of journals, ledgers, trial balances and balance sheets will be referred to as the debit side; and the right-side columns as the credit side. If you will remember to ascribe no further meaning to these terms, they will cause you no confusion.

The Forms of Transactions: Journal Entries

In Chapter 2, we described the nine basic transactions that may affect assets, liabilities and net worth, and we explained the effects of those transactions on the Fundamental Equation. The basic transactions are:

1. Increase Assets, Increase Net Worth.

2. Increase Assets, Decrease Assets.

3. Increase Assets, Increase Liabilities.

4. Decrease Assets, Decrease Liabilities.

5. Decrease Assets, Decrease Net Worth.

6. Increase Liabilities, Decrease Liabilities.

7. Increase Liabilities, Decrease Net Worth.

8. Decrease Liabilities, Increase Net Worth.

9. Increase Net Worth, Decrease Net Worth.

Using the same transactions as those in Chapter 2, Joan Wisdom will make the following entries in her journal:

1. Increase Assets, Increase Net Worth. Wisdom establishes a consulting business with $4,000 of her cash:

Cash	$4,000.00	
Wisdom, Net Worth		$4,000.00

2. Increase Assets, Decrease Assets. Wisdom purchases $500 of office supplies for cash:

Office Supplies	$500.00	
Cash		$500.00

Note that in the first transaction, the debit to cash increased that asset by $4,000. In this second transaction, the credit to cash represents a decrease of $500.

3. Increase Assets, Increase Liabilities. Wisdom buys $5,000 of furniture on credit:

Furniture	$5,000.00	
Accounts Payable		$5,000.00

In this transaction, the credit (right-side) entry increases a liability.

4. Decrease Assets, Decrease Liabilities. Wisdom makes a $2,000 cash payment on the liability for the furniture in transaction 3:

Accounts Payable $2,000.00
     Cash $2,000.00

Aren't assets like cash supposed to be on the left, and liabilities like accounts payable on the right? They are, indeed, but in this transaction assets are *reduced* by a credit entry (right side) and liabilities are also *reduced* by a debit entry (left side). This transaction is the reverse of transaction 3, in which assets and liabilities were both increased.

5. Decrease Assets, Decrease Net Worth. Wisdom removes a $400 chair from the business for personal use:

Wisdom, Net Worth $400.00
     Furniture $400.00

Here again, the accounts at first glance appear to be on the wrong side; assets "belong" on the left, and net worth on the right. However, the transaction involves a decrease in both accounts, so the debit to net worth (reduction) and the credit to furniture (reduction) are both proper. Since we are preparing the books for Wisdom's *business*, the removal of the chair reduces assets and net worth even if Wisdom still sits on it at home.

6. Increase Liabilities, Decrease Liabilities. Wisdom gives a promissory note for the $3,000 unpaid balance on the furniture purchased in transaction 3:

Accounts Payable $3,000.00
     Note Payable $3,000.00

7. Increase Liabilities, Decrease Net Worth. Wisdom agrees to pay $500 medical expenses to an injured client:

Wisdom, Net Worth $500.00
     Medical Expenses Payable $500.00

This is a transaction in which the enterprise incurs a liability (credit entry) and receives nothing of continuing value in return; therefore, net worth is decreased (debit entry). We shall see many variations of this entry when we discuss expenses, below.

8. Decrease Liabilities, Increase Net Worth. The injured client forgives the debt for medical expenses:

Medical Expenses Payable	$500.00	
Wisdom, Net Worth		$500.00

This entry is simply the reverse of transaction 7.

9. Increase Net Worth, Decrease Net Worth. Wisdom sells Sharp $2,000 of her interest in the business:

Wisdom, Net Worth	$2,000.00	
Sharp, Net Worth		$2,000.00

These transactions are the building blocks for all that follows. Let us now illustrate what becomes of these journal entries in the bookkeeping process.

Posting to the Ledger

After making the entries above, Wisdom will *post* the entries, or transfer them, to accounts in the ledger. Since each entry involves two items, the posting process will involve transferring 18 items for the nine entries. The ledger accounts will be:

Assets	Liabilities	Net Worth
Cash	Accounts Payable	Wisdom, Net Worth
Office Supplies	Note Payable	Sharp, Net Worth
Furniture	Medical Expenses Payable	

The ledger is usually arranged with a separate sheet for each account and separate sections for assets, liabilities and net worth, as well as income and expenses. Each sheet is divided down the middle; debit entries are made on the left, and credit on the right. Each entry in the ledger identifies its source in the journal, so that all entries can be traced back to the original transactions that occasioned them.

We shall use a simplified ledger, in the form of "T Accounts", named for their appearance, as follows:

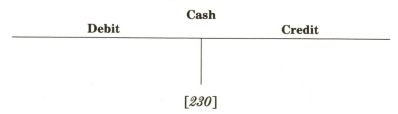

When the first transaction is posted to the ledger account for cash, it will appear as follows:

Cash

Debit		Credit
(1)	$4,000	

In other words, the debit entry in transaction 1 is transferred directly as a debit in the cash account. Similarly, the credit entry in transaction 1 will appear as a credit in the account Wisdom, Net Worth. After all nine transactions have been posted, the ledger accounts will appear as follows:

ASSETS

Cash			Office Supplies		Furniture		
(1) $4000	(2)	$500	(2) $500		(3) $5000	(5)	$400
	(4)	2000					

LIABILITIES

Accounts Payable		Note Payable		Medical Expenses Payable		
(4) $2000	(3) $5000		(6) $3000	(8) $500	(7)	$500
(6) 3000						

NET WORTH

Wisdom, Net Worth		Sharp, Net Worth	
(5) $ 400	(1) $4000		(9) $2000
(7) 500	(8) 500		
(9) 2000			

Preparation of the Trial Balance

If Wisdom now wanted to summarize her accounts, she would determine the balance of each account and list all of the accounts in a *Trial Balance*. The balances of each account are determined by adding the debit and credit columns and subtracting the smaller sum from the larger:

ASSETS

Cash		Office Supplies		Furniture	
(1) $4000	(2) $500	(2) $500		(3) $5000	(5) $400
	(4) 2000				
	———			− 400	$400
− 2500	$2500			———	———
———	———			$4600	
$1500					

LIABILITIES

Accounts Payable		Note Payable		Medical Expenses Payable	
(4) $2000	(3) $5000		(6) $3000	(8) $500	(7) $500
(6) 3000				———	
———				$500	− 500
$5000	− 5000			———	———

NET WORTH

Wisdom, Net Worth		Sharp, Net Worth	
(5) $400	(1) $4000		(9) $2000
(7) 500	(8) 500		
(9) 2000	———		
———	$4500		
$2900	− 2900		
	$1600		

Notice that the balance of accounts payable is zero. We can determine why this is so by examining the ledger entries and tracing them back to the original entries in the journal. Accounts payable were increased to $5,000 by journal entry 3, in which Wisdom recorded the purchase of furniture on account. Journal entry 4 reduced accounts payable by $2,000 to reflect cash payment of a portion of the account. In journal entry 6, accounts payable were reduced by an additional $3,000 (down to zero) when a note payable was substituted for the remaining balance due.

The trial balance is simply a listing of the balances in the ledger accounts. Of course, it also reflects the balance of the Fundamental Equation:

Joan Wisdom
Trial Balance
As of (date)

	Debit	Credit
Cash	$1,500.00	
Office Supplies	500.00	
Furniture	4,600.00	
Accounts Payable		$ 0.00
Notes Payable		3,000.00
Medical Expenses Payable		0.00
Wisdom, Net Worth		1,600.00
Sharp, Net Worth		2,000.00
Totals	$6,600.00	$6,600.00

Income and Expense

In addition to purchasing and selling assets and incurring and discharging liabilities, enterprises earn *income* and incur *expenses*. How would Sage, an attorney, record the receipt of $1,000 cash, representing a fee for services he rendered to a client? The increase in cash (an asset) is reflected as a debit. No other asset has been reduced, nor has any liability been increased. Therefore, Sage's net worth—his ownership interest in the business—has been increased. The entry:

Cash	$1,000.00	
Sage, Net Worth		$1,000.00

What entry would Sage make to reflect the payment of $300 salary in cash to his secretary? The decrease in cash is reflected as a credit. No other asset has been increased, and no liability has been decreased. Therefore, Sage's net worth has been reduced. The entry:

Sage, Net Worth	$300.00	
Cash		$300.00

Although the entries above are clearly correct, the recording of income and expense items as direct increases or decreases of net worth would be an unwieldy and unsatisfactory practice. Ordinarily, a business will have many income and expense transactions daily. A meaningful accounting system should maintain separate records of items of income and expense so that an adequately detailed *Statement of Income* may be prepared for the business. Therefore, income and expense are separately recorded in appropriate categories as part of the bookkeeping process.

Remember that income *increases* net worth and expense *decreases* net worth. Accordingly, the rules for entering income and expense items on the books are merely a variation of the rules for entering changes in net worth. They are:

Increases in income are recorded by credit (right-side) entries, and decreases in income are reflected by debit (left-side) entries.

Correspondingly, increases in expenses are recorded by debit entries, and decreases in expenses are reflected by credit entries.

Income and expense transactions will be entered in the journal and posted to the ledger in the same manner as all other transactions. Suppose that Smart opens his law practice on March 1, 1983, and that during the month Smart:

1. Deposits $5,000 into a bank account as his initial capital investment.
2. Purchases $1,000 of office equipment for cash.
3. Buys library books for $500 on credit from East Publishing Co.
4. Writes a will for Able and is paid a $400 fee in cash.
5. Prepares documents for Baker and sends Baker a bill for $1,000.
6. Receives partial payment from Baker of $700 cash.
7. Pays office rent of $300 cash.
8. Receives telephone bill of $100.

These transactions will first be recorded in Smart's journal:

1.	Cash	$5,000.00	
	Smart, Net Worth		$5,000.00
2.	Office Equipment	1,000.00	
	Cash		1,000.00
3.	Library	500.00	
	Accounts Payable—East		500.00
4.	Cash	400.00	
	Fee Income		400.00
5.	Accounts Receivable—Baker	1,000.00	
	Fee Income		1,000.00
6.	Cash	700.00	
	Accounts Receivable—Baker		700.00
7.	Rent Expense	300.00	
	Cash		300.00

8.   Telephone Expense   100.00

        Telephone Expense Payable   100.00

Note that in transaction 5, fee income has been recorded even though it has not yet been received. Similarly, in transaction 8, telephone expense has been recorded despite the fact that it has not yet been paid. These entries reflect the *accrual system of accounting*, discussed in Chapter 3. Under accrual accounting, items of income and expense are reflected in the books when the economic events giving rise to the right to receive income or the obligation to pay expenses have taken place.

Note also that in transactions 3 and 5 the entries identified the particular account payable (East) and account receivable (Baker). Separate accounts must be maintained for each receivable and payable so that Smart will know who owes him how much, and how much he owes to whom. The separate accounts are maintained as subsidiary ledgers. When the financial statements are prepared the total of accounts receivable will appear as a single figure, as will the total of accounts payable.

When Smart posts his journal entries to the ledger and calculates the balances, the accounts will be as follows:

ASSETS

Cash		Office Equipment		Library	
(1) $5000	(2) $1000	(2) $1000		(3) $300	
(4) 400	(7) 300				
(6) 700					
$6100					
− 1300	$1300				
$4800					

Accounts Receivable	
(5) $1000	(6) $700
− 700	$700
$300	

LIABILITIES AND NET WORTH

Accounts Payable		Telephone Expense Payable		Smart, Net Worth	
	(3) $500		(8) $100		(1) $5000

INCOME AND EXPENSE

Fee Income		Rent Expense		Telephone Expense	
	(4) $400	(7) $300		(8) $100	
	(5) 1000				
	$1400				

Preparation of the Balance Sheet and Income Statement

Smart is now ready to prepare his trial balance. However, since the trial balance will contain assets, liabilities, net worth, income and expenses, he will arrange it in a worksheet format. The first two columns will be the original trial balance, and the next four columns will be used to develop Smart's balance sheet and income statement.

Smart, Attorney
Trial Balance Worksheet
March 31, 1983

	Trial Balance		Income Statement		Balance Sheet	
	Debit	Credit	Debit	Credit	Debit	Credit
Cash	$4,800.00				$4,800.00	
Office Equipment	1,000.00				1,000.00	
Library	500.00				500.00	
Accounts Receivable	300.00				300.00	
Accounts Payable		$ 500.00				$ 500.00
Telephone Expense Payable		100.00				100.00
Smart, Net Worth		5,000.00				5,000.00
Fee Income		1,400.00		$1,400.00		
Rent Expense	300.00		300.00			
Telephone Expense	100.00		100.00			
Totals	$7,000.00	$7,000.00	$400.00	$1,400.00	$6,600.00	$5,600.00

The worksheet separates the items that will appear on the income statement from those that will appear on the balance sheet. Notice that the trial balance columns are in balance, but the balance sheet and income statement columns are not. The reason is that the net income has not yet been calculated and transferred to Smart's net worth account. From the worksheet, we see that income (credit) totalled $1,400 and expenses (debit) totalled $400. Net income for the month is the excess of income over expenses, or $1,000. We will add an additional columns two to the worksheet to provide space for adjusting entries; in those columns, we will reflect the transfer of net income to Smart's capital. (This transfer is further explained below under closing entries.) The items marked with the asterisks represent the transfer:

[*236*]

Smart, Attorney
Trial Balance Worksheet
March 31, 1983

	Trial Balance Debit	Trial Balance Credit	Adjustments Debit	Adjustments Credit	Income Statement Debit	Income Statement Credit	Balance Sheet Debit	Balance Sheet Credit
Cash	$4,800.00						$4,800.00	
Office Equipment	1,000.00						1,000.00	
Library	500.00						500.00	
Accounts Receivable	300.00						300.00	
Accounts Payable		$ 500.00						$ 500.00
Telephone Expense Payable		100.00						100.00
Smart, Net Worth		5,000.00		$1,000.00*				6,000.00
Fee Income		1,400.00				$1,400.00		
Rent Expense	300.00				300.00			
Telephone Expense	100.00				100.00			
Net Income: Transfer to Smart, Net Worth			$1,000.00*		1,000.00			
Totals	$7,000.00	$7,000.00	$1,000.00	$1,000.00	$1,400.00	$1,400.00	$6,600.00	$6,600.00

From the worksheet as adjusted, we may now prepare the financial statements for Smart. The income statement columns provide the information for preparation of the following statement:

Smart, Attorney
Statement of Income
For the month ended March 31, 1983

Fee Income		$1,400.00
Less Expenses:		
Rent Expense	$300.00	
Telephone Expense	100.00	
Total Expenses		400.00
Net Income		$1,000.00

The balance sheet columns yield the following statement:

Smart, Attorney
Balance Sheet
As of March 31, 1983

Assets		Liabilities & Net Worth	
Cash	$4,800.00	Accounts Payable	$ 500.00
Accounts Receivable	300.00	Telephone Expense Payable	100.00
Office Equipment	1,000.00	Total Liabilities	$ 600.00
Library	500.00	Smart, Net Worth	6,000.00
		Total Liabilities and	
Total Assets	$6,600.00	Net Worth	$6,600.00

Accruals and Deferrals: Accrued Expense

Accrual accounting, as discussed in Chapter 3, requires that the books reflect income and expense when the economic events giving rise to realization have taken place, irrespective of cash receipts or payments. Most expense accruals involve expenses not paid directly in cash, such as services or supplies obtained by incurring accounts payable. Some accrued expenses, however, gradually build up over time, and require adjusting entries for proper reflection in the books. These adjustments frequently arise in connection with leases and interest-bearing promissory notes.

Suppose Laertes borrows $10,000 on December 1, 1982, giving his 12% one year promissory note. The loan will be recorded by him as follows:

Cash	$10,000.00	
Note Payable		$10,000.00

As of the date of the loan no interest is payable and therefore none will be recorded. However, as of December 31, 1982, when Laertes closes his books and prepares his financial statements, one month's interest will have accrued on the note. Therefore, despite the fact that no *payment* is required, Laertes must make an adjusting entry:

Interest Expense	$100.00	
Accrued Interest Payable		$100.00
(To record accrued interest for one month, $1/12 \times 12\% \times \$10,000 = \$100$)		

The effect of this entry is to record an expense in 1982 for the interest that accrued in 1982, and to show a corresponding liability. On November 30, 1983, when Laertes pays the note and the interest, he will make the following entries:

Note Payable	$10,000.00	
Cash		$10,000.00
(To record repayment of promissory note)		
Interest Expense	$1,100.00	
Accrued Interest Payable	100.00	
Cash		$1,200.00
(To record payment of interest on promissory note)		

The second of these entries shows that a total of $1,200 interest (12% of $10,000) was paid. However, not all of the $1,200 was expense in 1983, since $100 had been reflected as expense in 1982. Therefore, the $1,200 payment represents a discharge of the $100 accrued liability for 1982, plus $1,100 interest expense for 1983. We have combined these two items in a single *compound entry*. Whenever a transaction has multiple effects, the bookkeeper has the choice of separating the effects into multiple entries or, as we have done above, combining the effects in a single compound entry.

Accruals and Deferrals: Deferred Expense

Deferral is the opposite of accrual. Suppose that Gibraltar Co. purchases a one-year casualty insurance policy for $2,400, paying for the policy in full as of its effective date of June 1, 1983. The entry on June 1, 1983 will be:

Insurance Expense	$2,400.00	
Cash		$2,400.00

As of December 31, 1983, when Gibraltar prepares its annual financial statements, seven months of the policy's coverage will have expired. However, five months of coverage will remain for 1984. Accordingly, Gibraltar will make an adjusting entry to defer the appropriate portion of the insurance expense, so that it is recognized as an expense in 1984. The entry on December 31, 1983 will be:

Prepaid (or deferred) Insurance	$1,000.00	
Insurance Expense		$1,000.00
(To record prepaid insurance expense for five months' unexpired coverage: $5/12 \times \$2,400 = \$1,000$)		

Notice the effects of the entry. The debit creates an asset, Prepaid (or deferred) Insurance. Clearly, the prepaid insurance is an asset, since as of December 31, 1983 it has continuing value to Gibraltar. The credit *reduces* insurance expense, because the original entry showed the entire $2,400 as expense for 1983, whereas only seven months' coverage applies to 1983. Since the expense was originally recorded at $2,400, the reduction of $1,000 leaves a balance of $1,400 ($7/12 \times \$2,400 = \$1,400$) as expense for 1983.

In 1984, the prepaid insurance will expire, and it will be shown as insurance expense. The entry to reflect the expiration of prepaid insurance should be made on May 31, when the policy term runs out:

Insurance Expense $1,000.00
   Prepaid Insurance $1,000.00
   (To record expiration of prepaid insurance)

Accruals and Deferrals: Accrued Income

Similar accruals and deferrals are recorded for income items, but—as you must by now expect—income entries are the reverse of expense entries. Suppose that Polonius makes a six-month loan of $5,000 on October 1, 1983, and receives in return a promissory note bearing interest at the rate of 10%. Suppose also that the loan and interest are paid in full on the due date of March 31, 1984. The following entry will be made by Polonius on October 1, 1983:

Note Receivable $5,000.00
   Cash $5,000.00

No entry is made to record interest, since none is due as of October 1. The entry simply reflects the disbursement of cash (a reduction of an asset) and the receipt of the note (an increase in another asset).

If Polonius prepares financial statements on December 31, he will make an adjusting entry to reflect the interest on the note that has accumulated without payment—*accrued*—for the preceding three months:

Accrued Interest Receivable $125.00
   Interest Income $125.00
   (To record accrual of three months' interest:
      $3/12 \times 10\% \times \$5,000 = \$125$)

The entry shows an asset, accrued interest receivable, since Polonius has earned three months' interest. Correspondingly, a credit is made to interest income to recognize the income that has been earned.

When Polonius receives payment on the note on March 31, 1984, he will make the following entries:

Cash $5,000.00
   Note Receivable $5,000.00
   (To record receipt of payment on
      promissory note)

Cash $250.00

  Interest Income $125.00
  Accrued Interest Receivable   125.00
  (To record receipt of interest on promissory
      note)

The second of these entries shows that a total of $250 of interest was received. However, only $125 has been reflected as income in 1984, since $125 had previously been accrued as income in 1983. The combined effect of all the entries made by Polonius has been to record the interest income when it was earned, $125 in 1983 and $125 in 1984.

Accruals and Deferrals: Deferred Income

Income that has not yet been earned must be reflected as deferred income, a liability. Suppose that Landlord leases an office to Tenant on November 1, 1983 at a monthly rent of $1,000, and that the terms of the lease call for rent to be paid six months in advance. Accordingly, Landlord receives $6,000 from Tenant on November 1. Landlord's entry will be:

Cash $6,000.00

  Rent Income $6,000.00

On December 31, 1983, before preparing its financial statements, Landlord will make the following adjusting entry:

Rent Income $4,000.00

  Deferred Rent Income $4,000.00
  (To record deferral of 4 months' unearned
      rent income)

The debit to rent income reduces income, to reflect the fact that Landlord has not earned the full $6,000 it received. The credit to deferred rent income establishes a liability, representing the obligation to make the office available for the next four months at the agreed rate of $1,000 per month. On April 30, 1984, when the six months have expired, Landlord will make the following entry:

Deferred Rent Income $4,000.00

  Rent Income $4,000.00

This entry reflects the fact that the income previously paid has now been fully earned.

Inventories and Cost of Goods Sold

To this point, we have illustrated service businesses, in which net income is the difference between revenues from services and expenses. Calculation of net income for manufacturing or merchandising businesses involves additional accounts and entries for inventories and cost of goods sold. Inventory accounting is introduced in Chapter 3 and explained in detail in Chapter 4, both of which should be reviewed before studying this section.

Under the periodic inventory system, which is the most widely used system, separate accounts are maintained for Sales, Purchases and Inventory:

Sales is a revenue account. As each sale is made, it is recorded at the selling price. The increase in assets (cash or accounts receivable) is recorded as a debit, and a credit is made to sales.

Purchases is an asset account that will become expense as the purchased goods are sold. As the company buys inventory items, a debit is made to purchases for the purchase price. The increase in liabilities (accounts payable) or decrease in assets (cash) is recorded as a credit.

Inventory is maintained unchanged in amount throughout the accounting period, usually one year. Since the taking of inventory is *periodic*, inventory is recalculated only at the end of the period.

Suppose that you are preparing the books for Mercenary Merchants, Inc., a very small business. A summary of Mercenary's transactions for the year 1983 is as follows:

1. Mercenary's ledger shows that Inventory as of January 1 was $1,000.

2. Mercenary purchased $1,500 of goods for cash from various suppliers.

3. Mercenary sold goods to various purchasers for $3,200 cash.

4. A physical count of the inventory as of December 31 revealed goods on hand, at cost, of $1,400.

5. Operating expenses for the year totalled $500, all of which were paid in cash.

The first four items above represent each of the principal transactions involved with inventory and cost of goods sold for a merchandising business. The fifth item represents expenses other than the purchase of merchandise. The items will be entered in the journal as follows:

1. No entry. The January 1 inventory—known as the *Opening Inventory* or *Beginning Inventory*—already appears in the ledger, having been entered on December 31 of the previous year.

2. Purchases $1,500.00
        Cash $1,500.00

3. Cash   3,200.00
        Sales   3,200.00

5. Operating Expenses   500.00
        Cash   500.00

Item 4, the year-end inventory—known as the *Closing Inventory* or *Ending Inventory*—is recorded in the journal as part of a series of year-end entries known as *Closing Entries*. To illustrate these entries, we must first review the status of certain of Mercenary's ledger accounts as of December 31:

Inventory, 1/1		Purchases		Sales	
(1) $1000		(2) $1500			(3) $3200

Operating Expenses	
(5) $500	

Since Mercenary had $1,000 of inventory on hand at the beginning of the year and purchased an additional $1,500 of merchandise, it had a total of $2,500 of merchandise available for sale during the year. And, since the physical inventory count showed $1,400 of inventory remaining at year-end, a total of $1,100 of merchandise ($2,500 – $1,400 = $1,100) was sold or otherwise consumed (by spoilage, theft, etc.) during the year. The $1,100 is known as *Cost of Goods Sold*, and a separate summary account is set up in the ledger at the end of the year to bring together all items of cost of goods sold.

With sales of $3,200 and cost of goods sold of $1,100, Mercenary had a *Gross Profit* of $2,100 on its sales for the year. A summary account for gross profit is also established in the ledger at the end of the year.

Closing Entries

Closing entries will be made by Mercenary as of December 31 to reflect cost of goods sold, gross profit, and net income. Each entry eliminates (or closes) the balance in an account and transfers it to a summary account. The closing process will begin with transfers of all items relating to cost of goods sold to the summary account *Cost of Goods Sold*. Next, sales and cost of goods sold will be transferred to the summary account *Gross Profit*. Then, gross profit, operating expenses, and all other income and expense items will be transferred to the summary account *Profit and Loss*. Finally, the balance of the profit and loss account will be transferred to Net Worth.

Mechanically, an account is closed by determining the debit or credit balance of the account and making an entry equal to that balance on the *opposite* side of the account. For example, in entry (a) below, Inventory has a debit balance of $1,000; the account is therefore closed by making a credit entry of $1,000. This leaves a balance of zero. The original $1,000 debit does not disappear, however, since it is *transferred* as a debit to the Cost of Goods Sold account.

The process of closing, or transferring, accounts applies only to income and expense, since these items are determined on a periodic basis. Assets and liabilities, as well as the net worth account, are never closed: their balances are carried forward from year to year.

Mercenary's closing entries begin with the following:

a. Cost of Goods Sold $1,000.00
        Inventory, January 1 $1,000.00
        (To transfer opening inventory into Cost of
           Goods Sold)

b. Cost of Goods Sold $1,500.00
        Purchases $1,500.00
        (To transfer purchases for the year into
           Cost of Goods Sold)

c. Inventory, December 31 $1,400.00
        Cost of Goods Sold $1,400.00
        (To remove from Cost of Goods Sold the
           unsold ending inventory)

Since cost of goods sold is an expense account, entries (a) and (b) *increase* expense and entry (c) *decreases* expense. This is just as we would expect under the periodic inventory system.

Cost of goods sold is determined by adding all merchandise that was available for sale during the year (beginning inventory + purchases) and subtracting whatever merchandise was left at the end of the year (ending inventory).

Now that entries have been made for cost of goods sold, entries must be made for gross profit:

d. Sales $3,200.00
    Gross Profit $3,200.00
    (To transfer sales to Gross Profit)

e. Gross Profit $1,400.00
    Cost of Goods Sold $1,400.00
    (To transfer cost of goods sold to Gross
       Profit)

Let us now post these entries to the ledger and analyze what we have done:

Inventory, 1/1		Purchases		Sales	
(1) $1000	(a) $1000	(2) $1500	(b) $1500	(d) $3200	(3) $3200
(c) $1400					

Cost of Goods Sold		Gross Profit	
(a) $1000	(c) $1400	(e) $1100	(d) $3200
(b) 1500	(e) $1100		

Posting of the entries reveals that the process of closing the books has transferred all items related to cost of goods sold to the summary account called Cost of Goods Sold. Similarly, cost of goods sold has itself, along with sales, been transferred to the summary account called Gross Profit. We must now transfer gross profit, together with operating expenses, to the summary account for Profit and Loss:

f. Gross Profit $2,100.00
    Profit & Loss $2,100.00
    (To transfer gross profit to Profit & Loss)

g. Profit & Loss $500.00
    Operating Expenses $500.00
    (To transfer operating expenses to Profit &
       Loss)

These entries have the following effects on the ledger accounts:

Operating Expenses		Gross Profit		Profit & Loss	
(5) $500	(g) $500	(e) $1100	(d) $3200	(g) $500	(f) $2100
		(f) 2100			

The final closing entry will transfer the balance of the profit & loss account to the net worth of Mercenary, Inc. Since Mercenary is a corporation, the transfer will be to the net worth account called *Retained Earnings:*

h. Profit & Loss $1,600.00
        Retained Earnings $1,600.00
        (To transfer net income to Retained Earnings)

This last entry has the following effects:

Profit & Loss		Retained Earnings	
(g) $500	(f) $2100		(h) $1600
(h) 1600			

We can chart the flow of information in this process of closing and summarizing as follows:

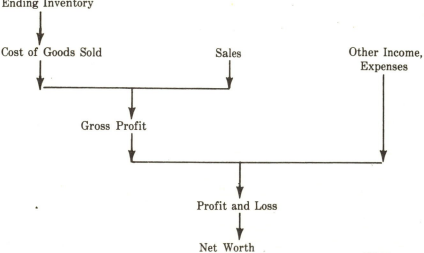

[C6890]

The chart demonstrates that the process of closing the books represents a series of steps in which increasing amounts of fi-

[*246*]

nancial information are summarized.   Ultimately, all income and expense items are "closed", or transferred to net worth.   However, each intermediate step generates summary information that will appear on the financial statements.

Note that once the income and expense items are transferred, a double line is drawn at the bottom of the ledger accounts.   The balance is then zero, and the account is ready to be started over again in the new year.   One account, however, does not become zero: the ending inventory for 1983 becomes the beginning inventory for 1984.

Mercenary's income statement may now be constructed, based on the summary information that was transferred to the accounts for cost of goods sold, gross profit and profit and loss.

Mercenary Merchants, Inc.
Statement of Income
For the year ended December 31, 1983

Sales		$3,200.00
Cost of Goods Sold:		
Beginning Inventory	$1,000.00	
Purchases	1,500.00	
Goods Available for Sale	$2,500.00	
Ending Inventory	1,400.00	
Cost of Goods Sold		1,100.00
Gross Profit		$2,100.00
Operating Expenses		500.00
Net Income		$1,600.00

Depreciation and Fixed Assets

Depreciation and fixed asset accounting are discussed in Chapter 5, which you should read before studying this section.

Fixed assets are recorded on the books at their cost, and separate accounts are maintained for accumulated depreciation. We will illustrate the entries with a single asset, but the same principles apply to groups and classes of assets.   Suppose that Heavy Haulers Co. purchases a truck for $35,000 cash on January 1, 1983.   The truck has an expected useful life of five years, and an estimated scrap value of $5,000. On January 1, 1983, Heavy will make the following journal entry:

Truck	$35,000.00	
Cash		$35,000.00

If Heavy uses straight line depreciation, on December 31 of each year from 1983 through 1987, Heavy will record the following journal entry:

Depreciation Expense	$6,000.00	
Accumulated Depreciation—		
Truck		$6,000.00

(To record annual depreciation:
[$35,000 — $5,000] ÷ 5 = $6,000)

Therefore, as of December 31, 1983, the ledger accounts relating to the truck will appear as follows:

Truck	Accumulated Depreciation, Truck
$35,000	$6,000

The two accounts are really subdivisions of a single account for the truck. In fact, the truck is being carried on the books at $29,000 ($35,000 — $6,000). Two accounts are maintained, however, in the interests of providing more informative disclosure of assets acquired and of accumulated depreciation. The account for accumulated depreciation, truck is maintained in the same location in the ledger as the account for the truck itself. It is known as a *contra asset* account, or a *valuation account*, since it reflects a reduction in the book value of an asset.

The same depreciation entry will be made to accumulated depreciation, truck, for each year in which it is owned until it is fully depreciated down to its scrap value. After five years, the ledger accounts will appear as follows:

Truck	Accumulated Depreciation, Truck
$35,000	$6,000
	6,000
	6,000
	6,000
	6,000

Since the two accounts are separately maintained and disclosed, Heavy's balance sheet, at the end of five years, would show the truck as follows, under the heading of fixed assets:

Truck, at cost	$35,000
Less accumulated depreciation	30,000
	$ 5,000

When the truck is ultimately sold or otherwise disposed of, both accounts—Truck and Accumulated Depreciation, Truck—must be appropriately adjusted. Suppose that following the fifth year Heavy sells the truck for $6,000. The following entry will be made:

Cash	$ 6,000.00	
Accumulated depreciation, truck	30,000.00	
Truck		$35,000.00
Profit on sale of truck		1,000.00

The entry removes the truck from the books and also the related account, accumulated depreciation, truck. Since the difference between the two was $5,000, the sale at $6,000 produced a profit of $1,000.

Partnership Capital Accounts

Partnership and corporate capital accounts are discussed in Chapter 8, which should be reviewed before studying this section.

Contributions of capital to a partnership are recorded in the same manner as capital contributions to a proprietorship, except that the contributions are separately credited to the capital account of each partner. Suppose A and B each contribute $10,000 cash to the AB Partnership. The journal entries will be:

Cash	$10,000.00	
A, Capital		$10,000.00
Cash	10,000.00	
B, Capital		10,000.00

Similarly, when a partner withdraws capital, a debit will be made to that partner's individual capital account. Often, a separate *drawings* account is maintained for each partner, which shows the withdrawals of capital made by each partner during the year. At the end of the year, the drawings account of each partner will be subtracted from that partner's capital account.

If A withdraws $2,000 of capital in cash from the AB Partnership, the entry will be:

A, Capital (or A, Drawings)	$2,000.00	
Cash		$2,000.00

After the net income of a proprietorship is determined, it is credited directly to the capital account of the proprietor. In a partnership, the net income (or loss) must first be divided in accordance with the partnership agreement. Each partner's capital account is then credited with that partner's share of net income (or debited with the appropriate share of net loss). Suppose that A and B agreed to divide profits and losses 60% to A and 40% to B. If at the end of the year the Profit & Loss Account shows a credit balance (net income) of $10,000, the following entry will be made:

Profit & Loss	$10,000	
A, Capital		$6,000.00
B, Capital		4,000.00

This will be the last closing entry, and it divides the net income of the partnership in accordance with the agreement of the partners.

Corporate Capital Accounts

Corporate capital accounts, as we noted in Chapter 8, are generally divided into at least three separate categories. These include the *Capital Stock* account, the *Capital in Excess of Par* account, and *Retained Earnings*.

Contributions of capital to a corporation take the form of issuance of stock by the corporation to stockholders. If the stock has a par value, the total of the par value of the shares issued will be added to the capital stock account and any excess will be added to capital in excess of par. Suppose A Corp. issues 100 shares of its $100 par stock for $15,000 cash. The entry:

Cash	$15,000.00	
Capital Stock, par $100		$10,000.00
Capital Contributed in Excess of Par		5,000.00

Since the total par value of the issued shares was $10,000 (100 shares × $100 par value per share), that amount is credited (added) to the capital stock account. The remainder represents capital contributed in excess of par.

If the Stock is without par value, the entire amount is generally credited to the capital stock account. If A Corp. issues 100 shares of no-par stock for $15,000 cash, the entry will be:

Cash	$15,000.00	
Capital Stock, no-par		$15,000.00

A corporation may issue several classes of stock. A separate account is maintained for each class of stock, and each class is separately disclosed on the balance sheet.

After the net income of a corporation is determined, it is transferred to a separate capital account, *Retained Earnings.* Suppose that as of the end of 1983, A Corp. shows a credit balance (net income) of $2,500 in its Profit & Loss account. Its final closing entry will be:

Profit & Loss	$2,500.00	
Retained Earnings		$2,500.00

In Chapter 8, we indicated that retained earnings represents not only the accumulated and undistributed net income of a corporation, but also the usual financial and legal measure of the corporation's ability to pay dividends. The payment of dividends by a corporation to its shareholders represents a distribution (or reduction) of its net worth, analogous to drawings by partners. If A Corp. pays a cash dividend of $5 per share on each of its 100 outstanding shares, the journal entry will be:

Retained Earnings	$500.00	
Cash		$500.00
(To record distribution of a cash dividend of $5 per share)		

*

INDEX

†

EDUCATION
Still under Siege

Critical Studies in Education and Culture Series

Teachers As Intellectuals: Toward a Critical Pedagogy of Learning
Henry A. Giroux

Women Teaching for Change: Gender, Class and Power
Kathleen Weiler

Between Capitalism and Democracy: Educational Policy and the Crisis of the
Welfare State
Svi Shapiro

Critical Psychology and Pedagogy: Interpretation of the Personal World
Edmund Sullivan

Pedagogy and the Struggle for Voice: Issues of Language, Power, and Schooling
for Puerto Ricans
Catherine E. Walsh

Learning Work: A Critical Pedagogy of Work Education
Roger I. Simon, Don Dippo, and Arleen Schenke

Cultural Pedagogy: Art/Education/Politics
David Trend

Raising Curtains on Education: Drama as a Site for Critical Pedagogy
Clar Doyle

Toward a Critical Politics of Teacher Thinking: Mapping the Postmodern
Joe L. Kincheloe

Building Communities of Difference: Higher Education in the Twenty-First
Century
William G. Tierney

The Problem of Freedom in Postmodern Education
Tomasz Szkudlarek

EDUCATION
Still under Siege

Second Edition

Stanley Aronowitz and Henry A. Giroux

Critical Studies in Education and Culture Series
Edited by Henry A. Giroux and Paulo Freire

BERGIN & GARVEY————————————————————
Westport, Connecticut • London

Library of Congress Cataloging-in-Publication Data

Aronowitz, Stanley.
    Education still under siege / Stanley Aronowitz and Henry A. Giroux. —
2nd ed.
        p.   cm. — (Critical studies in education and culture, ISSN
1064-8615)
      Includes bibliographical references and index.
      ISBN 0-89789-310-7 (alk. paper). — ISBN 0-89789-311-5 (pbk. :
alk. paper)
      1. Education—United States—Aims and objectives. 2. Educational
equalization—United States. 3. Education, Humanistic—United
States. 4. Academic freedom—United States. I. Giroux, Henry A.
II. Title. III. Series.
LA209.2.A76   1993
370′.973—dc20   93-15183

British Library Cataloguing in Publication Data is available.

Library of Congress Catalog Card Number: 93-15183
ISBN: 0-89789-310-7 (hb)
     0-89789-311-5 (pb)
ISSN: 1064-8615

First published in 1993

Bergin & Garvey, 88 Post Road West, Westport, CT 06881
An imprint of Greenwood Publishing Group, Inc.

Printed in the United States of America

The paper used in this book complies with the
Permanent Paper Standard issued by the National
Information Standards Organization (Z39.48–1984).

10 9 8 7 6 5 4 3 2 1

This book is dedicated to our children:
Nona Brett Willis-Aronowitz
Brett Brady Giroux
Chris Brady Giroux
Jack Brady Giroux